— *NELLIE FRANCIS* —

Also by William D. Green
Published by the University of Minnesota Press

A Peculiar Imbalance: The Fall and Rise of Racial Equality in Minnesota, 1837–1869

Degrees of Freedom: The Origins of Civil Rights in Minnesota, 1865–1912

The Children of Lincoln: White Paternalism and the Limits of Black Opportunity in Minnesota, 1860–1876

— *NELLIE FRANCIS* —

FIGHTING FOR RACIAL JUSTICE AND WOMEN'S EQUALITY IN MINNESOTA

WILLIAM D. GREEN

UNIVERSITY OF MINNESOTA PRESS
MINNEAPOLIS
LONDON

The University of Minnesota Press gratefully acknowledges assistance provided for the publication of this book by the John K. and Elsie Lampert Fesler Fund.

Published by the University of Minnesota Press
111 Third Avenue South, Suite 290
Minneapolis, MN 55401–2520
http://www.upress.umn.edu

ISBN 978-1-5179-1070-9 (pb)

Library of Congress record available at https://lccn.loc.gov/2020023708

Printed in the United States of America on acid-free paper

25 24 23 22 21 20   10 9 8 7 6 5 4 3 2 1

To my loving wife, Judi, who reminded me time and again
of the true meaning of love, patience, and wise counsel

Contents

Prologue

On the afternoon of November 25, 1962, the Nashville chapter of the National Council of Negro Women paid tribute to "a [local] woman" for her many contributions in her church and civic life. Held at the Student Union Center at Fisk University, Mrs. Marie B. Johnson, founder of the Nashville chapter and wife of the university president, had organized the recognition and had worked with the honoree's husband in 1929 as a member of a special commission to document forced labor operations in Liberia, and she may have been the only person present who knew the larger story of the honored guest. Few others, including the reporter covering the event, seemed to realize that Nellie Francis was more than "the widow of William Francis, ambassador to Liberia, West Africa, and niece of the late Mrs. Frankye Pierce, one-time supervisor of the Girls Vocational School here in Nashville."[1]

Fewer still knew what this frail, diminutive lady in darkened glasses, now deaf and blind, had accomplished in the distant northern city of St. Paul, Minnesota, earlier in the century. Nellie Francis had conferred and dined with the most noted black leaders of the twentieth century: Ida B. Wells-Barnett, W. E. B. Du Bois, Mary Church Terrell, and Margaret and Booker Washington. She had met three U.S. presidents as well as persuaded one of the nation's wealthiest men, Andrew Carnegie, to make a sizable donation to her favorite cause, her church's organ. She had served as one of the leaders of the 1919 women's suffrage campaign in Minnesota and had drafted and successfully lobbied for passage of the state's antilynching law in 1921. Few knew of her highly noted speech on race relations as a seventeen-year-old high-school girl in 1891, delivered to thousands of white people.

But that day at Fisk University in 1962, as had long been the case over the past several decades, she was perhaps fine with their lack of knowledge of her distant past. After all, she had never talked about the St. Paul years, as it was a place and time of both triumph and pain—and those few who could had long since passed away. She was alone now. As nice as this recognition was, she felt, as her cousin would later write, that it was more somehow for those needing closure and who would survive her own nearing demise. An additional source of peace came from knowing that a younger generation of activists had already taken the baton.

Her dignified and watchful younger cousin, Dr. T. G. West of Meharry Medical College, her aunt Alice's son, accompanied her that day, providing her with a steady arm, making sure that she was comfortable in her chair, positioning her as he must have known she wanted—not so much so that she could gratefully acknowledge the august council for giving this generous recognition but where she could luxuriate, perhaps in her memories, and certainly in the warm and life-affirming shaft of afternoon sunlight that defied the chill of the encroaching winter, her ninety-second and counting.

Introduction

> "He is recognized as a leader of his people. He is very light. I am told you would hardly know he is colored. His wife is also very light in color. They are both educated and refined."
>
> —*U.S. Senator Thomas Schall to President Calvin Coolidge, in an endorsement of William Francis for the position of U.S. consul and minister to the Republic of Liberia, 1927*

Not long ago I served on a committee of the Minnesota Historical Society charged with the task of drawing up procedures for selecting art that was to hang in the state capitol. Two criteria we settled on for selecting the pieces were that they would reflect the full diversity of the people of the state and illustrate how Minnesotans participated in the political process. As a committee member, it wasn't my role to make recommendations—certainly not at that stage of the process—but I could not resist thinking that an image of Nellie Francis would be ideal. Within the majestic structure designed by noted architect Cass Gilbert, the capitol's art had long primarily displayed white men who had served as governors and as soldiers during the Civil War and the Dakota Conflict. On the four floors of marble-and-plaster walls, with soaring arches laced in gold leaf, there were only two likenesses of women—one, the wife of a governor; the other, a fanciful image of a bare-breasted Dakota woman standing off to the side with a basket hoisted to her head as Father Hennepin blessed St. Anthony Falls. That was it. I (and a few others) thought we could do better, starting with the portrait of an African American woman who had walked those very halls, lobbying legislators in 1921 for passage of an antilynching bill that she drafted. It wasn't just that a portrait of her was not on display, but that no one had even heard of her. I wanted to correct this.

In fact, I had wanted to write about her for some time. But her story, quite frankly, intimidated me. There are so many unwieldy and enigmatic dimensions to it. I knew that any in-depth review of the many significant things she did would be a useful addition to the canon of our history, but I always felt that such a treatment would merely gloss over the more important subject—namely, Francis herself. To fully understand her story, I also knew that it was necessary to interpret her character through the strictures of the many expected roles prescribed to her because of her gender, social class, political affiliations, legal status, her marriage, and especially the juxtaposition of her racial identity and physical appearance, all examined within the propriety of Victorian discretion of the late nineteenth and early twentieth centuries. So much of who she was compelled her to simultaneously defy as well as embrace convention and succeed in efforts that black and white men alike could not or would not achieve.

Nellie Frances Griswold Francis (this was indeed her name) was firmly grounded in an identity of blackness. Yet she seemed to understand at an early age the disarming—even disorienting—effect she had on white people because she was black, and refined, pretty, intelligent, articulate, and white-looking, and she used it all to openly promote the interests of her people. She must have recognized, if not fully in her youth then in adulthood, that white people wondered why she didn't make her life easier by simply passing for white. By the same token, her racial affiliation along with all the other attributes she possessed allowed such men as Andrew Carnegie and President William Howard Taft to grant her private audiences, led suffrage leader and soon-to-be mentor Clara Ueland to call her "a flame," and later inspired Senator Thomas Schall to endorse Nellie and her husband Billy to President Calvin Coolidge for government service. In an age when her race was commonly reviled, she made it palatable, even virtuous when some whites found in her the opportunity to further elevate themselves above the white rabble who spewed racial epithets and registered their hatred with the lynchers' noose. As such, she was a person who belied the nineteenth-century trope of the "tragic mulatto," a racially mixed person rejected by both white and black communities who as a result met a terrible end due to self-loathing. Francis, on the contrary, feeling equally at home in either world, was not inclined to compromise her identity as an "Afro-American," the term that race-conscious blacks used at the time to label themselves. She was indeed very clear as to who she was. She inherited that sense of clarity from her grandmother, born in antebellum Tennessee from parents who were master and slave, and after whom Nellie got her name, and she was nurtured by strong parents both listed by census takers as "mulattos"—an imprecise label for light-skin African Americans. Indeed, her parents grounded her within a stable, close-knit family, and she was mentored by an aunt who remained in the South to be active in education, women's suffrage, and civil rights. Nellie was, in short, imbued with the spirit of generations of strong women.

Often when she is mentioned in histories, her story is woven, and more often subsumed, within her notable marriage to William Francis, as illustrated in part in the epigraph of this Introduction. While I feel that their marriage was and remains an extraordinary subject of exceptional people who became even more so in the course of time as a mutually supportive couple, it is a singular treatment of Nellie Francis that I feel is long overdue, for the character that compelled a petite seventeen-year-old girl to speak about race before a white audience of thousands, within a city and time when racism and mob violence would soon erupt, was on full display before she married Billy, before, even, she had matured into adulthood. However, it would also be wrong to dismiss Billy's significance, for, despite his own accomplishment and strong political ambition, he fully supported his wife in her work, never seeing it as a threat to his own needs. He wasn't the reason why her story was subordinated to his own. In the interest of her race and gender, Nellie made her own way, just as she did in walking the halls of the state legislature to meet with lawmakers. She brought black and white women together even when she was discouraged to do so by the larger caucuses of both races. At considerable emotional expense, she was a woman with a mind of her own.

Even so, she always worked with others, and so to really know Nellie is also to know the other women around her of whose lives she was a part.

No one was closer to her than her older sister Lula. Born two years apart, she and Nellie were virtually inseparable for the remainder of their lives. Growing up as girls with talent during the tumultuous years of postwar Nashville and navigating through the inevitability of sibling rivalry, they seemed to settle into roles that they long played for each other—sharing the attention as Nellie sang and danced to Lula's accompaniment at the piano. It would be in Nellie's home, which Lula and her husband shared, that Lula would spend her final days. But other women as well left significant impressions on Nellie, both good and bad: from her deep affection for Maggie (Mrs. Booker T.) Washington, Maggie Payton, and Hallie Q. Brown, to an uncertain accord with Mary Church Terrell and Mary Talbert, to enmity with fellow state club leader Ione Gibbs. All of them, and many others with whom she interacted, illuminated Nellie's life, work, and personality and help to round out a full portrait of this most remarkable and complicated person.

Indeed, Nellie lived during a time that was deceptively complicated. Few women of her race and social class self-disclosed their deepest feelings, induced in large part by the strictures of their membership in church-oriented, proper society. Few even used their first names in public, identifying themselves instead with the honorific "Mrs." followed by their husbands' full name. In the tightly corseted conventions of the day, discretion ruled. As Nellie matured into middle age, her images in photographs typically captured her looking askance, demure, even melancholy, which, in part, befitted the fashion of the day. Yet her pose reflected someone who also seemed to favor keeping the world at arm's length. I came to realize that it was her privacy that was for her both recuperative and freeing. We are thus left with "seeing" Nellie perhaps in the manner that she preferred: not for the purpose of self-promotion but through her actions and her impact on the people, friends and rivals alike, who inhabited the world in which she lived and their impact on her. Although she rarely left in her own voice a record of her thoughts, I was able to piece together a portrait culled from her speeches and newspaper accounts—principally, *The Appeal,* which usually was the only record of note for much of the period of black St. Paul, a community that otherwise was largely ignored by white newspapers and opinion makers, and often overlooked by historians. With this,

I interpreted the evidence of her life within the context of racial and women's history during the late nineteenth and early twentieth centuries; and I acknowledged those moments in this record where I was left to speculate. I hope this book does Nellie Francis justice, as it allows us to see her more closely.

— 1 —

No Flowers

On Thursday, June 11, 1891, the twenty-first annual commencement of St. Paul Central High School was held in the People's Church, a massive structure of unique stone and brickwork whose architecture defied the conventions of church design for the late nineteenth century. People's Church was a three-story brick box that lacked a tower or steeple and had little in the way of religious symbolism: as one historian would later note, "It resembled more a giant clubhouse or school than a place of worship." But the true marvel, especially perhaps to anyone in the two-year-old church for the first time that June day, was the church's cavernous auditorium: one of the largest in St. Paul, holding 2,500 people. Situated in the heart of the edifice, the massive room consumed the upper two floors and dwarfed the more than one-thousand proud parents, family members, and friends who for the day, at least, could feel the collective sense of excitement, pride, and hope.[1] It was a fitting place to celebrate the largest class in school history, reflecting both the school's growth and the city's population that it served.[2]

Adding to the spectacle of the grand stage was the massive pipe organ situated to the rear of the seated class, fringed with palms. Surrounding the greenery, Seibert's Orchestra played its finest airs. Down from the organ front hung the class banner of silk with the Latin words "Aut viam inveniam aut faciam," meaning roughly "no smooth, easy pathway through the jungle of life, will bravely proceed to clear away the rubbish and make a pathway for themselves."

"How clear and conclusive the motto sounded last night," reported the St. Paul *Dispatch.* To the left of the stage sat the school dignitaries,

The People's Church Sanctuary, as it would have looked in 1891. Courtesy of the Minnesota Historical Society.

including board members, the superintendent, and the principal, and to the left was seated the class of 1891: eighty-four in all, of whom thirty were "clear eyed, manly young fellows, and fifty-four vivacious, ambitious and good-looking girls." Every girl wore a pretty white gown with a cluster of flowers on her belt and a smile on her face. "It was a brave and inspiring spectacle."[3]

The young people, within a short time of receiving their diplomas, would be in a position to attain a life better than their parents had experienced and thought possible for their own futures. For many, recent arrivals from several European countries—or, as *The Appeal* noted, "representing various Americanized nationalities"—this was what it meant to be an American.[4] Clarence Wells Halbert, the last student to speak and a future St. Paul attorney and political leader, argued that "brains were worthless without strong wills, and that ability was necessarily second to determination," and when he finished he dramatically turned to the school superintendent and principal and gave, as reported in the *Globe*, a "loving good-bye to them and the class. He then made his farewell to the teachers, and in a simple and manly fashion addressed the class with a robust 'Anglo-Saxon God be with you,' he bid the assembly adieu."[5] The reporter from the *Dispatch* felt that Halbert "was easily 'first,' both in style and matter."[6]

In a city so ethnically diverse, white skin predominated, and for most it was the emblem of being, or potentially being, a true American, if not in their time, in coming generations. To many of them, it was the rarely seen yet often-denigrated Negro who was foreign—indeed, none appeared to be present in the auditorium to experience this most American of rituals.[7] And yet the novelty of one certain colored girl, of whom many had heard so much and who would this day not only share the stage with their sons and daughters but dominate it, must have filled them with a measure of curiosity and ambivalence.

The attractive colored girl with light skin, just then stepping forward to deliver her speech, seemed positively exotic. Standing there now, erect, poised beyond her years, and seemingly quite at ease in front of the large watchful crowd that filled the seats on the main floor and balcony wrapping around her, she captured and held their focus. Nellie had often performed before the school throughout her years at Central as a star of the debate club, which staged plays, dramatic readings and musicals. The performances became a popular venue for a wider audience seeking wholesome entertainment, as well as a successful fund-raiser for the school's most ambitious projects. In 1888, her first year as a student at the renamed "St. Paul Central," the club raised enough funds for a fourteen-room annex for laboratories, a domed turret for an astronomical observatory, and a fixed telescope, making Central the only high school in the nation to have a lens ground and polished by the noted telescope maker Alvan Clark, whose company built some of the largest and best telescopes in the world, including the telescope for the renowned Lowell Observatory in Flagstaff, Arizona. "Miss Griswold," reported the *Pioneer Press*, "possessed an attractive and intellectual face, and a petite figure." Dressed in a soft cream-colored gown, noted the reporter, Nellie held no flowers, departing from the nineteenth-century custom for recitation by girls. Instead, her hands would be free "to company her words with suitable gestures."[8]

Nellie in 1891 while at St. Paul Central High School. Courtesy of the Minnesota Historical Society.

She was the only black graduate in her class, and the only black student to participate in the commencement's recitation competition.[9] And, it would seem, she was the first colored girl to enjoy the privilege she acquired as the embodied intersection of racial pride and beauty, for the fashion sense of the day seemed to prefer physical traits that appeared more white than African. It opened doors to opportunity; and with talent, as in Nellie's case, the world was possible. The attention she received from teachers, counselors, and the press, who all recognized her extraordinary gifts and ambiguous racial qualities, led to her being encouraged to attend the University of Minnesota and the Minnesota School of Dramatic Arts, which both offered her scholarships.[10]

The experience of most black students at Central High School was not as positive. "You must understand," wrote Lorenz Graham of the days when his mother attended Central, "that Negroes, as they were called at the time, and Indians were not encouraged to go to school. At Central High, faculty people advised black boys and girls to drop out. If they did not drop out voluntarily, they were given low grades and severe discipline by which they were literally forced out." Lizzie M. "Etta" Bell, the writer's mother, refused to drop out. In spite of challenges, she stuck with her studies. At the end of four years, she was deemed not ready to graduate. The principal told her that she knew enough that she would not need a diploma. "The principal told her, 'The others aren't getting diplomas. Why do you have to have one?' My mother had to stay an extra year, with her father constantly in arguments on her behalf. In 1894, she was graduated."[11]

The prejudice would last into the twentieth century. Estyr Peake, a dark-skinned, African-featured woman who would become a well-known newspaper writer in the Twin Cities area, reported that, because she was black, there had been many problems for her in her years at Central, from which she graduated in 1928. The counselors did not

St. Paul Central High School, circa 1888. Courtesy of the Minnesota Historical Society.

want her to take typing and bookkeeping; instead they told her to take home economics, because they all thought she would probably become a cook or maid. But she took her business courses anyway. When the seniors graduated, their typing teacher found jobs for them. Peake was the only one they could not place in a job, even though she could type seventy-five words per minute and take shorthand at 175 words per minute. She was the only black person in the class. Despite the problems, the one thing she remembered that was good was that the school had a very good English department—"one of the best in the country."[12] Janeabelle Taylor, a 1939 graduate and honor roll student, wrote that at the time of her graduation, "black students were discouraged from taking college-prep courses . . . The counsellors did not foresee black students as successful college graduates." It was her father who encouraged her to take courses at the university.[13]

But in Nellie, the teachers felt they saw something special. Her topic to be delivered that day before a roomful of white people, within a venue so clearly dedicated to their joy and sense of accomplishment, was titled "The Race Problem," which to some may have seemed incongruous to her obvious intelligence, budding refinement, and evident breeding, all elements that led some to conclude that Nellie was somehow above racial concerns. The visage of the seventeen-year-old colored girl, breaking rules by her very presence sharing the same grand dais with their own children, was as paradoxical as her message, which was both provocative and yet somehow nonthreatening. This was a big task for a petite girl, and, for that evening, the "best of her race."[14] The sanctuary grew silent.

As the *Pioneer Press* reported, "Speaking with a clear, silvery musical voice, soft, yet perfectly distinct and supplemented with faultless enunciation," Nellie reviewed briefly the former condition of the Afro-American, which had made him "less favored in his surroundings than the domestic animals on his master's plantation." She could not see where the white American derived the feeling of superiority that prompted him to refuse the Negro that panoply of citizenship equal to his own. She argued that in light of these facts it cannot be denied that should the Negroes be accorded the same rights and privileges as other people and given the same opportunities, there is no cause for apprehension as to the solution of the race problem.[15]

Nellie continued: "They have the highest respect for good government; they do not disturb the order of things by consolidated strikes and constant threatenings. In all the struggle against the rights of the Negro he is not found to be an enemy of society. He aims no deadly blows at the welfare of our government, nor does he attempt the overthrow of our laws under the cover of a Mafia or a Clan-na-gael.[16] He is no anarchist, no socialist, but thoroughly American, patriotic and law-abiding. May the people of this country, North and South, East and West, early awake to the sense of their duty in this matter and thoroughly realize that the race problem must be settled right, and then will the early rays of the morning sun kiss the fair land of a happy, peace-loving, justice-doing people; and then can all, black and white, American and foreign-born, shout with one glad shout that shall sound and resound from pole to pole, and from sunrise to sunset, this is the land of the free."[17] And further, "When the negroes are given equal rights and chances the race problem will solve itself. Let color be forgotten, and merit be the standard, and the race problem will disappear as mist before the rising sun."[18]

The *Pioneer Press* later reported that "No speaker of the evening was more enthusiastically received than Nellie Frances Griswold . . . She charmed the audience." Seeming to dismiss the meaning of her remarks to focus on the dramatic performance in which they were delivered, the reporter wrote that her "production" was greatly appreciated for its "freshness and naturalness that all enjoyed . . . [U]ndoubtedly there were many in the audience who would have given her first place."[19] The *Globe,* in noting the "remarkable oration" that she delivered "with great spirit and feeling in a clear, low-pitched voice," observed: "That the thunders of applause which rose as Miss Griswold finished did not raise the roof was a surprise to everybody. It seemed as if the audience would never [stop] clapping."[20]

Nellie, a seasoned performer even at age seventeen, was active in various cultural activities in her church, frequently—despite her young age—appearing in, directing, and even writing productions. One week after graduation, she played the mother in "Little Red Riding Hood;" the following January managed "Magic Mirror," for which she also wrote the dialogue, and two weeks later, at age eighteen, performed in a mock trial as a lawyer arguing for women's suffrage.[21] That evening at People's Church, she projected the full extent of theatrical presence and it was in the service of a more important message—her prescription for the welfare of her people. The proud editor of *The Appeal,* the state's only black newspaper, saw in her the voice of a new generation and was more succinct: "She proved to be a host within herself."[22]

But the evening was not St. Crispin's Day, and the charmed audience was hardly about to be rallied into a heroic charge against Jim Crow and Judge Lynch. This was St. Paul, Minnesota, where racial discrimination reigned and black men—even her father—were not safe to be in many neighborhoods. Nellie was graduating from high school in the advent of the last decade of the nineteenth century, when, nearly four years hence to the day, and only blocks away from where they now sat, black men on two separate occasions would come within a hair-breadth of being lynched, one at the prompting of the *Pioneer Press* and the *Globe,* both of which now sang her praise.[23]

And this audience would surely not rally on behalf of black people against the so-called Republican friends of the race, let alone confront Minnesota's black leaders for their timidity. This was a time in history when both enemies and the friends of the black people preferred the race to be docile. While lynchings were commonplace throughout the old Confederacy, northern friends of the race chastised and ostracized blacks who rose up to protest those horrible spectacles. Less than two years earlier, in November 1889, the fiery black editor T. Thomas Fortune had issued a call for a national organization to address the nation's racial problems, insisting controversially that only black men be allowed to become members. After the conference met on January 15, 1890, the *Pioneer Press* and the *Minneapolis Tribune* chastised the all-black group for nefariously being "a secret organization." Minnesota delegates John Adams, editor of *The Appeal,* and Fredrick McGhee, mentor to the future husband of the precocious Nellie Griswold, who had both already been punished by their Republican friends because of their affiliation with Fortune, felt uncomfortable with the "antiwhite" atmosphere of the convention. Because of a small black population with minimal community wealth, the Minnesota group tended to be less demanding and more fraternal with white patrons than the more aggressive national leadership of Thomas Fortune.[24]

Indeed, many of the leaders of Nellie's community cloaked their loyalty to the party within the conservative trappings of the Victorian middle class. While forming a rich, albeit complex, cultural expression that celebrated the Emancipation Proclamation and the advancement of their people in all corners of the nation, the black social elite partook in the infamous cakewalk. While advocating for political and social equality as defined by access to public accommodations, most of the black leaders would soon support Booker T. Washington's call for accommodation to black subjugation and white rule.[25] It was a community of mixed messages, and its leaders, especially those seeking a wider constituency as they sought elective office, set the tone. "The Afro-American," *The Appeal* stated, "must learn that when he aspires to a position that will place him over white men as well as those of his own race, his fitness must be judged, not by his own, but by the white man's standard."[26] It was a city—indeed, a nation—without black champions, a reason why Nellie, the only Afro-American of eighty-four graduates that evening, spoke, and on this topic in particular.

She did not win the competition, yet it is hard to imagine she thought that she would.

After the diplomas were conferred by Superintendent Gilbert, the judges of the competition announced the winner of the George Benz Prize, named for the successful German immigrant who had established a St. Paul restaurant and wholesale liquor business. Despite a "bearing on stage [that] was a little stiff," the award winner—giving a speech with the less than provocative title "Don't Be a Clam"—was a quiet boy with a misleading Brahmin-sounding name, Walter Bradford Cannon: "Do not despise your day and generation, do not destroy your life with pessimism or cultivate a fealty to a dead and buried and less excellent past; be a true citizen of these, our modern times, the best and noblest that have yet dawned in the world."[27]

Having arrived and lived in St. Paul for a shorter time than Griswold—shorter still at St. Paul Central, having recently transferred from Milwaukee, graduating valedictorian and editor of the school paper, matriculating from a four-year course in three years—he had little time for a social life. Given his interests, perhaps clearly referenced in his speech, he had little time and interest in being popular. He was a freethinker: as noted by one of his biographers, "a man of advanced ideas had in former years suffered for the opinions they entertained. The world is slow to adopt new ideas."[28]

Cannon's was an inspiring speech, though without the same oratorical appeal as Nellie's; yet it was the work of the quiet boy with few if any friends, an interest in science, and a promising writing talent, all crying out to be nurtured. Miss M. J. Newson, his high-school teacher of English literature and faculty adviser to the school newspaper, had discovered that talent and worked with him to give it a voice. The result was that the power of his words, which had impressed the judges of the competition for "its originality and style" more than Griswold's more popular presentation, won him top honors.[29] It was Newson who persuaded him to apply to Harvard and helped secure financial aid for him so that he could take a postgraduate year to prepare for the college entrance examination before departing for Cambridge in 1892. They would continue their correspondence until he graduated from medical school.[30]

Because of Newson's effort, Walter Cannon had the opportunity to become a noted and much-published scholar of anatomy and physiology, the burgeoning X-ray technology, and what later would be called posttraumatic syndrome.[31] He would teach for the entirety of his career at Harvard Medical School and turned down opportunities to head the medical school, the University of Minnesota Medical School, and Mayo Hospital. As the twentieth century experienced war and massive deprivation in all corners of the globe, Cannon would become an active participant in international relief efforts in Russia, Spain, and China, and in national organizations for civil liberties, democracy, and intellectual freedom.[32] But, no doubt to the satisfaction of Miss Newson, who retired in 1925, he never lost his muse for writing, submitting his bound volume "Letters Home from France and England, 1917–1918," to the *Atlantic Monthly* nonfiction prize contest of 1935.[33]

This was a stellar example of what a teacher could do for a student. In the least, with the same kind of mentoring, one wonders how many black students with aptitude and talent could have participated in this most American of pageants, the commencement ceremony at Central High. The lesson seemed to be that if the student was black, success was likelier to come if the student was a girl, talented, pretty, and fair. Absent those features, they would not be a part of the festivities, leaving whites with the conclusion that academic success was only possible for white children and exceptional white-looking blacks. Considering the speech that she elected to deliver, Griswold understood this fact of life in which she was the embodiment of absolution for white racism and she chose to reject its rewards by declining scholarships to the university and the Minnesota School of Dramatic Arts. She had wanted a high-school education, but she would not sacrifice the sense of herself in order to be what white people wanted her to be for their sense of redemption. Nellie Frances Griswold, St. Paul's "talented daughter, received honorable mention."[34] But it was their reward. Hers, as the *Pioneer Press* seemed to predict, would be on her own terms. "This young woman evidently has or ought to have a mission in life where she may be heard on behalf of the American colored people for whom she spoke so well last evening."[35] *The Appeal* agreed prophetically: "[O]ne who can produce such an oration has that within which will bring her before the public again and again, for a light set upon a hill cannot be hid, and [this editor] predicts for Miss Griswold a notable, brilliant career 'ere life's fitful dream in o-er."[36]

It was her spirit and not her skin color that would dictate her destiny. Yet, as a race person Nellie would not deny the bloodline of the people who bore her, nurtured her, and protected her from harm, and through all of this gave her an unwavering sense of who she was and what she had to give. To know her, who she was and who she would become, we must go further back and to Tennessee, where her grandmother, for whom Nellie was her namesake, was born.

– 2 –

The Legacy

Nellie's grandmother was born in slavery. Colonel Robert Allen, the man from whom she received her surname—her father—had served under General Andrew Jackson during the War of 1812 and had done well for himself. After the war, when he settled in Carthage, Tennessee, Allen took up the mercantile business as well as a law practice and later farmsteading, and soon established himself as a man of considerable standing in Smith County, leveraging his social position to serve four terms in Congress. He died in 1844 at age sixty-six, leaving a substantial sum to his second wife, Alethia VanHorn (his first wife, Rebecca Greer, had died in 1822), and his sixteen children.[1] His fortune grew between 1820 and 1830, if the ownership of slaves was any indication, for during the period he owned from twenty-seven to forty-one men, women, and children. One of them was a girl named Nellie, born in 1814 on the Allen's Carthage estate, where she grew up to be a servant in the colonel's home. Her surname, light skin, and features would be her only legacy from the influential family.[2] By 1840, the colonel had completely transformed his business into commerce, employing only a number of white skilled and unskilled laborers and selling off, freeing, or giving away all of his slaves—including Nellie, who went to his son Dixon just before the young Allen moved to Nashville to begin his tenure in the state legislature. In 1832, a year before Dixon's legislative term ended, he married Louisa C. Brown. In two years' time, he was dead.[3]

It is unclear whether his bride set Nellie free in the wake of his death, but it does appear that she was at least afforded a degree of autonomy when, in making Nashville her home, Nellie became a member of the white First Baptist Church in 1839. It was a logical spiritual home for her as it ministered to the black people of Nashville before, during, and after the Civil War, having had ordained in 1853 a freedman, Nelson Merry, as pastor of its African American congregation, a position he held until 1884.[4] The church's reputation for receiving free and enslaved blacks and "mulattoes" attracted one freedman named Frank Seay who met and eventually wedded Nellie Allen by the newly ordained Merry.[5] In 1856, their first child, a daughter named Maggie, was born.[6] Four years later, their second daughter, Alice, was born.[7] Four years after Alice's birth, 1864, their third daughter, Juno Frankie, was born.[8] With them, and with the end of the Civil War and unquestioned emancipation, a new chapter for the young family had begun.

In the years immediately following the end of the Civil War, thousands of slaves throughout the South left their plantations for opportunities to live as free men and women, and to many, Tennessee was an attractive destination. It appeared to be on the forefront of social and political change, for slavery was legally abolished in Tennessee even before the war officially ended and the General Assembly, early in April 1865, unanimously ratified the Thirteenth Amendment to the U.S. Constitution. During the Reconstruction period, Tennessee's former slaves continued the transition to freedom that had begun during the war, establishing communities outside the rule of slavery. They created churches, cemeteries, and schools, including the First Beale Street Baptist Church in Memphis, Tennessee's oldest surviving African American church edifice, and Jubilee Hall of Fisk University in Nashville, the nation's first permanent building for the higher education of black citizens. Black Tennesseans also commemorated their new status by holding annual Emancipation Day celebrations in communities throughout the state.

In 1866, Tennessee became the first former Confederate state to ratify the Fourteenth Amendment, which specified that no state should "deprive any person in life, liberty, or property, without due process of law." And shortly afterward, Tennessee became the first former Confederate state to return to the Union. Black men gained the state franchise in 1867, one year before Minnesota and two full years before Congress passed the Fifteenth Amendment. A small number of black citizens took positions in local and state government, including Sampson Keeble, a

Nashville barber who in 1872 became the first black citizen elected to the Tennessee House of Representatives. From 1865 to 1872, many former slaves in Tennessee took advantage of local offices of the Freedmen's Bureau, created by Congress to help manage the transition from slavery to freedom. Seeing these positive changes, former slaves and freedmen alike, many streaming in from neighboring states, were drawn in particular to Nashville, one of the few southern cities whose economy had not been reduced to shambles. By 1865, eleven thousand blacks settled in Nashville, up from four thousand in 1860.[9]

It was during this time that a teenage boy named Thomas H. Griswold arrived from Georgia, a state that had been devastated by war and that would be the last former Confederate state to reenter the Union. His parents were listed in the census only as "mulattoes" and Georgians, but otherwise unidentified in the unsettled postwar period when African Americans could rename themselves and reinvent their past. But as far as is known, Thomas was born approximately in 1852, and he would meet and soon marry the adolescent Maggie Seay on February 14, 1868. He found them a place at 125 McLemore Avenue in Nashville that would become their home, which they would share with Maggie's parents Nellie and Frank. To make a living, Thomas sold goods door-to-door, making friends and soon emerging as a community leader. In April 1869, responding to an urgent need for a final resting place for black Nashville residents, he joined other black leaders to found Mount Ararat Cemetery, later renamed Greenwood Cemetery, the future burial site of his yet-to-be-born daughter Nellie and her husband, the future consul to Liberia.[10] Frank, in turn, worked as a porter on the Nashville–Chattanooga line. They would live at the McLemore address until 1885.[11]

The Nashville in which they lived during those days was a place of great transition. After occupying the city for much of the last two years of the Civil War, by the end of 1866 the Union army disbanded and soldiers mustering out of service returned to their homes in the North, leaving a large urban black population to make its own way into an uncertain future. Prior to the war era, blacks lived with whites in close proximity throughout the city, though under a social code governed largely by the unwritten rules of white benevolence and paternalism—blacks knew their place. But the Civil War and the postwar urbanization of freedmen attracted more blacks to Nashville, making the old antebellum system of relatively benign racial controls unworkable. The sudden growth of a population of "unknown" Negroes in their midst compelled city officials to increasingly enact procrustean laws that banned "talking too loud," "using bad language," "speeding in a wagon," "having a party without permission," and "running and drumming." Social control for a nervous white population included the creation of residential concentrations of blacks around the periphery of Nashville proper. But these neighborhoods also provided a degree of security for new black arrivals, for residents raised money to establish orphanages, soup kitchens, employment agencies, and poor relief funds. Five black neighborhoods took form: Edgefield, which formed from the contraband camp, Black Bottom; Edgehill contraband camp; Trimble Bottom, and northwest contraband camp. Living on McLemore Avenue (which would later become Ninth Avenue), the Griswolds lived virtually in the shadow of the state capitol.[12] Thomas and Maggie were making a home for themselves. With the right to vote, Thomas had good reason to believe the future was theirs.

With forty thousand black men holding the ballot, leaders like Rev. Nelson Merry of First Baptist Church, Thomas and Maggie Griswold's pastor, were now stepping forward, the largest number of whom came from Nashville.[13] "[N]ow is the time for Tennessee to show the world," the opportunistic Governor William Brownlow, a prewar racist and proslavery ideologue, declared in January 1867, "that she belongs to the advanced guard on the great question of equal suffrage . . . Without their votes, the State will pass into disloyal hands, and a reign of terror . . . will be the result." Thus, by early 1867, Tennessee became the first southern state to establish biracial democracy in the aftermath of slavery.[14] But the Ku Klux Klan had other plans in mind.

Throughout the Tennessee countryside, whites rebelled against black men getting the vote. Ex-rebels, excluded from the franchise, found expression in the politics of force and terror. Wearing robes and hoods and riding under cover of night, these men terrorized blacks and whites allied with them. They wanted to defeat Unionist control of state government and restore the dominion of white supremacy. Brownlow's Unionists responded to this threat by organizing their own army, the

Tennessee State Guard, whose purpose was to uphold the governor's administration and political allies, who now included black voters.[15] Another civil war—a latter-day "Bleeding" Tennessee—seemed in the offing. Yet it is likely that Thomas Griswold, the recent transplant from Georgia who likely had witnessed Sherman's brand of all-out warfare, kept his focus on making a living on McLemore Avenue. His ballot was yielding positive results in local matters. He joined other black voters to effect a change in city governance. From 1870 to 1874, Nashville's Republican mayor, Augustus E. Alden, expanded its medical facilities and provided, bread, soup and firewood to the poor.[16]

But Griswold could not ignore the awful stories of Klan terror coming in from the rural counties. Nashville, for now, seemed to be an island of safety, even as legislators brooded up the hill in the General Assembly over the threat of new civil war to be waged within their own state. Eventually, the hopes of black Tennesseans were dashed when moderates and a few prominent Brownlow Unionists joined the call by Conservatives endorsing universal suffrage as a solution to the problem. In this case, "universal suffrage" was code for returning the ballot to the ex-Confederates. In a move that only surprised observers who did not understand Brownlow's artful dance to maintain control at the expense of principle, he joined the chorus to bring the ex-rebels back into the political fold. Even the anti-Brownlow Nashville *Republican Banner* proclaimed in a banner headline, "The Devil Is Not So Bad as He Is Painted!" Soon, Unionists of all stripes called for coalescing with respectable white Southerners and to disband the State Guard in an effort to mollify the Klan. But the Klan only saw this, as at Bull Run, as an enemy in full retreat.[17]

The victory of the Klan-friendly Conservatives in the election of 1869 was significant enough to reverse the strides made to advance civil rights. Ex-rebels, not yet able to vote, rejoiced at the returns. But within months, the new Conservative majority was poised to reinstall the ex-rebels into seats of power. Intimidation and violence had paid off. Almost immediately the new majority called for a constitutional convention to be held in 1870 that ratified new laws, like the poll tax followed by literacy tests and open ballot, that cumulatively had the effect of disenfranchising thousands of black voters and weakening civil-rights protections. Another such reversal was a constitutional prohibition against intermarriage between blacks and whites "or descendants of Negro ancestors to the third generation," which had to be unnerving for the newly wedded Griswolds, who by virtue of being listed as "mulattoes" could have been viewed, in these most uncertain times, as people who violated the new law. Within one year's time, from getting married and being granted the vote, to becoming disenfranchised and possible criminals simply for being the offspring of their parents, Tennessee had become a dangerously unpredictable state in which to live. The new constitution was overwhelmingly approved by the voters in March. In November 1870, John C. Brown—a Democrat, former Confederate, and member of the Ku Klux Klan—was elected governor of Tennessee in an election that signaled the end of the Reconstruction Era in Tennessee.[18]

It was now open season on black people, particularly in the rural counties of the state where the Klan could intimidate and murder blacks and their white allies with impunity; such vengeance was intended not only to disenfranchise black men, but also to deny them the opportunity to own land and start businesses. It was a campaign to turn the clock back. Starting in the late 1860s, black Tennesseans began emigrating into Kansas to create all-black communities, and the movement continued into the next decade, reaching its zenith in 1879 when thousands left the state. By the 1870s, blacks in middle Tennessee counties—which included Davidson, where Nashville was located—had begun to join the exodus, inspired largely by one man: Benjamin "Pap" Singleton.[19]

Called "Pap" because of his advanced age and kindly disposition, Singleton was not an imposing man, but slender and shorter than most men, "a light mulatto with long, wavy iron-gray hair, gray mustache, and thin chin whiskers."[20] At various times a slave, a fugitive, and a self-proclaimed "scavenger," he had been on the fringe of society most of his life and so could more readily envision building a life that was wholly separate from a white-dominated society. In espousing the formation of all-black communities, Singleton, a trained carpenter and cabinetmaker, founded the Edgefield Real Estate Association, an organization that sought to secure land purchases for black Tennessee farmers, and

Activist and former slave Benjamin "Pap" Singleton, circa 1880. Courtesy of kansasmemory.org, the Kansas Historical Society.

he saw in Kansas a perfect opportunity. Singleton first began to take emigrants to Kansas in the late 1860s, although the highest numbers came during the economic depression of the early 1870s. Eventually, he helped found three farming settlements in Kansas: the Dunlap Colony in Morris and Lyon counties, Nicodemus Colony in Graham County, and the Singleton Colony in Cherokee County, comprised of some three hundred emigrants from Nashville. He reportedly said, "the whites [of Tennessee] had the lands and the [cents], and the blacks had nothing but their freedom . . . [Blacks] ought to be trying to get homes of their own, lands of their own, instead of depending on renting from their former masters or subsisting." Singleton had concluded that blacks who strove to better themselves while living among white people would inevitably face hostility. Emigration to form black colonies was the only solution for black development. He insisted that black people must be segregated from the whites. Whether whites were friendly or not, he felt that blacks should be separated for the good of black people.[21]

This campaign would likely have caught Griswold's eye, because posters that promoted emigration to Kansas could be seen in every black community, distributed by preachers, porters on railroads, and employees on steamboats, and emigration was the subject of much conversation. At meetings, Pap would excite the crowd by asking his people to stand together and understand their duty to the race. Now was the time to go, or, as he more colorfully exhorted, "Place and time have met and kissed each other." He wanted emigrants with "muscle in their arms," and rejected "political negroes" and "educated negroes" for whom he had a profound and bitter contempt, likely because they generally opposed his emigration movement. Singleton claimed that most northern blacks who were well situated feared that Negro migration to the North would undermine the positions of those already there.[22] Neither Nashville nor the North could be a secure home for black folks.

Nevertheless, the Griswold family stayed in Nashville within the relative security of the city's Fourth Ward, even though the city had its own Klan chapter founded by John W. Morton, who had notably performed the service that initiated Nathan Bedford Forrest into the organization.[23] Although their man—in a perverse twist of history, named John Brown—occupied the governor's house located just blocks from Edgefield, rural areas remained particularly at the mercy of white terror.[24] Although darkness seemed to be descending all over the state, by 1870, even with the reenfranchisement of Confederate veterans and a new draconian constitution, northern funds for educational institutions flowed into the city, establishing Fisk University, Central Tennessee College, Roger Williams University, and Meharry Medical School for the freedmen, and to Vanderbilt University and Peabody College "for the reconstruction of the white minds of the South."[25] Opportunity was everywhere, for the area around their neighborhood included churches, houses of industry, offices of daily newspapers, free schools, banks, hotels, foundries, spectacular homes, and restaurants that catered to well-heeled white clientele and provided enterprising blacks with opportunities to acquire skills to augment their income.[26] In this environment, Thomas acquired and refined the courtly manners of black men who could enter the class of the black elite and work well with white men of influence. Learning to wait tables while selling goods door-to-door would provide for his young wife and children-to-come and get them educated. Working hard, taking advantage of every opportunity day after day for the good of the family, was what a man did. And it all laid the groundwork for its own reward, for in 1873, the same year Pap Singleton led three hundred Nashville emigrants to Kansas, the first of two lights shone over 125 McLemore with the birth of Maggie and Thomas's first daughter, Lula—and a year later, on November 7, with the birth of Nellie Frances.[27]

— 3 —

Mr. Griswold

Very little is known about Nellie's childhood years in Nashville. But what can be pieced together is a likely portrait not just of that period in her life but of the specific moments that seemed formative to the budding future leader, moments that were not principally experienced by this little girl but by her father—Thomas Griswold—who, without even being aware that he was doing so, perhaps modeled her future choices in life. Already showing signs of precociousness, and before even becoming of school age, young Nellie may have noticed, if not fully comprehended, traits that would later set her in the direction of public service, traits that etched within her an undeniable sense of duty, a drive to lead and give voice to the underserved. She was her father's little girl.

Every day, he went forth into a city that, despite its advances from an untamed frontier settlement at the beginning of the century, was still, in part, a raucous waterfront town along the Cumberland River with its share of taverns and brothels catering to transient longshoremen and dockworkers. During the 1870s, Nashville's prosperous commercial sector had attracted a large number of poor Irish and black laborers, many of whom were quartered in crowded housing along the waterfront and on the fringes of the downtown business district. A sizable black community called Black Bottom was located in the low-lying area south of Broadway between downtown and the elite neighborhood of Rutledge Hill. A growing red-light district existed on the other side of Capitol Hill, a few blocks from the stately residences of Vine and High Streets. Saloons sprang up in these neighborhoods as well as along the river and on lower Board, and these areas became centers for gambling, vice, and crime. Because walking was the primary form of transportation and the city's streets were shared by all residents, opportunity for contact among the different social classes was constant—much to the discomfort of the middle and upper classes.[1]

On McLemore, located farther away from the waterfront and just beyond the shadow of the state capitol that loomed high on a hill, the Griswolds lived close to but not within the tawdry busyness of the downtown area, where they could safely shelter the girls under the watchful eyes of their mother and grandmother. Mr. Griswold, just a few short years after arriving in Nashville, had already remarkably transformed himself from laborer to vendor to successful merchant and community leader. Like other black men of the times who strived to bring their families into the middle class, he worked hard to afford for Mrs. Griswold to stay home with the girls. With her parents living with them and the added income that Grandpa Frank Seay brought home, the girls spent their first few years within the protection of a black family fast becoming middle class. To them—unlike the attitudes of white America that correlated race with deprivation—class and racial pride were one and the same, as one of Griswold's cohorts had proclaimed at the dedication of Mount Ararat Cemetery on May 1, 1869: "We must have education, valuable property, and plenty of money; and we should labor to secure colored teachers in the colored schools of the city."[2] Until that day, the Griswolds would shield their girls from public school, where they would first encounter, then continue to encounter, the blunt and soul-crushing force of racism from school segregation, inferior education, and a steady regimen of low expectations fostered by patronizing white teachers who only saw the futures of their colored scholars as a continuation of their parents' degraded lives. Griswold, along with attorney James Napier and their cohorts, would try to change this for the good of their community and hopefully, especially where Daddy was concerned, before Lula and Nellie were old enough to enroll. Until then, in all probability, they were schooled at home even at a young age.

In fact, the refined talent that both sisters would display as early as the first few months after their arrival in Minnesota suggests that they were exposed during their preschool years to books and music. Their mother likely provided this part of their education. Because a majority of free blacks in Nashville were literate by 1850, it is likely that Mrs. Griswold was one of that number.[3] Thomas's business acumen and the prestigious commercial district location that he was able to acquire for his business suggest that he also had some education as well as a fluent use of proper English. In fact, both parents probably made it a point to routinely speak in this manner as a way of reinforcing diction with their girls, which would prove beneficial because that would tend to signal to white people that the girls were exceptional. But knowing that talking like white people could trigger the wrong reaction, and even spark resentment from some black folks who might feel that the girls were putting on airs, their parents worked to instill in them the idea that so-called proper speech did not replace racial pride. Yet, the parents may have taught them that even though one could not control what others thought of them, ultimately it was only the family that would keep them both self-aware and levelheaded, and that only the family could be relied on for enduring love, support, and understanding. They were raised with a strong sense of a family identity. In years to come, and through much adversity, Lula, who would graduate from high school the year before Nellie to no fanfare and was destined to forever live in her shadow, would "never be separated in life" from her younger sister.[4] One imagines that the whole family recognized Nellie's special budding talent and they nurtured it—her ability to carry a tune and dramatize the sentiment of the lyric at a young age, possess a captivating stage presence, and, above all, exude self-confidence. Yet, it seems that with all this nurturing, they did not let it go to her head, for she would exclusively place her talents for the rest of her life, and without pecuniary reward, in the service of the church and the black community.[5]

What additional formal instruction the girls may have received came from either a church-sponsored school, a benevolent society, or a northern-sponsored missionary school whose numbers markedly increased immediately after the war.[6] Still, as historian Bobby Lovett notes, "the blacks wanted [free] public schools."[7] And not just "public schools" per se, but schools of quality, schools equal to those offered to white children, schools taught by teachers of their own race who saw the children's future as their own. It would be this work that Nellie's father would undertake. By the time she was born in 1874, he had already established a name for himself within their immediate community of Nashville's Fourth Ward, starting with addressing strikingly its most rudimentary need—disposing of its dead—and doing so in association with an emergent racial elite.[8]

With the end of slavery, black men were able to form secret societies, which allowed them to discuss progressive issues in detail and security, set and maintain codes of ethics, and develop strategies for black uplift. One such group of men of note was comprised of thirty-seven members of Nashville's black civic and business leadership, as the (white) Nashville *Republican Banner* called them, "the more intelligent [elite] portion of their race."[9] These "elite" men made it a point to be present at every dedication of new structures in an effort to impress the freedmen with the ideas of socioeconomic progress and give credence to the existence of a Negro elite. Through Masonic lodges and mutual aid societies, they learned to pool their resources and solicit money from the masses to start businesses and even cemeteries.[10] Being a principal in establishing a cemetery launched Griswold into becoming a community leader, and a crucial first step it was.[11] In April 1869, the members of the Sons of Relief and the Colored Benevolent Society organized Mount Ararat, the city's first black cemetery. Through a prominent white Republican, wealthy and influential black men led a community-wide effort to pay for the necessary property. "Thomas H. Griswold, the owner of [53 Marketplace] in the prestigious City Market, became secretary of the Mt. Ararat Cemetery."[12] Nellie's father, a successful merchant in the eyes of the black elite, had been entrusted with the welfare of the community's first black institution.[13] Immediately upon Nellie's birth, his focus turned to education for his infant girls and black teachers who would nurture them.

As late as 1875, there were no blacks among the seventy public-school teachers in the system. Yet, black residents made up 35 percent of the city's students. Black teachers were only permitted to work in county schools. Between 1878 and 1885, when Griswold and Napier consistently won elections from the overwhelmingly black Fourth Ward to the city council, both men demanded that qualified blacks be hired as public-school teachers, insisting to white officials that black teachers would provide incentives to colored pupils. In his 1877 annual report, an irate superintendent wrote, "I have devoted this chapter to discussing them [blacks] because some of our leading colored citizens are agitating the question of substituting colored for white teachers." The "leading colored citizens" were right, as Lovett noted. "[T]here local freedmen's colleges already produced teachers."[14]

But these were not the only concerns. Few black children reached the top grade (8th), and there were no black high schools in Nashville and the entire county. At a time when the county Negro public schools were no more than one-room shacks with a wood- or coal-burning stove in the middle of the floor, Napier introduced a city council resolution to open a Negro high school in Nashville. With the support of local reformers, Napier and Griswold persuaded the council to approve the resolution. But the school board took no action. Although black schools, along with principals and teachers, would be added in time, white school authorities continued to openly discriminate against black parents, children, and staff, paying principals, teachers, and employees less than their white counterparts and allowing white teachers in black schools, but not allowing black teachers in white schools.[15] By 1880, the paltry conditions of the colored schools drove desperate black parents to consider the incendiary step of sending their children to white schools where they surely would be refused admission. One year later, the Nashville Board of Education opened Pearl High School.[16] It seemed that the efforts of Nellie's father had paid off.

One can only speculate when or even whether children become aware of the respect that the community holds for the parent, a respect that enhances in their eyes the father's stature beyond that of simple breadwinner and authority figure within the household. In this instance, so much possibly relied on the extent to which he brought them along into the larger world, especially the one daughter who did not shy away but seemed rather to hold the greater fascination for the adult realm of ceremony, celebration, and protocol. In this moment the proud but protective father may have noted that his younger daughter was growing into an appealing little girl who appeared at ease while being on display before a charmed gathering, as may have happened in 1879 when the five-year-old Nellie was held by her father as he was about to assume his seat on Nashville's city council in his first of five years of service, representing the largely black Fourth Ward.[17] Whether or not he later explained what the attention was all about cannot be known. But what is evident is that his perspicacious second-born would carry over some of the traits he used for political success into her future work, traits that would first appear in the spring of 1891 as she practiced the speech that she would deliver at her high-school graduation, traits that likely confirmed what he probably always felt: that Nellie was his favorite child. Yet, there was nothing too big for him to sacrifice for either daughter if it was for their welfare. They, his family, would always come first.

In 1881, with Lula already in public school and Nellie eligible to attend, her parents were no more confident than before that she and sister Lula would receive a good education. The girls were fast outgrowing what their parents could provide and they were desperate to look elsewhere. The opportunity presented itself in 1883. While traveling as part of a delegation from Nashville to Chicago to inspect the gas plant, Thomas learned of the educational advantages of the schools there. and in St. Paul, a place noted for its progressive relations with its black residents and its integrated schools—black and white children would receive the same educational opportunities. Within the year, in a similar move that would create problems for Nellie when she chose family over civic duty to the women's organization that she would later be leading, her father resigned his seat, sold his business, and relocated his family to Minnesota, where they would temporarily share a house with a family who had also moved there from Nashville.[18] The change that left Napier alone to battle the city council and school board may have felt like abandonment as the momentum for the equitable opportunity for black schoolchildren came to a halt. Three years later, in 1886, James Napier lost his bid for reelection to the city council. The political climate had indeed changed. No blacks would be elected to the council again until 1911.[19] But that could no longer be Mr. Griswold's primary concern.

★ ★ ★

Since the mid-1880s, many leaders of black society in St. Paul and Minneapolis did not welcome the arrival of southern blacks into the state for they were viewed as unfamiliar with urban living and with the subtle nuances of northern racial détente. As a result, these new black arrivals were relegated to the bottom of the social hierarchy.[20] The Griswold family was part of the migration that inflated the black population of about 490 African Americans in 1880 to 3,150 by 1910. But they were soon considered exceptional, and in the early years, Thomas Griswold held a spot among the patriarchy of black St. Paul, as illustrated in the prominent role he was asked to fill during the national education convention that convened in St. Paul in 1890.[21] It had seemed then that he was about to assume a leadership role in his adopted community, perhaps resuming that which he had walked away from seven years earlier in Nashville, as a business owner and politician. But leadership in both spheres required financial stability and, at least for the time being, he had to settle for what jobs he found.

It had to be unnerving for this proud man who had uprooted his family to take a leap of faith by moving to an unfamiliar northern city, having severed ties with extended family members, friends, and business and political contacts in Nashville; but their future now was in Minnesota. By March 1884, one year after he had resigned his seat on the Nashville city council, he relocated the family to St. Paul and spent the next few months in a cramped apartment with old Nashville friends, unable to find work. Finally, that summer, Griswold heard of an opportunity in the nearby town of White Bear Lake, where he worked as a waiter at the Ghat-o-Gay Hotel. It was here that the considerable talents of his daughters were put on display. Lula accompanied Nellie on the piano while she sang and danced, and the girls "were frequently included in the hotel programs arranged for the guests." By fall, they had returned to the city, where Tom Griswold would never again be without work.[22]

His continuous employment helped the family's standing within their adopted community. He was a clear provider as well as a generous donor to community activities; but it was as much, if not more, the family's active and tithe-paying membership in Pilgrim Baptist Church that had placed the imprimatur of respectability on the Griswold name. The good works of Maggie and the girls more than made up for his absences from church affairs. Nellie, by now a precocious teenager, had begun writing plays and directing "entertainments" for the church, while the older Lula was pressed into service at Pilgrim and St. James African Methodist Episcopal (AME) church in Minneapolis, eventually becoming much in demand as the preferred accompanist in the life of colored folks of the two cities. In her twenties, Lula became the organist at Pilgrim; she turned down the check they paid her.[23] The family's selflessness, the cornerstone of the public service that Thomas had preached to his girls, now elevated the Griswold name even higher within their adopted community. In 1890, Nellie could take note of her father's growing stature when he served as a committeeman for the National Education Convention.[24] Less evident was that he had to leave the festivities early to wait tables, and it was waiting tables that kept him from attending Nellie's high-school graduation.[25]

By now, Nellie had become accustomed to her father's absences. Indeed, she understood the arrangement all too well and considered it his sacrifice to the family and to the community; and she especially recognized his devotion to her when he afforded the dress she wore for her big moment. But still, the words she spoke meant more to her than any that she had recited in previous performances, for he had been the source of her inspiration, and she hoped that he would be there in the audience to witness her ability to sway a white audience that was undisposed to racial equality. But in his absence, Lula would later write, "[S]he felt something missing. He wasn't there to see what she learned from him, and share in her triumph . . . [It was like] those words did not mean as much to him."[26] But Nellie apparently chose not to share these feelings with Thomas. In years to come, she would better understand just how much the words that she delivered at her graduation ceremony had meant to him. But until then, his presence in her life increasingly became both spectral and incommunicative; she saw the unarticulated toll on him as his powers ebbed, and she seemed to fritter her potential away.

She would never know how he felt about her declining the scholarships that were offered to her, choosing instead to work in the stenographer pool of West Publishing Company. However, the girls did know that he wanted them to have a better education in the North than in Nashville, which he felt they would get in Minnesota—access to opportunities that could refine their talents and expose them to the larger world that came with attending a school with different races and classes of children, and in doing so, become a leader of her generation. The fact that the lynching of Eph Gizzard, a black man lynched for supposedly raping a white woman in Goodletteville, Tennessee, in 1892, could still happen at the end of the century, just blocks from their former house in Nashville, showed that her willingness to speak out against the national problem of racism would be needed more than ever.[27]

From Nellie's childhood on, he could see that she had special qualities to move people, reaffirmed in laudatory accounts from the white newspapers that had covered her speech. She was articulate and at ease in public, personable yet strong-willed, poised yet motivated by a sense of right and wrong, and with the ability to connect with all sorts of people—qualities that he had nurtured in Nashville by taking her along to political gatherings and later talking about what they had seen. Now, no longer in that arena, he was not in a position to teach her anything. The magic he felt in the early days in Nashville had dissipated in the grueling need to provide for his family while both his age and a growing sense of irrelevancy were catching up to him. The powerful father figure he had once been was no more, and, one imagines, he saw his decline every time he looked into her eyes.

In 1893, two years after her high-school graduation, Tom Griswold walked his nineteen-year-old daughter down the aisle to marry her fiancé Billy Francis; a year later, Lula married Thomas King.[28] Befitting the role of a proud father, he sought to provide her with the proper send-off. To afford these expenses, he took a job as a porter on the railroad, which seemed to offer more income and prestige. He had brought the family to Minnesota in the mid-1880s, at the time when the railroad era had begun in earnest in St. Paul. The two great transcontinental lines, the Northern Pacific and the Great Northern Railways, linked with regional companies to make freight and passenger transportation readily available, offered a certain type of black man—courtly, well-heeled, well-spoken, with a light skin, which always seemed to be an asset for the servant class—a chance to make a reasonable wage while traveling to the nation's big cities. The job seemed made to order for a man like Thomas Griswold.[29] But more: judging from other black men who served as porters, it seemed that through his new associations he might become a part of a new black elite, not unlike what he experienced during the early days in Nashville. Black men of high quality were already lining up in his city. As the Minneapolis *Afro-American Advance* would later report, "St. Paul has more Afro-American graduates of law and other departments of science, in the railroad service, than Minneapolis."[30] But in short time, Thomas found that the experience as a railroad porter was not as rewarding as he had hoped.[31]

By 1895 Pullman coaches acquired a standard-size car fully equipped by an elegant interior of black walnut furnished with Axminster carpets and beautiful chandeliers. The men hired to be porters were required to be indefatigably courteous to their passengers while tending to their every need and desire. Each day the porters had to break down and make up as many as 22 berths while being careful not to inconvenience the passengers. Porters received passengers and helped them to board, carried their baggage, saw that their clothes were brushed, and their berths made up and pulled down when requested, and served food and beverages from the dining car. Each night they were also required to shine all shoes left in the aisle outside the berths. All were ordered to answer to the name "George," custom from slavery day when slaves were called by their master's name.[32]

The Pullman rule book limited porters to only three hours of sleep the first night out and none for the remaining days. Stationed in the men's smoker where they could be reached by sounding a buzzer, porters were expected to be at the beck and call of passengers at all hours of the night, standing by for any emergency and ensuring that their charges got off at the proper destination. While they tried to sleep on the leather seats of the smoker, they were often awakened when passengers went to the bathroom or when those who had trouble sleeping merely wanted to talk. Their meager wages, for which, in 1883, they were paid twelve dollars per month, made them dependent on tips, compelling them to always be obsequious. When one passenger who remembered Thomas's true name called out for "Uncle Tom," he jumped to it as was expected of him. Porters received no overtime pay until they had logged at least four hundred hours a month or eleven thousand miles, whichever occurred first.[33] It was getting harder coming home bone-tired with little to show for his labors except for the unspoken toll of both having to be thankful, courtly, and demeaned by people who didn't bother to learn his name. But even more troubling was what he learned in the course of his work, and what it suggested about Nellie's line of work.

Only days after she married Billy Francis, having completed her course in stenography, she found employment in the office of West Publishing Company, which published law books. Her color was not an obstacle. She demonstrated that she had good concentration and language skills, as required for the position, a quiet intellect, as well as providing an eye-catching addition to the male-dominated stenographer pool. Yet, if she had any regrets, after her years of transcribing business meetings, taking dictation, and preparing legal documents, she apparently never said so. It was good steady work with a future, if she wanted it, and she and Billy certainly needed the money. Although she was the only Afro-American in the pool, she thought it feasible to work herself into a position where she could help someone else of her race land employment. But the fact that she was employed at all seemed to revive her father's misgivings, though it soon proved to be based on more than that. In his work as a porter, cleaning up behind male passengers traveling on business, he would have seen the lascivious postcards businessmen left behind that depicted coquettish women in secretarial roles, sitting on their employers' laps or positioned more compromisingly—the so-called prerogatives of bosses.[34] It would be hard for this father to imagine that his lovely daughter would not fall prey to the carnal desires of her employers, and he was impotent to protect her.

In neither case as a father of a married woman with a mind of her own nor as a railroad porter did he dare say a word. The events that occurred earlier that year of 1895 reinforced the reticence of the Afro-Americans of St. Paul to say anything other than to be agreeable to white men. In April, and later, in June, the city became the staging area of two separate attempted lynchings of black men accused of raping white women. The *Pioneer Press,* Minnesota's newspaper of note, which four years earlier had sung its praise for Nellie Francis and the speech she delivered on the topic "The Race Problem," called the mob's attempt to lynch one of the men "a burst of righteous wrath." Another newspaper, the *Globe,* which had likewise sung his daughter's praise, called the second attempted lynching "thrilling and remarkable."[35] It was therefore logical for Thomas to conclude that just treatment for black men and for women was chimerical. He seemed to withdraw more into himself. As his older daughter Lula would later note, "He kept his judgments to himself."[36]

Thomas worked the rails one more year, then once again, in 1896, found a job as a waiter at the exclusive Aberdeen Hotel located just three blocks from the prestigious Summit Avenue that catered to a well-heeled clientele. Governor John A. Johnson would call the hotel home from 1904 to 1910 and the St. Paul Cathedral architect Emmanuel Masqueray lived at the Aberdeen for several years.[37] Thomas knew how to do work the employer needed done, but he no longer had the stomach for it. Even the energy to keep alive the memory of the man he had once been, with aspirations to do great things, had waned from the fatigue of working hard in a string of demeaning jobs. After a year at the hotel, he moved into the kitchen to do work that did not require that he have personal contact with customers who felt a sense of privilege over his race. Meanwhile, his illness, which had been coming on for two years, was getting the better of him. In November 1899, he was bedridden, waiting for his time to come, wordlessly lying in a room full of well-wishers whom he did not want to see.

With all the prestige that Pilgrim Baptist enjoyed, its noted membership, and its educational and cultural programs, it had made little effort to help the city's poorest and most destitute Negroes, which he now must have feared was Maggie's fate the moment his pay stopped coming in. In fact, none of the black churches in St. Paul and Minneapolis ever developed a systematic program of social welfare for their members. Aid to the destitute and impoverished was more often spiritual than material, and usually only came through visits from ministers and members of the congregation. Church historian Jon Butler notes: "Occasional contributions apparently were made to poor members of the congregation but Pilgrim Baptist seldom spent more than sixty dollars a year on such efforts, about 5 percent of their yearly budget in the late 1890s." The church had raised far more to pay for its new structure, sometimes through methods that seemed heavy-handed.[38] How would any of that pointless activity keep a roof over his wife's head when he was gone? It must have angered—even shamed—him to know that he would not leave her in better straits after his lifetime of hard work and sacrifice. No longer the provider, no longer the protector of his girls: memories served only to measure his fall from grace. His encroaching demise was turning him into the sort of man he never respected—someone hoping that others would carry the responsibilities for his loved ones. It was his wife and girls at his bedside who seemed to most draw from him, Lula later noted, "the hint of a tear."[39]

But as for the rest—the ministers and church friends most concerned—Tom Griswold, ever unrepentant, seemed to care little for God's grace. A churchgoer in Nashville, he refused to join any church in St. Paul, until finally, after several days, *The Appeal* reported, "light broke into his soul," perhaps finally in deference to Maggie and the girls' wishes, the only thing he had left to give them—a certain peace of mind. On November 9, too tired to carry on, and "assured that [God's] forgiveness was his," he passed away.[40] Later, as the Griswold women went through his things, they found an old folded clipping from a newspaper. Nellie recognized the words. They were hers from her 1891 commencement speech. He had kept them all this time.[41]

Billy

He could not be at her father's bedside in the end. He had to work. For as long as Nellie had known her husband since they married in 1893, he must have seemed to her to understand how the world worked and he was a man on the move. Like her father in his younger years, Billy was filled with ambition and knew how to work hard to achieve great things, from being a messenger for the Northern Pacific Railway to becoming an office boy—which brought him closer to the action, where he could see at least the workings of the outer office—and then working as a stenographer in the legal department, which brought him inside the executive office. Working assiduously for a corporate office at least gave him a chance to grow, mastering skills that the office needed, always presenting himself as eager to learn and perform and to show himself to not be just dependable but trustworthy, while expertly managing the delicate balance of ambition and modesty. And, especially for a black man, he understood the right way to carry himself: to the extent possible, not so much to minimize as to deflect the distraction of his race, skirting along the line between good manners and obsequiousness; he would not carry the white man's bags, but he would carry his attaché case.

These were promising traits to catch the eye of the boss, and Billy felt it within his grasp to become the first black man to become a junior executive. The very fact that such opportunities existed in this otherwise white-only office suggested the presence of a crucial and rare fact: Billy had lucked into working for a boss who was willing, for now, to give him a chance. It was thus easy to imagine—despite the racism that governed society—that there were certain white men who, if the corporation could afford it, would do the right progressive thing, men who deserved to be highly regarded, men who wanted to reward the "useful" Negro, but who were not deterred by the aggressive racial politics of radicals like Ida B. Wells-Barnett, W. E. B. Du Bois, and Monroe Trotter, white men who respected Booker T. Washington and all he stood for—Billy's man.

Billy was, in other words, a man who understood it all, agile enough to take an alternate route to success, if need be, as reflected in his acquiring a certificate in osteopathy.[1] Yet, he could not hope to go as far without the right partner, someone with charm, intelligence, talent, and beauty and commitment to him—a companion and confidant. This was Nellie. The partnership they forged would be based on communication. There would be no gulf between his job and their home, no long periods of silence and brooding fatigue, no Sunday services without the head of the household, no more witnessing of a patriarch who had loved, provided for, and protected his family fade wordlessly away. Nellie would be for Billy, he for her, and they would talk about everything.

Thus, in 1901, they likely discussed his next move when the opportunity presented itself—a clerkship, the same kind of position that the company's president, Charles Sanger Mellen, had held when he began his railroad career in 1870. But this job would be in the legal department, in the heart of the company's activities, for these were the days of antitrust litigation. Both Billy and Nellie, by now a stenographer of ten years at West Publishing, which specialized in law books, could see the job as a promotion. In March, Billy began his new assignment.[2]

Nellie was thirteen years old when she first saw Billy at a friend's birthday party in 1887. He was eighteen and sang in a quartet that called itself the "Little Four" and had been retained to perform that evening. He had a refined manner, was slim and handsome, and he sang and danced in a way that sparked the girl's imagination. She was, of course, too young for him, so, constrained by the rules of polite society, she kept her attraction to herself. But her mother noticed. Billy had a good job with the railroad company—one that exercised his brain rather than his brawn—and he was a churchgoer, which was of crucial importance to Mrs. Griswold. Mr. Griswold, always at work, had ceased to attend church, which in itself was not unusual. In the St. Paul of that time, black churchgoers tended to be female.[3] Thus, it greatly impressed Mrs. Griswold when she learned that one of the first things the young man did after moving to the city with his mother, just a few months earlier, was to establish himself as a dedicated Christian by joining Pilgrim Baptist. This provided her with the added benefit of having more sets of eyes to scrutinize his sincerity. Later that year, in October, at Nellie's fourteenth birthday party, the Little Four was hired to perform in their home.[4] Six years later, in 1893, after a proper courtship, her daughter and the young man married in splendid fashion.[5] They were now Mr. and Mrs. William T. Francis, but Nellie called him Billy.

It is hard to imagine that Mr. Griswold had much to say in the matter, not because he disapproved or that his opinions bore no weight around the house, but because he was always working to serve the white-owned establishments that were always seeking "col'd" help, often holding down two jobs so his wife could stay home with the girls, just as he had done in the early days in Nashville, except that in addition to meeting the basic needs of the household as he had then, he now needed to earn the most to afford his daughters' weddings—Nellie's in 1893, Lula's in 1894.[6] A wide gulf divided his "work" world, which often abraded his dignity, from the world he and his loving wife and daughters inhabited. Although they understood his devotion to them, he never let on the toll it took on his soul. Men didn't do that. His family recognized ennobling qualities in Billy, especially his inclination to appeal to Nellie's lighthearted side.

Over the next few years, Billy Francis acted in a comedy, sang in an Irish trio and a Mozart quartet, played a nobleman disguised as a peddler in the Gypsies' Festival, danced the schottische at a Christmas event, and even starred as "Knight Francis William" in a play called under the direction of his wife (five years his younger) and speaking the words that she had drafted. The many theatrical and musical performances at their church, Pilgrim Baptist, thrust them together time after time. When he played the prince in *The Magic Mirror,* she played the bride. When he starred in a comedy called *Betsy Baker* in September 1892, Nellie was his costar. They hosted parties and dances, gave speeches, served on committees, and convened clubs. By the end of the century, they were each taking significant leadership roles in social and cultural affairs, politics and civil rights. Attractive, musical, strong-willed and smart, they were not just companions but equals in virtually every way, breaking from the conventions of the day. They were the golden couple, and as such, they brought the best out in each other.[7] Early on, Billy seemed to know that the beauty of his bride went far deeper than the skin.

Billy was born in Indianapolis, Indiana, on April 26, 1869, to James and Hattie Francis. His mother, listed as a "mulatto" from Kentucky, and his father, a black man from North Carolina, met in Indianapolis as part of the westward exodus of escaped slaves using the Ohio River as a means westward to freedom. By 1880, James had suffered a violent death at the hands of white men, forcing Hattie and Billy to make it in the world on their own. In time, they moved into the home of Jane Bell, Hattie's mother, and stepfather William Bell, a clerk in a railroad office. It did not seem to have been a happy time. Though William Bell held down a steady job that paid a comfortable wage, Hattie was still expected to take in laundry to support herself and her son, who was expected to work after school to defray the monthly cost of room and board. The ages of the adults living under the same roof may have been enough to create an awkward relationship among them: Jane was forty-two, William was thirty-two, and Hattie was twenty-eight.[8] Billy never mentioned his stepgrandfather or the days he and his mother lived under his roof.

What is apparent, however, is Bell advised Billy that work was available in St. Paul and that Bell, as a railroad clerk, may have had contacts that could lead to work for the young man. St. Paul was in the middle of the second of three great waves of railway expansion. Following the Civil War, railroad mileage in the United States more than quadrupled, primarily from 1868 to 1873, 1879 to 1883, and 1886 to 1893. After the first period of expansion, a vast rail network extended from the Atlantic Coast to the Twin Cities and to Kansas City, with connections to the West Coast by way of the Union Pacific line. During the late 1870s to the early 1890s, railroad construction expanded the existing rail systems east of the Mississippi River and extended railroad service into the less developed areas in the West. In addition, companies completed the Northern Pacific and Great Northern transcontinental routes, plus

The first known photograph of William T. Francis, from *The Appeal,* May 2, 1903. Courtesy of the Minnesota Historical Society.

connections to the Canadian Pacific transcontinental line by way of the Minneapolis, St. Paul and Sault Ste. Marie (Soo Line) and the Union Pacific by way of the Chicago, St. Paul, Minneapolis, Omaha or Omaha Road, which was part of the Chicago and North Western system. From the 1870s and through the 1880s, the mainline routes were completed and numerous branch lines were built to provide interconnecting networks.[9] There were great opportunities for a bright and hard-working young colored youth with the right recommendations and skin color. It was also a great opportunity for Bell to reclaim the privacy of his home. By 1887, two years after the Griswolds fully settled in St. Paul, Hattie Francis and her son Billy relocated to the city, where he got a job as a messenger for the Northern Pacific Railway. Despite not having a high-school diploma, he moved up to office boy, then into the legal department as a stenographer, a position still largely dominated by young men who were often groomed for a junior executive position and thus an incredible job for a young black man.[10] He stayed in that position throughout the 1890s.[11] Now, in 1901, he was offered a promotion.

Billy had clearly made as good an impression on his employers as he had on both Mrs. Griswold and Lula, as a family friend would later report: "Bill has been nearer and dearer than a brother since he came into their family."[12] He seemed now to be more philosophical about his father-in-law, a man, Billy would later write, who became increasingly harder to understand, "seeming to harbor his own darkness." Billy was showing himself to be a provider in the same manner as Mr. Griswold in those early years. By 1895, he, Nellie, and his mother Hattie, who still had to take in people's wash, all enumerated as "white" in the state census, lived together on 397 Rondo Street, then a predominately white neighborhood.[13] All that was missing in the household, he later said in an interview, was an opportunity to be a father of a son or daughter—he wasn't partial, coming home every night after work to a family with a sense of history, a family with a legacy.[14] This, too, may have been a part of the attraction to Nellie Griswold. Billy would make something of himself and, through his wife, inherit family roots. He would work very hard to make his bride happy in every way and vindicate his wife's choice of him to be her husband. He would become someone that his father never had the opportunity to be, and in Nellie he had found his perfect mate, and with her a chance to be the son-in-law whom her father would approve of, a son-in-law who wanted in turn to be a father. But on this score, he was running late. At Billy's age of thirty, Tom's second child, his favorite—Billy's wife—was eight years old.[15] But he came to understand that he could only control his will to work, and not God's Will and Providence.

In Billy's new position, he would be expected to attend administrative meetings, retrieve information and documents for legal staff, handle communications for the office, contact various local, state, and federal agencies to gather information, record all interactions and prepare documents, and provide any other administrative support to the office as needed. The range of litigation duties of the legal department had become quite complex, and the clerk had to be familiar with all of it. He had to be able to retrieve decisions and analyze court cases in which Northern Pacific found itself plaintiff, defendant, or appellant. The majority of the substantive cases were over freight rates, antitrust matters, applications for service changes and line abandonments, loss and damage claims, valuation of corporate properties, labor disputes, and court case reports documenting Northern Pacific litigations before the Interstate Commerce Commission (ICC) and all levels of state and federal courts.[16] Quickly realizing that he needed a formal legal education, in September he enrolled at the St. Paul College of Law, the predecessor of present-day Mitchell–Hamline School of Law.[17]

The St. Paul College of Law had been founded one year earlier, in 1900, by members of the Ramsey County Bar Association. At that time there was no law school in Minnesota that provided night classes for those who held day jobs. Classes began that year for "a modest enrollment of twenty students," convening nightly from 7:30 to 9. Faculty members were all practicing lawyers and judges, many of whom taught without salary. Entrance requirements were a high-school diploma or its equivalent, "requiring the applicant to be at least eighteen years of age—and breathing." The school professed to offer the same level of training as the University of Minnesota, and its graduates were immediately admitted to the bar.[18]

But washing out of the program was always a possibility. After ten or more hours of clerking in the office, learning the administrative machinations by day and studying the arcane reasoning of legal doctrine by night, Billy's grasp on the ring of opportunity was never secure, unless, late into the night, he studied harder still, laboring under the imperative to save face before his employer, his community, as well as what must have been his own fear of failure, and somehow having enough left in him to begin again the next day. The mood in the Francis household during that first year had to be filled with unanticipated isolation and anxiety. Although Nellie entertained visitors at their home and participated in church activities, her husband was seldom around, and this must have left her feeling alone. Then, in the spring of 1902, one year into his clerkship and only months into his legal studies, without consulting with his wife, who would inevitably be called on to do some of the work, Billy took on an additional assignment.

His friend and mentor, Fredrick McGhee, planned to hold the fifth annual National Afro-American Council (NAAC) meeting in St. Paul that summer, and he asked Billy to help coordinate the event. It was far more than a diversion from the intensity of his law work. The council was an organ of the powerful Booker T. Washington. If the event was successful—that is, brought within the Bookerite fold such noted radicals as Ida B. Wells-Barnett and W. E. B. Du Bois, both of whom were expected to attend—then McGhee, Washington's chief counsel, and by extension, the organizers, who would now include Billy, might be elevated to the forefront of Afro-American national leadership, not to mention showcase their fair city.[19]

Pleasing the Wizard of Tuskegee was no small matter, for the great man had cultivated an unapproachable and imperious demeanor to all but the most powerful white men in America. His philosophy of accommodationism enjoyed widespread support among philanthropists and business leaders such as Andrew Carnegie, as well as men in the highest reaches of the federal government. Washington had hosted President William McKinley when he visited Tuskegee, dined with Theodore Roosevelt at the White house in 1901, and would come to advise Roosevelt and later President William Taft. With such influence, he was not a man to be trifled with, known increasingly as one willing to use ruthless and duplicitous methods. Rival newspapers, intellectuals, and educators were frequently intimidated by his brand of boss politics; young black professionals risked ostracism and unemployment if they embraced political activism instead of Washington's accommodationist social policy. "Until his death," Richard Kluger noted, "Booker Washington would reign as the uncrowned king of black America."[20] But Billy was a true believer, for his story, like Washington's *Up from Slavery,* epitomized self-help, self-taught struggle out of a pecuniary state that afflicted so many of his people. It is likely that his Northern Pacific employers—certainly those who supported Washington's prescription for the race problem—may have spared him a few hours to work on the event.

And there was a lot to be done. Along with *The Appeal* editor John Q. Adams and photographer Harry Shepherd, Billy designed and printed stationery featuring photographs of Minnehaha Falls, St. Paul's new High Bridge, Fort Snelling, and Como Park. They used the senate chamber of the old state capitol for business sessions, Central Presbyterian and House of Hope Presbyterian churches for education and entertainment sessions, and the University of Minnesota Armory for the banquet. They arranged guest lodging, mainly in private homes, and organized parties, receptions, and musical programs featuring the best local talent. As Nelson writes, "By the time June gave way to July, it is likely that every middle-class black family in the Twin Cities had contributed time, effort, or talent to the enterprise. For three days,

July 9–11, St. Paul would be the political and intellectual capital of black America."[21]

The three men were, of course, not likely to be the only people doing the work. In fact, if convention held, as it did for all social, cultural, educational, and religious functions in St. Paul's black community, women often anonymously did the lion's share of facilitating the event. Men took the stage and spoke from the podium, but it was the women who ensured that there was a stage and podium from which to speak; and one of the most energetic organizers was Nellie Francis. Coordinating her activities with her husband may have been the only time in more than a year that they did much together, itself a serendipitous outcome considering that taking on the added stress of organizing the conference initially seemed overwhelming, ill conceived, and maybe even, at least for Billy, a little selfish. The routine during these days had to be hectic, with Billy preparing for the conference while carrying his workload at the office and in law school. But Nellie's days were just as exhausting, for in addition to assisting her husband, she would have held down her own job, received visitors at their home, and snatched quiet moments when she could spend time with Hattie, "her other mother."

At last, after successfully navigating a few choppy waters during proceedings in which the Radicals had unsuccessfully but raucously challenged Washington's man for council leadership, for the most part the convention was peacefully coming to an end. Enjoying the fruit of their hard work, in his only visible leadership role during the three-day conference, Billy presided over the banquet on the final evening and introduced the speaker, Archbishop John Ireland. He then announced commencement of the grand march, led by Fredrick McGhee dressed in a tuxedo and his wife Mattie in pink silk and diamonds, followed by Billy and Nellie Francis, who wore a turquoise crepe de chine, duchess lace, and pearls.[22] As reported in *The Appeal,* "The evolutions of [the grand march] were artistic and the long lines and curves of the column filled with handsomely gowned ladies made a scene long to be remembered."[23] Later that evening, Billy prepared for the next day of work. There had to be some comfort for both of them in knowing that in two years this routine would be over. They had no reason to know how much more complicated their lives would become.

In 1904, Billy graduated from law school in a class of 150 students.[24] With the degree under his belt, he was promoted to chief clerk, which implied supervisory authority over the other clerks—all white—many presumably scrutinizing his capacity to lead and direct their work. He could not afford to get it wrong, for the eyes of employer and subordinates alike were always on him. It was as if he was still on trial. To the black community, he was every bit the star that his wife was in high school. Back then, she brilliantly spoke about the potential of the Afro-American, if white people gave him the chance to succeed. Now, he embodied that dream. Through hard work, he was an attorney in the legal department of a prominent railway company. It was a position of prestige. All the other black professionals were independent and relied on black patronage, whereas Billy enjoyed a responsible position in an enormous, white-owned corporation. "At a time when it was a plum for a black man to be appointed a courthouse janitor or statehouse messenger," Nelson notes, "Francis' achievement was unprecedented."[25]

But it was also evident that his future with Northern Pacific as one of its lead attorneys had grown dim. He was a lawyer performing clerk duties. The grind that came from meeting the clerical needs of the legal department had improbably diminished, for Northern Pacific permitted him to practice law privately on the side.[26] It seems that through a gentlemen's agreement to use face-saving discretion, Billy Francis, with his head held high and the resounding adulation from the black community to which he was about to return, was being eased off the track to an executive position in the company. His boss was not pushing him out, just freezing him in his present position of employment. In other words, his trajectory had plateaued and he looked for a different way in which to move forward. He was young, fair, a talented singer, once again a busy member of Pilgrim Baptist Church, an active Republican, and a follower of Booker T. Washington; possessing all the traits needed to inspire a hero's welcome, he would land on his ennobled feet. Although he had worked in a privileged world of powerful white men, he was returning to serve his people. Soon he seemed to be everywhere—making speeches, chairing committees, presiding over events of all kinds.[27]

How much he shared with Nellie about what transpired between him and his employer behind the corporate doors of Northern Pacific

The National Afro-American Council met in St. Paul in 1902. Among the attendees pictured here were Booker T. Washington, Fredrick McGhee, Ida B. Wells-Barnett, Emmett Scott, and W. E. B. Du Bois. Photograph from *The Appeal,* July 19, 1902. Courtesy of the Minnesota Historical Society.

is open to speculation. Pride sometimes filters candor into different shades of clarity. In any case, during the months he made the rounds, she was being the proper wife of a husband who was becoming a public figure, keeping the home, entertaining guests and visitors, and, even as she began to nurse her mother who had just fallen desperately ill, supporting him as best she could as he charted his next course of action, which included courting support from the city's Republicans. Two years later, in February 1906, he announced his plan to run for a seat on the St. Paul City Assembly in the election scheduled for May.[28] But on April 11, sadness descended on the Francis household: after two years of steady, bedridden decline, Maggie Seay Griswold, Nellie's mother, "peacefully passed away."[29] However, buoyed by the recent party endorsement—"His vote [of support among the delegates] was quite flattering as it was greater than five other candidates, some of whom were old politicians and well-known to the voting public"—Billy escalated his campaign.[30]

Over the course of the following weeks before election day, Billy spoke in every venue available to him. Sometimes he spoke in multiple places in one evening, after which he met with organizers and well-wishers.[31] The Citizens' League reassured white voters that Billy was a safe bet: "W. T. Francis . . . is a lawyer in the employ of the legal department of the N.P. railroad; is 35 years of age. He is quiet, modest and unassuming. His word is good and the League believes he could be depended upon to vote for what is right."[32] Nellie had reason to question some of these traits, considering how he seemed to flippantly draw attention to the baby who would never be born, a nerve deep within her that surely had remained sensitive, because their household had been and would remain childless.[33] Meanwhile, as it routinely did during the final weeks before an election, *The Appeal* plastered the third page normally reserved for society and church news with photos and events of Republican candidates for city and legislative offices, highlighting during this campaign season Billy's likeness and candidacy. It does not appear that he took much or any time off to grieve for the passing of his mother-in-law, who was instrumental in first bringing him and her daughter together in 1887.

The results on election day were disappointing, despite all of Billy's hard work. When the votes were tallied, he had come in last.[34] Nonetheless, recognizing the long-term benefit of striking a positive note on the otherwise disappointing return, he published a message of appreciation to those who had supported him: "While my name does not appear among the list of the elected to secure the result attained on last Tuesday—(9080 votes polled for me, almost 800 of which are estimated to have been Afro-American votes)—indicates strenuous and untiring efforts on the part of my friends in my behalf." He gave credit to "the faithful men who assisted me from first to last," then specifically "To the big committee whose organized movement and plans did so much to bring about the success we attained; to each individual worker who rendered service by interesting another voter; to each man who cast his vote for me on last Tuesday; to Mr. Orrie Hall (a prominent black St. Paul barber) who first perceived the idea of entering an Afro-American in the race; to the ministers who so ably championed my cause; and last but not least, to the noble women of St. Paul who took up the work with a will and purpose and vim that meant success in itself, and to whose efforts no small part of the handsome vote I received is to be attributed, I desire to express my earnest and sincere thanks."[35] Although he had included the "noble women of St. Paul" who had helped him in his campaign, notably absent from this list was any reference to his wife, Nellie, which would have been at least customary. It would seem that Billy and Nellie's partnership was fraying.

The use of the phrase "peacefully passed away" to characterize the circumstance of Momma's death belied the ordeal that she endured for two years: "Mrs. Maggie Griswold, one of our long time, well-known and highly-respected citizens was taken ill suffering a complete nervous breakdown over two years ago, and after a struggle long and painful has at last been compelled to succumb to the irresistible power of the King of terrors."[36] For two years she had been bedridden, and there was very little indication that doctors or medical treatment gave her relief. Her condition throughout her infirmed state seemed far too severe for any kind of available remedy. Given how the term "nervous breakdown" was broadly used during the late nineteenth and early twentieth centuries, without a present-day diagnosis it is hard to know exactly with what Maggie was afflicted.

That said, it would seem that at least part of what she was dealing with was some form of depression, likely not the result of one incident but a number of causes for stress that had a cumulative effect on her emotional health. She had been married to Thomas for the entirety of her adult life, working exclusively within the home, keeping it orderly with limited resources, and maintaining the welcoming appearance of being members of proper society. Their daughters were never wanting. The year 1894 was the last time the girls would be living at home, for they had married good men and were now off on their own.

Thomas, who had always been a hard worker, would not be home until late, and when he worked on the railroad he would sometimes be gone for days, leaving Maggie alone in their home. And even when he was home, he, a man accustomed to keeping his own counsel, seldom provided the kind of companionship that would help lift her from her isolation. Yet, with his death she experienced a different kind of loneliness that placed her face-to-face with her own mortality, for she had never imagined a life, even in his quietude, without him, the scent of his clothes, the smell of his shoe polish, the fragrance of his shaving cream, his brush and comb, all that provided in their own unique ways unrecognized comfort, had become cruel reminders that he was forever gone, and with him, a part of herself that had begun to beckon her to join him in the great black void.

Her lifeline had been her church and the sisters of the Eastern Star and the Household of Ruth, and the good works that brought her the high esteem of her community, until her grasp weakened right before their unmindful eyes: the black taffeta lace and ribbons that she wore as she sat at a corner table, watching absently as the grand march at the end of the National Afro-American Council (NAAC) conference and the superb multicolored "confections" of the ladies' gowns processed by, a possible sign of her fate to the furies to come.[37] Her midcentury body was about to go through the change, as she recognized fewer friends, day by day, until she was totally out of reach, leaving only the whispers.

On the same page and in the same column that Billy's letter to the voters appeared, *The Appeal* printed the following note of gratitude:

> To all those who so faithfully and devotedly assisted us, whether by acts of kindness to add to her comfort, or by prayers and well wishes for her recovery, all through the past two years and one month during which our beloved daughter and mother Maggie Griswold, was afflicted, and since her death, we desire to tender our sincere thanks and express our heartfelt appreciation. These will always lend a touch of brightness to the sad memories of her sufferings and stand as a monument of a true friendship which you bore for her.

The note was signed by the Griswold women: Maggie's mother Nellie Seay ("Gramma"), in town in time for the end to come, Lula H. Chapman, and Nellie Francis—the only people who daily had been with Maggie during her long decline.[38] Billy, who had been "nearer and dearer than a brother since he came into their family," had not recently been as much.[39]

– 5 –

A Bitter Taste Still Lingered

For the remainder of 1906 and well into 1907, Nellie and Billy did not appear in public together. Since the election, while Billy went unaccompanied to various events usually in the role of master of ceremonies and committee chair, Nellie seemed to drop out of sight. It would be logical to assume that she was still in mourning, and in light of the nature of Maggie's decline, there was reason to feel concern for her emotional well-being. It is just as likely that in the wake of her mother's passing and the domestic isolation she must have felt as Billy's participation in civic and political affairs increased, she may have taken this moment to make an accounting of her own life, hearing echoes perhaps from her high-school triumph telling of recognized yet unrealized potential: *"This young woman evidently has or ought to have a mission in life where she may be heard on behalf of the American colored people for whom she spoke so well last evening."*[1] But what was her "mission"? To be an asset to Billy's ambitions? To serve as an ornament on her husband's arm? And what was she to do with the cloying sense that all of the societal affairs seemed trivial compared to what was happening to her race on the national stage? At thirty-three years of age, there was so much yet to learn and understand, so much life to live—indeed, so much about herself with which to be reacquainted; and how would she begin from within the velvet constraints of her very safe and proper home and very safe and proper society? It would begin from reading of a horrific event that was reported within the very safe and proper pages of *The Appeal.*

Before midnight on September 22, 1906, approximately ten thousand white people, most of them under twenty years of age, beat and murdered every black person they found on the streets of Atlanta,

Georgia. The mob burst into the post office, train station, and all white-owned businesses, seeking out every black employee they could find. Black passengers were dragged from trolley cars and beaten to death. "In some portions of the streets," reported the *Atlanta Constitution,* "the sidewalks ran red with the blood of dead and dying negroes." Stopping short of venturing into the tough black ghetto near the Morehouse College campus, the mob cowardly shifted its focus onto the prosperous black community in the far southeast corner of the city, destroying property and attacking people in their homes. A Memphis newspaper, joining the opprobrium that would rain down on the city by the national press, wrote, "Atlanta brought shame to the South." As this horrific tragedy occurred, President Theodore Roosevelt, whose likeness routinely appeared in *The Appeal* as a friend of the colored race and Booker T. Washington, said nothing at all.[2] Neither, it seems, did Billy, whose first public appearance since the massacre in Atlanta was to appear as toastmaster at a banquet for Joe Gans, lightweight boxing champion.[3]

These were some of the stories in the same issue of September 29 that would have caught Nellie's eye and set in stark contrast the dire conditions of black Southerners and the priorities that Billy seemed to hold dear. When *The Appeal* reported that "[a]mong the novelties sent out by our Southern brethren are postcards [that were] embellished with lynching scenes," the paper announced that Billy would soon be going to Richmond, Virginia, to represent the state in persuading the national Order of Odd Fellows to secure the next meeting of the convention to be held in St. Paul. In another column, *The Appeal* reported, "The massacre of Afro-Americans at Atlanta Saturday night was the most horrible that has ever occurred in this country and rivals in atrocity the massacres of the Jews at Kischineff (1903), Bialystok (1906) and Siedlce (1906). For hours, with the apparent connivance of the police, who were evidently in sympathy with the mob, the slaughter continued and many men and women were killed for no reason except that their skins were black."[4]

In October, Billy returned from Richmond, but apparently with no good news about the prospects of bringing the next national Odd Fellows convention to St. Paul, nor of a meeting to be held in St. Paul where he was to report on his trip.[5] And in November, Billy chaired a gathering for Republican candidates at Pilgrim Baptist Church, never once bringing up the recent horrors of Atlanta, though he did publish an article, not on the race problem in America but as a correction to the "misconception that [Democratic] Governor John Johnson appointed a number of blacks to the capital, when in fact he made no such appointments."[6]

Yet Billy did not criticize the Democratic governor of Georgia for the bloody events that started on September 22. The massacre in Atlanta had lasted for two days, egged on by city newspapers that reported four sexual assaults on local white women, allegedly by black men. The fact was that there was no substantiation of the allegations, but white gangs formed and grew into thousands, commencing to destroy property and murder innocent black bystanders. Even the insinuation of a black man having sex with a white woman was justification for his murder. A white man, on the other hand, who had sex with a black woman was only carrying out a time-honored southern custom. *The Appeal* article would be especially poignant concerning the hypocrisy of southern white men and their sexual practices, a topic that told the story of her family line: "Many of the Afro-American women have been despoiled of their virtue and made unwilling rivals of their white sisters. Of course, it is one of the conditions of existence and inseparable from the institution of slavery that the women of the enslaved race have no legal protection and are at the mercy of the masters . . . The evil effects of slavery have survived the institution itself and are still prevalent throughout the entire South."[7]

It was to such a world that all Afro-Americans were to accommodate, with, it seemed, no brighter day in sight. The January issue of *The Appeal* reported: "In the United States, in 1906, scores of Afro-Americans, including one woman, and two whites were murdered by mobs—all in the South. Of these, 23 were for assault or attempted assault, 21 for murder, and the rest for such grave crimes as miscegenation, carrying a pistol, theft of calf, theft of $1, and disorderly conduct. Only one was burned alive, but several of the corpses were burned. The above shows an increase of seven cases over 1905."[8] And the chief proponent of accommodating to all of this was the offspring of a white man and black woman, Booker T. Washington—Billy's man—who soon would receive a lifetime pension from his largest donor, Andrew Carnegie.

To the most committed of Bookerites, it only seemed fitting considering Washington's pledge at the 1895 Exposition in Atlanta, which first brought him national notice: "In your effort to work out the great and intricate problem which God has laid at the doors of the South, you shall have at all times the patient, sympathetic help of my race."[9] The race problem, in other words, was not the fault of white men, but of God. A seventeen-year-old high-school girl named Nellie Griswold would have disagreed: racism was not a problem of God's making, but of men; and not just Southerners, but all white Americans, native- and foreign-born.[10]

She had said then what she felt now. She had affiliated with the Bookerites because Billy had, and it made sense in his case to do so. His life was a variation of Washington's up-from-slavery story, except that his had its origins in poverty, not slavery. Still, it was hard to deny that his hard efforts to make his life *useful* to society, and to Northern Pacific in particular, was vindicated by his apparent inclusion within the white dominion of Republican power brokers as an attorney in the company's legal department and an office seeker. Both opportunities brought him stature to lead his people to a place of respectability. Indeed, Washington's words from the Atlanta Exposition defined Billy's life: "No race that has anything to contribute to the markets of the world is long in any degree ostracized."[11] The door to opportunity, owing in no small part to his affiliation as a Bookerite, opened for Billy every day he arrived at work and, of course, when he was leading the community by facilitating some festive occasion.

Yet one can wonder whether the events that Billy officiated were truly useful to Afro-American advancement or mere "ornamental geegaws," as Washington so derisively termed the superficial.[12] What was especially disturbing was that, with all of the opportunities to do so, Billy, like his hero Washington to a large extent, uttered and wrote not one public word of condemnation of the violence done to his southern brethren. It is ironic that he did not take to heart the central lesson of *Doctor Huguet,* a novel that he approvingly reviewed for the Pilgrim's Men's Sunday Club, of which he was president.[13] Written by former Congressman Ignatius Donnelly (under the pseudonym "Gilbert Boisgilbert"), the story was about a South Carolina aristocrat who felt guilty for his failure to do more to improve race relations in the South and declared that it was his duty as a man seeking redemption to speak and act against evil.[14] For the fictional doctor it was simply a matter of character.

Not so for the Wizard. During the aftermath of the murderous chaos of the Atlanta riot, the Bookerite press insinuated that Du Bois found a place to hide until calm was restored while the heroic Wizard of Tuskegee had hurried from New York to defend his people. Neither report was true. As Du Bois biographer David Levering Lewis noted, "Washington stayed put [in New York] for several more days, issuing deeply pained, even-handed condemnations of non-unsubstantiated black rapists and white rioters. Du Bois rushed to the city by train to sit on the steps of [his Atlanta residence] to protect Nina [his wife] and Yolande [his daughter] with a shotgun."[15]

It was interesting to contrast the image of this heroic gun-wielding Du Bois with that of a dashing young university professor, whom Nellie first met at the NAAC conference in 1902. He had already delivered his address on Wednesday afternoon, and was free to leave later that day. The problem was that two of the three most prominent Afro-Americans attending the conference—Ida B. Wells-Barnett and Booker T. Washington, the man who the conference was intended to please—had already left town. The image of a successful conference now rested on Du Bois sticking around until its conclusion on Thursday, and he had to be given a reason to stay. A dinner was organized to honor him, and Nellie, a contralto, accompanied by her sister Lula, entertained and hosted the professor throughout the afternoon.[16] Whether it was out of solidarity for the convention or the attractiveness of the hostesses, it worked, for he stayed until the end, and attended the grand reception on Friday evening.[17]

Three years after the conference, Du Bois's name, which held such high value to the conference organizers—and presumably to Billy as well, who probably encouraged her to host the by now controversial civil-rights leader—sparked an argument between two old friends. The Francises, the McGhees, and Dr. and Ms. Valdo Turner were on vacation on Sturgeon Lake in the summer of 1905. Fredrick, fresh from the inaugural meeting of the Niagara Movement—he had jumped to the Du Bois camp, which he had helped to form—got into a heated argument with Billy, his closest friend who was still a staunch Bookerite. The issue was the viability of the platform of the new organization: freedom to speak and to criticize; an unfettered press; full manhood suffrage, though gender limitation would soon be an issue for Nellie; the abolition of all caste distinctions based simply on race and color; the recognition of the principle of human brotherhood as a practical, present creed; compulsory common school attendance for all Americans and an increase of high-school facilities in the South; the recognition of the highest and best human training as the monopoly of no class or race; a belief in the dignity of labor; and a united effort to realize these ideals under a wise, pure, and fearless leadership. If the other principles were like kindling to a committed Bookerite like Billy, the allusion to the failure of Washington's accommodating leadership proved combustible, foretelling a deeper rupture that would later form between the men. Considering the steady rise of white violence against black men, how could anyone—including Billy—take issue with the platform?[18]

Except for Nellie, few seated around the table at Sturgeon Lake in late July 1905 fully understood just how much Billy needed this political moment to be governed by moderation, for he was already planning to seek Republican support for St. Paul assemblyman in the city election in May 1906. To that end, being labeled "radical" would not do. Although he would lose his bid, his ambition required that he be committed for the long run and, with the help of *The Appeal,* this meant staying in the public eye for proper and uncontroversial reasons. It would be a matter of course that extended into 1907, with the announcement in a February issue that the Lincoln Club "was making great preparations for its annual banquet, which will be held at the Ryan Hotel, Tuesday evening, February 12th. The Honorable E. L. Miller of Duluth, will be the principal speaker." The tickets were one dollar and could be "obtained from George F. Dix, clerk of the Municipal court or from W. T. Francis," along with T. H. Lyles, a black businessman and funeral director, and *The Appeal* editor J. Q. Adams, "who are members of the various committees" that endorsed the banquet.[19]

It was also time for Nellie and Billy to reemerge as the golden couple of black St. Paul society. That May, at the reception that was billed as "the largest and grandest private social function ever witnessed in the Northwest"—the celebration of the Crystal (or fifteenth) Wedding Anniversary of editor and Mrs. J. Q. Adams—"Doctor (the honorific coming from a course he had completed in osteopathy in 1900) and Mrs. W. T. Francis" were very much in attendance. It would have been difficult not to attend because the two families lived only a block apart.[20]

But the symbolism of domestic harmony seemed short-lived, for afterwards, for a time, Nellie and Billy stopped appearing in public as a couple, and it may have been because of something he did that indelicately revived what was a sensitive element in their marriage—childlessness. Years before, Billy had told a reporter writing a Christmas feature that all he ever wanted for the holiday was a child. History does not record whether this was just a throwaway line or whether Nellie was pregnant at the time or even wanted to have children. What is certain is that they would never become parents and neither of them would ever speak publicly about it. Still, one can only speculate whether she was experiencing the profound sense of loss from the absence of childbirth, and knowing that with her demise the proud legacy of her family, and in particular the Griswold–Francis line, would end with her, and whether all of their social, political, and cultural activities sublimated the emptiness of a childless home, or whether the work was its own satisfaction. In any event, in October Billy served as one of the judges in the great (and only) baby show at Pilgrim, "Babyland," where prizes would go to the prettiest baby. Billy alone represented the Francis household for the evening.[21]

On January 18, 1908, *The Appeal* announced that Booker T. Washington intended to visit St. Paul and that Billy Francis had assumed the role of organizing a grand reception for him.[22] Granted, it would not be of the scope of the NAAC conference of 1902, when housing accommodations had to be secured for delegates and guests from all over the country. Nor would he have to get speakers and mollify rivals who would attend, or plan entertainment and arrange tours to sites all around the Twin Cities region. And fund-raising would not be as onerous as it had been for other initiatives. But he had learned much from the organizational

W. E. B. Du Bois with his wife, Nina, and daughter Yolande, circa 1901. Courtesy of the Photographs and Prints Division, Schomburg Center for Research in Black Culture, The New York Public Library.

skills of his friend Fredrick McGhee who, at the time, was a prominent Bookerite and well understood the high currency of the Wizard's good name with prospective donors. This time, the reception that Billy envisioned would be smaller in scale. Still, it was to be a mighty task that would take virtually every spare hour he had to pull off.

Two weeks into the work, another wedding anniversary of a prominent black St. Paul couple was set to be held. *The Appeal* hyperbolically billed the festivity, as it was prone to do for such events, as "The reception of the Largest and Grandest Social Function of the Year." When it finally occurred, the paper dedicated two page-length columns to list those who had attended along with the gifts that they brought. Those present were a veritable who's who of proper black St. Paul society though their numbers were fewer than those who had attended the Adams celebration previously in May. Still, conspicuous in their absence were the names of "Mr. and Mrs. W. T. Francis." Often the paper printed the names of prominent individuals who were ill, had gone out of town, or were otherwise indisposed, as if to explain their absences, but for this occasion Nellie was absent without explanation and, seemingly, unrepentant. And this was the sort of occasion when it would not be fitting for Billy to attend without her. It was better that neither Francis attended than only one. In any event, he had much to prepare for the Washington reception.[23] Seven days later, *The Appeal* gave official notice of the reception to its readers and listed the officers of the planning committee and representatives selected by the various groups, clubs, and churches in St. Paul and Minneapolis. The person selected to represent Pilgrim Baptist Church, one of the major partners of the event, was Billy's wife.[24] Any other of the men and women in the church could have been given the assignment and, considering her absence from so many affairs, it would have been reasonable that any one of them would fill the post. But she was the person selected.

On Monday afternoon, February 10, the appointed hour of the public reception arrived. It was expected to be, as *The Appeal* predicted, "the largest and most representative function of its kind ever witnessed in St. Paul." At about 2:30 p.m., Billy Francis, Tom Lyles, John Adams, and the pastors of Pilgrim and St. James churches, all members of the committee of arrangements, called upon Booker T. Washington at his hotel and escorted him to the state capitol. The guest of honor and the committeemen were then directed into the private office of Governor Johnson, who extended to Washington an official welcome; they then sat down to talk "of matters of interest, both giving and receiving valuable intervention." Finally, it was time for Washington to be escorted to the reception.[25]

The hall of the House of Representatives of the old state capitol where he was to speak barely contained the large gathering of people who came to see, hear, and greet the great man. Once he appeared in the hall, the vast audience rose as one to give him "the Chautauqua salute." Amid a beautiful display of American flags, clusters of posies, ferns, and potted plants, a large bouquet of roses and carnations graced the speaker's stand. The program began with an invocation by Rev. W. D. Carter of Pilgrim, followed by singing. The Mandolin Club "discoursed very sweet music," and the soloist sang delightfully. Then Billy, who was quite pleased with his own remarks, introduced Washington to the jubilant crowd who delighted at a speech that lasted for more than an hour, "replete with words of wisdom and good sound advice, which fell upon willing ears and was roundly applauded as the speaker proceeded." *The Appeal,* however, did not report what he actually said, though the paper assured readers that the "exercises throughout were very pleasing." In the vestibule, young ladies served refreshments until nearly six o'clock, when crowds reluctantly left the hall.[26]

Washington later spoke at the People's Church, after which he was driven to the Francis residence, where a number of gentlemen had assembled to meet him "in a social way." Refreshments were served in the dining room, consisting of salmon salad, finger rolls, olives, ice cream and cake, coffee, and cigars, after which the party adjourned. Although this part of the evening was a man's affair—no women were apparently invited to the gathering—the host introduced his guests to the charming but reserved lady of the house. Before a silenced room, the good doctor took her hand and kissed the back of it as the men looked on as if seeing her for the first time. Later that evening, as *The Appeal* reported, Washington "expressed himself, highly delighted with the magnificent and cordial reception which was accorded him."[27]

To be sure, there was reason for the great man to hold these feelings for the event. St. Paul, as presented to the guest of honor by Billy's leadership of the grand reception, was a Bookerite town. And the qualities that characterized St. Paul this way were highlighted in the pages of *The Appeal.* Although not strictly accommodationist, for it decried Jim Crow laws, racist politicians, and the horrors that had played out on the streets of Atlanta, the newspaper clearly favored Washington, who cozied not as much to the Republican Party as to the philanthropic business community that influenced party leadership; and it was from such affiliations that benefits to his followers could be granted, something that no other Afro-American, prominent or otherwise, not even W. E. B. Du Bois, "one of the greatest scholars that the race had produced and interesting to listen to," could provide. Du Bois, after all, had proclaimed himself to be a radical, more recently a socialist, and therefore un-American.[28]

As portrayed in the pages of *The Appeal* that printed constant reminders of Washington's bounty, this Bookerite town rosily boasted a thriving black middle class with a very active social life and political involvement with the Republican establishment. There was no visibly embarrassing black underclass, at least judging from the stories that regularly appeared in *The Appeal.* Discrimination and racial tension from white Minnesotans were virtually nonexistent. A benevolent and accessible power elite ruled both city and state. And there was no mention of poor southern blacks who moved to the city in search of refuge and opportunity, for the existence of such a class would only invalidate the very prescriptions of the Wizard of Tuskegee who insisted that the solution to the race problem necessitated that black people remain in their ancestral home in the South. Their presence in Minnesota would also confuse unknowing Minnesota whites with the wrong image of black people. Within this Bookerite town, the strongest and most notable ties of its residents to Afro-Americans from other states who were celebrating in the press were with Afro-Americans of similar social status.

Proper women worked in the shadow of their husbands' surname and selflessly labored to facilitate civic and religious programs that the menfolk officiated, while keeping their opinions to themselves. An image of Mary Church Terrell, captured in an aristocratic profile, presented her as the first black appointee to the school board in Washington, D.C.,[29] but no mention was made of her work as president of the National Association of Colored Women Clubs, nor her collaboration with Ida B. Wells-Barnett (who had not appeared in the paper's pages since 1902), Frances Harper, Harriet Tubman, and Sojourner Truth, nor her efforts on job training, wage equity, and child care, antisegregation laws in transportation, and antilynching, all considered "radical." *The Appeal,* instead of revealing the mission of the Minnesota Federation of Colored Women's Clubs, mentioned only the activities of such polite affiliates as the Whist Club and the Art Club."[30] Readers learned more about how she entertained her husband's brother (a doctor) and wife who visited from Kansas City than of the work she did for the state organization.[31] But with *The Appeal* as the only source of information, readers had a roadmap of how to comport themselves as members of proper society in black St. Paul.

Indeed, in maintaining the state's image of being racially progressive, there was virtually no public outcry from community leaders over pressing issues of black Minnesota—unemployment, discrimination, limited education, poor housing. Rather, racial protest was directed against the latest outrage of southern white supremacy; and no politician in Minnesota was held responsible for racial inequities in the state. After the NAAC conference of 1902, readers could not follow the work of Ida Wells-Barnett, nor were they informed of the activities of the Niagara Movement after its inaugural meeting in 1905, or of successive efforts of the organization to promote women's participation, which had all been covered at the insistence of Wells-Barnett and Terrell. When speakers came to St. Paul, as in the case of Washington's reception, the reports provided greater detail on the decorations of the hall than to what was said, and the events were thickly glossed over with hyperbolic praise for the pageantry of the moment. In the case of Washington, who especially disliked being challenged, his reception, insulated from criticism, could not, of course, be anything but "delightful." When the committee on which Nellie served planned a reception for the state's Afro-American graduates later in September and asked Du Bois to speak, his appearance was canceled shortly after Billy—perhaps in service to his mentor, perhaps still smarting from memories that were now six years old—had taken over the leadership of the arrangements committee.[32] The host of the Washington event had secured a place within the Wizard's constellation of favored supporters.

Over the remaining months of 1908, Billy's star rose, as he frequently appeared at the center of most civic, social, and political affairs. With the inception of the Cosmopolitan Mutual Insurance Company, whose motto was "Let the Afro-American ORGANIZE the Expenditure of their money," Billy was both on the board of directors and general counsel, while retaining his post at Northern Pacific.[33] He was reported to have taken trips to Chicago and Wabash, Indiana, to represent the Northern Pacific Railway to give depositions in a suit against the railroad, as if to show the extent to which his employer valued his expertise.[34] As president of the Ramsey County Afro-American Republican Organization, he was called on to introduce Mayor Joseph McKibbens and other Republican candidates to black voters.[35]

Yet, throughout this period, unlike earlier, Billy and Nellie spent more time together.

When Billy left town to take depositions in Chicago, and later met his mother in Indianapolis while visiting his grandmother, who was then in declining health, Nellie was with him. Meanwhile, *The Appeal* posted a notice of the gala for the State Grand Lodge of the United Brothers of Friendship to be held at the Old State Capitol, an event at which Billy would ordinarily have officiated, that appeared in the report of Nellie and Billy's trip, as if to indicate why they were absent, assuring those who wanted to be in the know that the couple's absence was really in the spirit of domestic harmony.[36] Such notes, usually appearing in the left-hand column of page 3, though innocuous on the surface, served many such purposes. In late August, they returned to Indianapolis for his grandmother's funeral, then left in September for an extensive trip to the East, visiting Chicago, Pittsburgh, Washington, Philadelphia, New York, Atlantic City, and Boston, returning in October.[37] The tour was as much for business as it was a second honeymoon; but more still—it seemed to serve for Billy as a renewal of commitment to his wife's needs that would be manifested in his support of Nellie's maiden voyage into leading a widespread campaign in the interest of their community.

It was in the church that she had spent most of her life, and her family—or at least her mother, sister, and husband—had been mainstays in all of its functions. It was the place where she was married and where blessings were laid on her departed parents. But there was more than a personal connection, for Pilgrim, founded by slaves who had sought refuge in St. Paul, was the oldest and most respected black institution in Minnesota. This was a legacy that she was called on to nurture. Over the forty-four years of its existence, the church became the center of social, educational, and political activities for the black community, as well as the spiritual home from where a select group—McGhee (before he converted to Catholicism), Turner, Lyles, Adams, and Francis—would lead St. Paul's black community into the twentieth century. As Jon Butler observes, "Able, respected, largely self-employed businessmen and professionals, they were the major Afro-American spokesmen in the city and often dominated the affairs of the congregation to which they belonged."[38] The problem was that the spotlight that *The Appeal* cast upon them and the church created a distortion of the true sense of Pilgrim's financial viability. Far from being a bastion of the black middle class, notwithstanding the outer appearances and activities of the membership, "the bulk of the membership," Butler continues, "was found among less prestigious elements of the population."[39] Raising funds for a pipe organ would be quite challenging. But the times made it necessary to do just that.

Between 1900 and 1910, the black population in Minnesota grew markedly owing to an increase in the birthrate and the number of people seeking an escape to Minnesota and other northern states from the reestablishment of white supremacy in the South.[40] St. Paul showed a similar rate of increase.[41] Economic progress and the passage of favorable civil-rights legislation also contributed to Minnesota's reputation as a racially progressive place and further attracted blacks to the state.[42] It was hoped that many would be family-oriented churchgoers.[43] It was believed that the grand spectacle of music coming forth from a pipe organ, which no other black church provided, would draw new parishioners to the fold: "It is a common demand by a constantly growing population with an increasingly appreciative feeling for the best church music. It is an effort on the part of the church to properly value that appreciation."[44]

But acquiring a pipe organ was an expensive proposition and fundraising had not gone well. Reasoning that hosting a speaker of notable stature who also represented the self-help virtues of the day would help, in December the committee secured to keynote an event Mrs. Maggie Williams of Richmond, the only woman in the nation to be president of a bank.[45] However, on the day of the event, a large audience that had come expecting to see her was told, "owing to unavoidable circumstances she was unable to be present." The disappointed audience instead listened to an evening of selections by familiar choruses and soloists.[46] A second concert was hastily organized for which the tickets to hear Mrs. Williams would be honored: "Persons who bought tickets for the concert which was to have been given Dec. 17, 1908, for the benefit of the pipe organ fund of Pilgrim Baptist Church, will be admitted to the concert for the same purpose at Pilgrim Baptist Church Thursday evening, January 21."[47] But committee members could see that its fundraising was headed in the wrong direction, thereby placing the fund in an even deeper hole. It was time for a new leader—Mrs. W. T. Francis.

Minnesota Federation of Colored Women's Clubs in front of Pilgrim Baptist Church, St. Paul, 1907. Courtesy of the Minnesota Historical Society.

Nellie was the logical choice. She had creative plans to spark excitement among prospective donors, superb communication and organizational skills, a refined and attractive presence, and an audacious sense of urgency to see the project succeed: *The Appeal* reported, "The work of the pipe organ fund committee is going merrily on, and it is a certainty that the organ will be installed by Easter. Great praise is due Mrs. W. T. Francis and her corps of diligent workers for their untiring efforts in this direction."[48] But she also had a partner in Billy, who seemed to be picking up more litigation work while continuing his civic activities and contributing to her efforts.[49] She organized a mock debate that involved the larger black community.[50] "The members and friends are greatly elated, and very justly so, over the phenomenal success of the outcome of their pipe organ rally last Sunday. At the close of the services Sunday night the sum total of $1508.52 had been paid in cash and there is quite a neat sum still to be collected. Very much credit is due Nellie Francis, who as chairman of the Pipe Organ association has been indefatigable in her labors." Nellie had personally raised more than half of that amount. "The big pipe organ, which is to cost $2200 will be installed before Easter Sunday."[51]

But she knew that she had taxed all the resources in the community. To meet the goal of Easter Sunday, a different approach needed to be taken. It had been understood that philanthropist Andrew Carnegie would furnish half the money necessary but when a request from the previous chair of the pipe organ committee was made of him, "nothing came of it." This, beyond all of the community work she successfully would lead, became the central reason why church leaders selected her to take over, a person from all appearances who seemed comfortably suited for the trip to New York City where she would personally see the great philanthropist, a person who through her husband and, by extension, the Wizard of Tuskegee, was a very important contact. It was late March. "She was supplied with strong letters from Governor Johnson and others [as well as, most likely, Booker T. Washington] and [the letters] together with her own admirable personality, succeeded in securing $1100 from the great philanthropist."[52] There is no record of how the meeting between Mrs. Francis and Mr. Carnegie transpired but one hint may be found in a similar meeting that occurred years earlier among Washington, Du Bois, and Carnegie, an object lesson on how to appeal to the philanthropist's ego. Lewis writes:

> As [Du Bois] recalled it . . . he and Booker Washington had ridden together uptown on the Madison Avenue trolley to Carnegie's Georgian mansion on Riverside Drive before the conference [for black men] opened at ten o'clock that morning. As they stood together at the back of the car, Washington, "who very seldom said anything," turned to Du Bois and asked, "Have you read Carnegie's book *[The Gospel of Wealth]*?" Du Bois said that he never thought it worthwhile to do so. "You ought to read it," the Wizard gravely advised. "He likes it."

Du Bois pondered these words as they walked to Carnegie's, where, after retiring to the philanthropist's bedchamber for a brief discussion, the Wizard rejoined Du Bois in the anteroom, saying importantly, "Mr. Carnegie's coming to address us." Carnegie's money having paid for the conference, it was both courtesy and politics for the tiny personification of the Age of Steel to appear before this gathering of black men whose total assets, had they been tabulated that afternoon, would not have amounted to the cost of one of his smaller libraries.[53]

Whatever the circumstances, Nellie got the hearing she had hoped for and received the donation she had sought. It was probably helpful that her hometown newspaper and Pilgrim Baptist had for more than a year encouraged the community to purchase bound copies of a speech titled "Progress of the Afro-American" that Carnegie had delivered in Edinburgh.[54]

Before she returned to St. Paul Billy telegraphed her to make an unplanned trip to Washington. He likely had arranged a surprise for her through his contacts in Republican circles that he thought she might enjoy. One of his contacts was Minnesota's Senator Moses E. Clapp, who met Mrs. Francis and through an appointment he had made at the White House, personally introduced her to President William Howard Taft. About him, she reportedly said, "The President's big smile was in evidence and he was genial and kindly . . . and as big in heart and principles as he is in size." Later, by courtesy of Congressman F. C. Stevens, she was given a seat in the gallery of the House of Representatives during a session of Congress. "For these overtures of Senator Clapp and Congressman Stevens to his wife," reported *The Appeal,* "Attorney Francis has words of highest praise."[55]

On Easter Day, Pilgrim Baptist Church was crowded to the doors in the morning and packed in every available space—committee rooms, platforms, and aisles. The beauty of the new organ enhanced by the new hardwood floor put in by the Young People's Society; the flowers, the palms, the music, the lights, and the beautiful amber dome, the memorial to Mrs. Maggie Griswold who died three years earlier, given by her daughters, all combined to add loveliness and reverence to the occasion. As *The Appeal* reported, "St. Paul can now boast of a magnificent pipe organ in Pilgrim Baptist Church. The splendid instrument which is now installed in the choir loft was presented with a grand recital on Tuesday evening, April 8th at which time the grandeur and power and sweetness of the most up-to-date pipe organ in this city was on full display." Some of the leading musicians of the city's most prominent white churches joined in the celebration of Pilgrim's newest adornment by giving a recital all under Nellie's management, "whose work in connection with the Pipe Organ movement is so highly appreciated by the entire city." Billy Francis acted as master of ceremonies.[56]

Two months later, on Wednesday, June 9, the pipe organ was formally dedicated when Nellie officially presented it to the Pilgrim Baptist Church community. At a cost of more than three thousand dollars, "[i]t was a masterpiece. The audience was delighted, as was shown by the enthusiastic applause which followed each number." At the close of the program a magnificent cut-glass vase two-feet high was presented to Nellie by Reverend Carter as a token of appreciation of "her indefatigable labors." The evening was deemed as "one of the grandest in the history of the city."[57] And Nellie was the community's grand dame.

Yet, in light of the help Nellie received to get to this triumph—Billy's leveraging his contact with Booker T. Washington, who in turn secured an audience for her with the great industrialist, and the much-appreciated visits afterwards to the White House and Congress—she understood, as she considered her frustrations with racial tensions that seemed to deepen by the day on the watch of men who spoke not a word in protest, that she had deliberately sidestepped her ambivalent regard for these men who participated in managing the current body politic. She had compromised, not entirely unlike what she did in the face of certain advances that warranted diplomatic deflection. Her job, through compromise, was to steadfastly remain charming. She had a taste for leadership, and compromise was indeed its flavor, and with this, as her aunt would later note of the moment, "a bitter taste still lingered."[58] She was now determined to do the work at hand in the company of women.

Sisterhood

Nellie had entered a new phase of her life that for the time being seemed to take her in a different direction from Billy and into the larger and increasingly familiar world east of St. Paul. Just weeks after she and Billy returned from a four-week tour of Baltimore, Brooklyn, and New York City, she left again on a solo trip to New York City, where for two weeks she, with Mrs. Booker T. Washington, whom she had come to know over the previous year at the urging of the Wizard, who had remained charmed since they first met at his 1908 reception in St. Paul, were guests of Mrs. Maggie A. Payton.[1]

Maggie's husband Phillip, who had been featured in Washington's compendium *The Negro in Business,* was a real-estate entrepreneur, known as the "Father of Harlem" for his work in renting and selling properties in the Harlem neighborhood of New York City to African Americans.[2] In 1893, two years before Washington's national debut at the Atlanta Exposition, he had come to Harlem, insisting that home ownership remained key to racial uplift. He returned the next year and called on his listeners to take advantage of the recent burst of speculative housing begun in response to plans for a metropolitan subway system, urging them to "Stop staying here and there and everywhere and begin to live somewhere."[3] Payton would soon take up the challenge and his "up-from-poverty" story that validated the Wizard pronouncements was the type of success that drew the Wizard's admiration.

At the turn of the century, a greater number of southern blacks, largely relegated to quasi-slave conditions as sharecroppers, began migrating to the North to escape racial violence and the Jim Crow laws, to find sanctuary in cities only to confront the consternation of whites who lived there or nearby. In New York, the interracial tension forced migrating blacks to find a community in which they could safely live. Harlem, which had already become a melting pot for new communities, became for black arrivals their promised land, and for the Paytons, owing in part to his groundbreaking use of billboards and subway advertising, it was the perfect time to corner the African American real-estate market. By 1905, Payton and his wife had become members of New York's nascent black aristocracy, with their light skin color, distinguished bearing, and beautiful home on West 131st Street.[4] But it was not an easy road, as he would report to Washington:

> When we were first married we lived in three rear rooms in a tenement on West 67th street where we paid $12 per month rent. During the first two weeks of our married life, we slept on the floor . . . When I started in the real estate business I secured the agency of a flat on West 134th street, so we moved up there. Things seemed to go from bad to worse. It just seemed impossible for me to make any money. I recall one Sunday morning we awoke without a cent or anything to eat in the house. My wife hunted around the kitchen and found some Indian meal. She boiled this, cut it up in slices, fried it, and melted sugar for syrup and this constituted our day's meal. Like all very poor people we had both a dog and a cat. I will never forget how the poor things sat and watched us eating it. They . . . had nothing. Shortly after this both our cat and dog died. I have always claimed they starved to death, but Mrs. Payton won't have it that way.
>
> We remained in this house until April passed. We were dispossessed for not being able to pay our rent, and our entire scanty belongings were set out on the sidewalk. I managed to secure charge of another house after a while in the same street, and we moved in there. Seemingly this was the turning point in my business career. One fine day I made a deal that netted me nearly $1,150. I could hardly believe it true. My wife refused to credit it, until I showed her the check. From that time, things grew better.[5]

He had started his business as a janitor and handyman, and through the industrious sensibilities of Maggie, who sewed to make ends meet, the

Payton fortune in the real-estate business grew until they were making, through more investments in real estate, profits of thousands of dollars per month.

Payton formed the Afro-American Real Estate Company, for which he wanted only to attract black investors. Appealing to their sense of racial justice as well as profit motives, he drafted an advertisement that read: "Today is the time to buy, if you want to be numbered among those of the race who are doing something toward trying to solve the so-called 'Race Problem.'" But the claim in his prospectus was much more pragmatic: "The very prejudice that has heretofore worked against us can be turned and used to our profit." This northern ghetto with a ready-made customer base, in short, would be the source of black opportunity.

By 1914, *The Outlet*, a weekly magazine, published an article stating that three-quarters of the black population of New York City, including all blacks of prominence, lived in Harlem; it called Payton "the father of the Negro community." The success of Payton's enterprise could be seen in the neighborhood of 13 West 131st Street, the house he had bought in 1903. The entire street was white in 1900; by the time of the 1915 New York State census, the block was almost completely inhabited by blacks. If indeed, as it was said, Phillip Payton was the "Father of Harlem," Maggie, Nellie's new friend, was the "Mother," which Payton acknowledged:

> The hardships that my wife and I went through before things broke for us would fill a book. If I have gained any success, to my wife belongs the major portion of the credit. No man ever had a more faithful, patient helpmate than I. Many were the days we were compelled to live or rather exist on ten cents a day . . . Had it not been for her help, I fear I would have given up.[6]

From the Harlem address, Nellie, Maggie, and Mrs. Washington visited Philadelphia, Baltimore, and Washington, D.C. Whether it was simply to see the sights or to meet with women whom it would be useful for Nellie to know is uncertain, though events in the coming years would suggest that it was the latter: in Nellie, Maggie Washington saw her protégée. But, in Maggie, soon to be president of the National Association, Nellie saw not only a mentor but someone whose ambitious national and international agenda vastly outshone the provinciality of her accommodationist husband. After visiting the nation's capital, Mrs. Payton and Mrs. Francis visited the fabled Tuskegee for a few days as Mrs. Washington's guests.[7] "Then after a week [at Tuskegee]," *The Appeal* reported approvingly, "Doctor Washington joined the ladies in their return trip to New York where they were the guests of honor at an afternoon reception given by Mr. and Mrs. Andrew Carnegie at their palatial home in New York City . . . Mrs. Francis is having a very swell time generally from what can be learned."[8]

Meanwhile, during his wife's absence, Billy had hosted almost weekly a variety of functions, and traveled to Glenwood, Breckenridge, and Morris, Minnesota, where he was engaged in the trials of several lawsuits for Northern Pacific. He was elected to the board of directors of Galloway Investment Company, formerly known as "Small" Loan and Investment Company, and sought but failed in his bid for national office with the Odd Fellows fraternity, the second-oldest black secret society in the country.[9] In St. Paul, Billy collected his things to meet his wife in Chicago on her return home from "visiting in the East since Thanksgiving."[10]

A week later, *The Appeal* again reported that after a six-week tour, "Mrs. W. T. Francis . . . was the recipient of many social courtesies. She was very highly delighted with her trip."[11] On January 9, she was celebrated for her travels with a heroine's welcome. "About 50 friends of Mrs. W. T. Francis gathered at her home last Monday night, without having advised her of their coming, for the purpose of welcoming her upon her return from the East and to congratulate her upon the pleasures and honors received by her, and the reflections upon St. Paul, in New York. Many pleasant things were said of Mrs. Francis by several speakers, among whom included Mrs. Ione Gibbs, [president of the Minnesota Federation of Colored Women's Clubs] . . . The occasion was a very pleasant one. Refreshments were served by the well-wishers of Mrs. Francis' home." It was a women's affair and Billy was not present during the evening.[12] St. Paul, it now appeared, belonged to Nellie. And just as important, it must have been a sign of support for his wife when he debated in the affirmative for women's suffrage, an issue that Nellie had more openly embraced.[13]

Phillip and Maggie Payton, 1912. Courtesy of the Photographs and Prints Division, Schomburg Center for Research in Black Culture, The New York Public Library.

Things were falling in place. Members demonstrated a commitment to do substantive work for the advancement of black people. African American club women in Minnesota were interested and invested in self-improvement through literary and historical studies, but were also deeply concerned with honoring achievements by African Americans and with improving social conditions for members of their race. As early at the 1896, Ione Gibbs, then president of the Ada Sweet Pioneer Club, reported to the National Association of Colored Women's Clubs at their 1896 convention that her club's goals were to pursue "literary and musical culture, social unity, and [direct] domestic economy," and stated that "its work, so far, has been largely historical in nature, with musical and literary programs," and that "the fundamental and ultimate object of this club at its formation was philanthropic."[14]

Because of job discrimination, African American families in Minnesota typically did not have as much disposable income as their white, middle-class counterparts. Between 1870 and 1915, as David V. Taylor reports, "Discrimination in employment, the failure or inability of Blacks to support Black businesses, and the indifference of the white community to them prevented the accumulation of surplus capital. For Blacks, St. Paul was a working-class community."[15] Most African American men living in Minnesota during the early decades of the twentieth century worked as railroad porters, waiters, busboys, janitors, or barbers. African American women typically worked as domestics if they worked outside the home. Despite these discriminatory conditions, a small African American middle class arose in the Twin Cities, and its club women did all they could for local African Americans in need.[16]

By the 1890s, black Minnesota had deepened its connection with nationwide networks. Having first convened in Boston in 1895, the National Association of Colored Women's Clubs encouraged and inspired African American club women to organize on the state level. In response, Mrs. Ione Gibbs of Minneapolis initiated the Minnesota Federation of Colored Women's Clubs in 1905, originally representing twelve clubs. They added the state slogan "Our Men, Women, and Children" to the national motto "Lifting as We Climb."[17] Under that banner, in addition to supporting the Crispus Attucks home for the young and elderly, and granting college scholarships to African American students, the Minnesota Federation sponsored a legal department to help African American defendants receive justice. Despite its relevance, the work nonetheless went unnoticed from the public's eye.[18] But Nellie, with her star status, could change this.

Nellie had decided not only to get involved with the Minnesota Federation of Colored Women's Clubs but to seek the leadership post. But in the genteel world of women's organizations, such a bid was based on consensus rather than the unseemly manners of political competition. If one could persuade a rival for her support, thereby avoiding rancor that at best only festered until the next occasion when unsightly grievances spilled outward, one should. The way the organization and the next leader looked to the membership, not to mention the public, mattered. To the extent that the transfer of leadership went smoothly earned the new leader acclaim that would only garner the organization higher standing. And in the oldest tradition of office seeking—one that had clearly worn off since the Bull Moose campaigns of Teddy Roosevelt—the candidate let others do the campaigning, and Nellie had many friends.

She had never been involved with the state federation since its inception in 1905. In a sense, the organization was Lula's, for she had been an office-holder since the second year of operation, as well as the associate editor of its publication, which had a lot to report about the work of its national affiliate.[19] But her contacts went back further. In 1902, as an officer of the Adelphai Club of St. Paul, she hosted a reception at her home for eminent Josephine St. Pierre Ruffin, cofounder of the American Woman Suffrage Association with Julia Ward Howe and Lucy Stone, editor of *Woman's Era,* a journal that promoted equal rights for black women, and organizer of the National Federation of Afro-American Women, the precursor to the National Association of Colored Women's Clubs: she was in town to deliver a speech at the conference.[20] It was her vision, together with Mary Church Terrell, who set the broad scope of the organization's purpose, that most attracted Lula. In 1905, the national association had reviewed the work of its charitable effort—travelers' aid in cities for working women from the South, health conditions in Africa, and Belgian atrocities in the Congo.[21] In Minnesota, two women were in the graduation class at St. Paul College of Law.[22] But the readers of *The Appeal,* which did not report the various reform efforts of the national group, had no sense of these accomplishments. Instead, despite the various essays that Lula edited, the state organization was trivialized as yet another woman's social group.[23] The state federation had not yet gained its voice, nor had Nellie found her own: one week after the Minnesota Federation of Colored Women's Clubs was founded in Duluth, when Billy delivered a speech at Pilgrim titled "Prepare Yourself to Take Advantage of your Opportunities," Maggie Griswold, though ill, felt well enough to receive visitors.[24] Nellie chose to be with her; this was Lula's time to be in the world.

But it also seemed to be the time of the woman. In addition to the two female students who were part of the 1906 St. Paul College of Law graduating class, Irene C. Buell, a 1907 graduate, became the thirty-sixth woman in the nation to be admitted to practice before the U.S. Supreme Court. In Boston, where the Niagara Movement held its third meeting, nearly half of the attendees were women. It seemed to be the colored woman's hour, though it was not reflected by *The Appeal,* which ran on the front page of the January 18, 1908, edition a sensual photograph of a maiden under the banner: "The Woman with a Flat Chest: Quite Easy to Have a Good Figure in These Days of Advanced Physical Culture."[25] It was not just an advertisement for personal enhancement but a statement to the readers that women were supposed to be ornaments, not political actors, and it had been published, not by an avowed misogynist but a friend of women's rights, and it had appeared not on page three or four, where advertisements normally appeared, but on the front page, normally reserved for national and international news. There was no hue and cry by *The Appeal* readers. Yet, it is hard to imagine that many women readers viewing the image did not feel, if not degraded, at least awkward, for it served as a reminder of how women were to be measured.

At the 1908 national convention of the National Association of Colored Women's Clubs (NACWC), the association examined the New York settlement movement, domestic training, burial clubs, female industrial placement, thrift, morality and racial attitudes of domestics, black children in the Georgia penal system, teachers' salaries, social purity, Liberia, housing for female industrial workers, tuberculosis, child labor, temperance, antilynching, and "rescue" work among youth.[26] By 1911, through her travels to eastern cities, and no doubt during the quieter moments with her sister, Nellie had come to view this list of issues to be compelling and it seemed that with her success with the pipe organ, and her attained status from having met with Carnegie and Taft, not to mention a deepening association with Mrs. Margaret Washington, a senior officer in the national federation, Nellie's time was fast approaching.

Throughout 1911, the Francis household experienced a flurry of activity springing from divergent ambitions—the leadership of the state federation and Billy's ambitions for higher office in the Odd Fellows national organization. As Nellie must have paid close attention to the planning committee and executive board of the state organization as it conferred over issues and business items to be discussed at the next annual meeting, which met on June 21, Billy plotted out a strategy to methodically court officers in the nation's oldest and most prestigious black fraternal order.[27] He also began what would ultimately be a failed effort to become ambassador to Haiti.[28] Yet, admirably, when they could, they both seemed intent on supporting the other in their respective pursuits. For her part, Nellie entertained Mrs. William C. (Grace K.) McCard of Baltimore, whose husband was a civil-rights attorney, founder that year of the Baltimore chapter of the National Association for the Advancement of Colored People (NAACP), and senior officer of the Baltimore chapter of the Odd Fellows.[29] The following April, when Nellie could not host a dinner for Odd Fellow dignitaries, she asked her sister to represent her: "On last Monday evening," reported *The Appeal*, "Attorney W. T. Francis entertained at dinner [Odd Fellows supreme court] justices H. L. Davis and W. R. Morris, Revs. E. H. McDonald and H. P. Jones. Mrs. R. D. [Lula] Chapman presided at the table."[30]

All of his effort must have paid off, for Billy was elected to be delegate representing St. Paul's Mars Lodge at the next national Odd Fellows convention, hosted a local Odd Fellows banquet as master of ceremonies, and entertained dignitaries at his home.[31] Then, after taking depositions for a lawsuit in Thief River Falls, he sped to Chicago to attend the Republican national convention.[32] But through it all, he made it back in time to follow Mayor Herbert Keller in welcoming the delegates who had come to Pilgrim Baptist Church to convene the Eighth Annual Minnesota Federation of Colored Women's Clubs.[33] And he had done it for Nellie.

At the Eighth Annual Convention, twenty clubs from around the state were represented. There were reports on woman suffrage, juvenile courts, the responsibility of women, a roundtable on the role of the club women, and from the state Bureau of Labor a report on the Gordian Knot issues in which the "Club helped."[34] For the first time, *The Appeal* actually covered the work of the federation.

As cordial as the convention had been, the one issue that could disrupt the calm waters had yet to be resolved: the selection of president—whether to keep the incumbent president who had become accustomed to this station, or to select someone new and less experienced in the ways of the federation. But by the second day, it had been settled; and now all that remained to make the convention a total success was a commodious election. On that day, *The Appeal* breathlessly reported, "The State Women's Federation closed in a blaze of glory Friday evening at last week one of the most successful meetings in its history. The officers elected for the ensuing term are: Mrs. W. T. Francis, St. Paul, president . . . The retiring president, Mrs. Ione Gibbs of Minneapolis, becomes honorary president."[35] Among the new officers, Lula was selected as chair of the literature department.

Referring to Nellie's predecessor, the new president graciously spoke, thanking the members of the local committee of the federation for their hearty support and cooperation in making the recent meeting the great success it was, which would not have been possible but for the very efficient and willing service of the women composing the committee. "It was a source of pleasure to her to know," reported the Minneapolis *Twin City Star*, "that she was elected without opposition." In a show of harmony, the retiring president—never to be forgotten, forever to be needed—would be accompanying the president-elect to the upcoming convention of the national association to be held in Hampton, Virginia, as delegates from Minnesota. But it would be Nellie Francis and not Ione Gibbs who would be on the program.[36]

Two weeks after the state convention adjourned, *The Appeal* published the following story about Lula:

> Lula, the efficient Chairman of the Program Committee of the Federation, is at St. Luke's Hospital where she is undergoing the "Rest Cure." Although very active in the recent Federation, and a club, church, and social life, Mrs. Chapman had been far from well and her friends are praying that this rest and the course of treatment which it involves will prove highly beneficial. Mrs. Chapman is a valuable member of the community and has its deepest sympathy.[37]

Three weeks later, her doctor said that she was doing well enough to be "now allowed to sit up a while each day."[38]

For this year's convention (1912), the major topics to be discussed would include the spread of segregation in northern and southern state branches of the YWCA; reports on the NAACP; domestic service

The third meeting of the Niagara Movement in Boston, 1907. Photograph by E. Chickerings, W. E. B. Du Bois Papers (MS 312). Special Collections and University Archives, University of Massachusetts Amherst Libraries.

training; antilynching; segregation in common carriers; destruction of a colored orphanage in Lexington, Kentucky; women's suffrage; an antisegregation resolution; and prostitution. But it was the call for a resolution to act against the execution of a seventeen-year-old black girl from the city in which their convention had convened that gripped the attention of the membership—the fate of Virginia Christian.

On March 18, 1912, a seventy-two-year-old white woman named Mrs. Ida Virginia Belote was murdered in her home at Hampton, Virginia, by her black seventeen-year-old employee Virginia Christian. Belote, known to have frequently mistreated Christian, on the fateful day accused the girl of stealing a locket and a skirt and an argument ensued with Belote hitting Christian with a cuspidor. The altercation escalated when Christian and Belote ran for two broom handles Belote used to prop up her bedroom windows. Christian grabbed one of the broom handles and struck Belote on the forehead. In an attempt to stifle Belote's screams, Christian stuffed a towel down Belote's throat, and the woman died by suffocation. When Christian left the house, she stole Belote's purse with some money and a ring. One newspaper reported that police found Belote's body "laying face down in a pool of blood, and her head was horribly mutilated and a towel was stuffed into her mouth and throat."[39]

Police soon arrested Christian, and during questioning she admitted to hitting Belote but was shocked that Belote was dead. Christian claimed she had no intent to kill Belote. With a lynch mob looming in the background, she was tried at the Elizabeth City County Courthouse and convicted of murder. The trial judge sentenced her to death in the state's electric chair. Charlotte Christian, the convicted girl's mother, begged for anyone who would listen for a chance to hear her "splain things to you better."[40] The National Association took up her plea. It would be the organization's intention to persuade the governor to suspend Virginia's execution to enable her attorneys to file an amended petition for a writ of error to the state supreme court. At once it sent two of its most able members from the conference to go to Richmond, the state capital. In terms of political temperament, they seemed to form an odd partnership, but it was one that characterized the profile of the national membership, which included women from both Du Bois and Bookerite camps, together working in the service of black women, and as reflected in their leadership. Association president Mary Church Terrell was an integrationist, early Du Bois supporter, and charter member of the NAACP, while her successor to leadership would be Maggie Washington, wife of Booker T. Washington.

The acclaim Nellie experienced from meeting with President Taft and, more notably in some quarters, Andrew Carnegie, was not limited to St. Paul. Mary Church Terrell, a national figure on the rights of black men and women, had surely taken a wary note of the new president of the Minnesota Federation of Colored Women's Clubs, elected just days before going to Hampton, Virginia, to attend the conference of the national federation. While Nellie had apparently curried favor with the powers behind Booker T. Washington's throne, Terrell, who had been a valued ally of W. E. B. Du Bois, joined the Niagara Movement and later, at Du Bois's suggestion, was elected a charter member of the NAACP. In short, she was decidedly not of the accommodationist camp.

"The Woman with a Flat Chest" from the front page of *The Appeal,* January 18, 1908. Courtesy of the Minnesota Historical Society.

Mary "Mollie" Church was the daughter of Robert Reed Church and Louisa Ayers Church, both former slaves prominent in the growing black community of Memphis, Tennessee. Both parents owned small, successful businesses and they provided "Mollie" and her brother with advantages that few other African American children of her time enjoyed. Robert became one of the South's first African American millionaires. Her mother, Louisa, owned a hair salon. She had one brother. Terrell's parents divorced during her childhood. Their affluence and belief in the importance of education enabled Terrell to attend the Antioch College laboratory school in Ohio, and later Oberlin College, where she earned both bachelor's and master's degrees. She taught languages at Wilberforce University and at a black secondary school in Washington, D.C. After a two-year tour of Europe, she completed a master's degree from Oberlin (1888) and married Robert Heberton Terrell, a lawyer who would become the first black municipal court judge in the nation's capital.

An early advocate of women's rights, Terrell was an active member of the National American Woman Suffrage Association, addressing in particular the concerns of black women. In 1896, she became the first president of the newly formed National Association of Colored Women's Clubs, an organization that, under her leadership, worked to achieve educational and social reform, seeking an end to discriminatory practices. Appointed to the District of Columbia Board of Education in 1895, Terrell, *The Appeal* had proudly announced, was the first black woman to hold such a position.

An early civil-rights advocate, educator, author, and lecturer on women's suffrage and the rights of African Americans, Terrell was a formidable character who apparently did not always get along well with others. In 1898, Ida Wells-Barnett, a strong personality in her own right, was struggling to manage her busy family life and career, but she was still a fierce campaigner in the antilynching circle. That year, Terrell's National Association of Colored Women's Clubs met in Chicago but did not invite Wells-Barnett to take part. When she confronted Terrell, then president of the club, Ida was told that the women of Chicago had said that, if she were to take part in the club, they would no longer aid the association. Wells-Barnett later learned that Terrell's own competitiveness played a part in excluding her. If Terrell had a competitive streak, she subordinated it to the urgency of the matter at hand, for the life of a seventeen-year-old black woman hung in the balance. Nellie might be of help.

That year, Terrell had retired from the national club presidency. Yet, she still had enough clout within the movement to authorize this last mission of mercy in the name of the federation. A life was at stake and she wanted Nellie, a person with style and presence—the likes of which an old Virginia cavalier would appreciate—to be involved. Just as important, Nellie had proven contacts that might come in handy—Andrew Carnegie, who propped up the race's chief proponent of accommodation, who in turn may well have been the governor's favorite Negro, and William Taft, who as a presidential candidate vigorously courted white Southerners of both parties, the very same men whom Taft proclaimed before a black audience in 1909 to be "your best friend." These were two men to whom Governor William Hodges Mann, the last Confederate veteran to fill the office, could relate, and Nellie had effectively been endorsed by both.[41] The prospect of saving Virginia Christian's life made the Terrell–Francis partnership necessary.

From their meeting with the governor, they were "satisfied that the death penalty will not be enforced."[42] But their satisfaction was short-lived. The facts of the crime and the racial climate imposed only one unmitigated outcome. The Virginia Supreme Court denied the writ and the governor declined to commute the execution despite the pleas from Virginia's advocates.[43] One day after her seventeenth birthday, on August 16, 1912, a short five months after the crime, Virginia authorities executed Christian at the state penitentiary in Richmond.[44]

Lady Principal

The 1912 convention at Hampton, Virginia, ended, as all of the annual conventions did, with a profound sense of purpose, considering the issues and debates over the previous two days. There was so much to be done for black women and children, so much to be done for the betterment of the race, and it was revitalizing to be with so many accomplished and learned black women assembled for mutual benefit. Although many of the issues examined focused more on the urgent needs of poor black women locked in poverty and racism, the attendees—some having escaped that wretched life during the early stages of their lives, others born into the good fortune of privilege—nonetheless talked of those desperate circumstances as if they had befallen on beloved family members. There was no sense of condescension or pity, but one of sincerity and grace. Still, there was nothing more to be done for Virginia. Some stayed after adjournment to follow the drama unfolding in Richmond over her fate, and some of them who were most deeply affected were just not ready to go home.

Days after the execution, Nellie and Maggie Washington, a person to whom she had grown closer, traveled to New York to visit their friend Maggie Payton, a side trip that Nellie seemed to need as a diversion that only her two special friends provided and that could not be found in St. Paul.[1] So much remained to be done, so much to be learned about the issues, about mobilizing her sisters in Minnesota to engage with more ambitious matters, and Maggie Washington, eleven years Nellie's senior and just elected the next president of the national association, would be her mentor. In September, Nellie and a recuperated but weakened Lula, accompanied Billy to Nashville to visit their grandmother, Nellie Seay.

From there, Billy went to Atlanta for the annual national convention of the Odd Fellows while Lula went to Texas to visit their aunt Juno. Billy later met Nellie to visit the Washingtons' home at Tuskegee, before returning to St. Paul.[2]

Ione Elveda Wood Gibbs. Photograph from *The Appeal*, September 24, 1910. Courtesy of the Minnesota Historical Society.

Margaret James Murray (her friends called her "Maggie") was born on March 9, 1865, in Macon, Mississippi, the third of five children. Her mother supported the family as a washerwoman. Her father, of Irish descent, is unknown. Noting her potential, around the age of seven her mother sent her to live with Quaker siblings, the Sanderses, who were teachers in the community who sent her to Fisk University's preparatory school in 1881 as a half-time student; she graduated in eight years. To cover expenses, she worked in the homes of faculty members and taught during the summer. W. E. B. Du Bois was a classmate and fellow member of the college's debate team, though it is unclear whether they were close. When she graduated in 1889, one year after Du Bois, Booker T. Washington delivered the commencement address. Cornering the great man at the senior luncheon, Murray boldly asked for a job, even though she had accepted a teaching position at Prairie View College in Texas. "Impressed with her effervescence and arrogance," writes historian Jacqueline Anne Rouse, Booker Washington decided to hire her."[3]

With the title "Lady Principal and Director of the Department of Domestic Service," she directly supervised female students and oversaw the department's curriculum, which entailed establishing lower and postgraduate divisions in sewing, laundering, basketry, millinery, soap making, table setting, cooking, and broom making. Handling all matters that the girls encountered, she came to be seen as a nurturing mother figure, a mentor, and a friend, traits that she perhaps carried

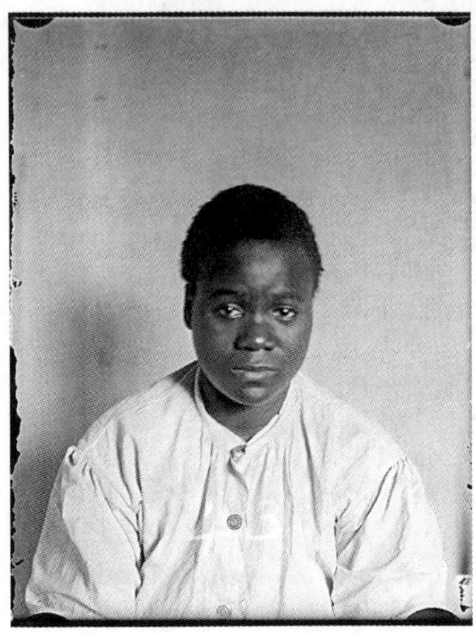

Virginia Christian, photographed most likely on June 3, 1912. Courtesy of the Library of Virginia.

over into her friendship with Nellie. Emergencies were usually handled by her and hence her advice was often solicited.[4] On a shoestring budget, she had many administrative duties ranging from arguing for more resources, equipment, and space to faculty relations, at times advocating Principal Washington to reconsider the issue of teacher salaries. She was his eyes and ears during his frequent absences from campus, monitoring the interaction of female students with male teachers, placing a high premium on values, tradition, and discipline. Graduates of her program easily secured employment, "though whites could not always understand the young ladies' desire to continue in college, when they could be working for them."[5] In 1892, the twice-widowed Booker T. Washington married Maggie Murray to make her the mother of three young children from his previous marriages.[6]

Maggie Washington's club activism began in Tuskegee when female faculty members and the wives of male faculty members formed the Tuskegee Women's Club (TWC). This small group of middle-class women saw the organization as a forum for their intellectual, educational, and spiritual growth, and as the college was located in a blighted area, members looked around for a reclamation project. They selected the Elizabeth Russell Plantation, located eight miles away and mostly populated by former convicts and those completing prison sentences, and where the dwellings were shabby, children undisciplined, and homes unkempt. For twelve years the Tuskegee Women's Club worked to transform the settlement. Margaret organized mothers' meetings and instructed women in home management, child care, and sewing circles, and she set up reading groups for the young and for older males. A day and evening school for parents was established with a Tuskegee graduate hired to teach. Sunday school classes were held and eventually a church was built. An abandoned cabin was donated by a local landowner to serve as the settlement's center.[7] But it was her belief in the strength of the home and a nurturing, God-fearing mother that served as the bulwark to social uplift. For all of their efforts, Margaret and her group measured their success by monitoring how quickly the poor conformed to the club's ideals and abandoned customs the reformers deemed demeaning or racially stereotypical, such as women wrapping their hair with cloth, a remnant of slavery.[8]

A final step in the struggle for black freedom, she felt, was landownership. Margaret Washington demonstrated a commitment to the mass cultural value of "black self-determination" and supported the attainment of black economic independence through property ownership. Annually, Tuskegee hosted agricultural conferences to train black independent and tenant farmers in the techniques for becoming economically successful, an emphasis she developed at the Russell Plantation. Financial solvency became a reality with a product the world needed. "It was the man and/or woman, free of economic reprisals from local whites, who was not afraid to challenge white supremacy in these racially divided small towns."[9] It would be a principle that later found itself part of the program of the Tuskegee's Women's Club, the Alabama Federation of Colored Women's Club formed in 1899 after a number of clubs formed across the state, and the National Association of Colored Women (NACW) that she would help establish.

Cultural uplift enriched the soul of former slaves. The Alabama federation pulled together wide-ranging projects such as purchasing property to build homes for girls and boys, creating libraries and reading rooms, providing shelters for the aged and infirmed, and organizing

Mary Church Terrell, circa 1900. Courtesy of the Library of Congress.

statewide programs that commemorated Negro history, particularly celebrations of the birthday of Frederick Douglass. The Sojourner Truth Club of Montgomery invited children in black schools to participate in an essay contest on famous black men and women, with winners presenting their essays at public programs around the state held during the second week of February, predating Professor Carter G. Woodson's "Negro History Week," which began in 1926.[10]

For Margaret Washington there was a need to improve the quality of segregated public spaces designated for blacks. Although they did not attack the political ideology and the everyday humiliations associated with legal segregation, Margaret and the Tuskegee Women's Club thought that it was important that the spaces provided be clean, comfortable, and pleasant. To these ends, the middle-class women of the

TWC cleaned segregated waiting rooms, hung curtains, secured modest furnishings, added reading materials on black people, and hung portraits and photographs of black leaders and progressive and political whites, such as John Brown and several presidents of the United States. In some places, as was the custom in some black homes, photographs of prominent Native Americans were also displayed.[11]

The Alabama Federation of Colored Women's Club's (AFCWC) most extensive work was in prison reform. Critical of the state's policy to incarcerate juvenile delinquents alongside hardened criminals, the federation was successful in getting the young black inmates released into the custody of its boys' school built in Mt. Meigs, the federation's center. Under federation president Cornelia Bowen and Margaret Washington, many young lives were saved from prison. The state eventually assumed responsibility for the boys' reformatory school and the federation began to raise funds to build a home at Mt. Meigs for young girls. Because prison reform was a national issue, the NACW's national office joined the program. By 1920, NACW's efforts to have black probation officers hired culminated in positions being created in several cities, including ones for Ida B. Wells-Barnett in Chicago and Alice Dugged Cary in Atlanta.[12]

Urgent though the matter of prison reform was, concern over the increase of lynchings and massive forms of mob violence shocked the conscience during the closing years of the nineteenth century and into the twentieth century, as reflected in Brownville, Atlanta, and Springfield that stimulated the formation of the NAACP. Soon, while antilynching bureaus and multiple investigations were launched, the antilynching crusade itself became associated with one woman, Ida B. Wells-Barnett, who took the campaign to Europe following her successful tours in the United States. The British enthusiasm for Wells-Barnett's movement could not be deterred by Francis Willard, leader of the temperance movement in America, then touring England, who suggested that the lynchings were a response to black men's attacks on white women. James A. Jacks, president of the Missouri Press Association, learned of Wells-Barnett's remarks to the British suffragists and antilynching crusaders and declared that black women's immorality caused black men to attack virginal white women. In letters to England

and before the annual conference of the press association, Jacks asserted that "black women are wholly devoid of morality, the women are prostitutes and all [are] natural thieves and liars."[13]

The defamation of the character of black women triggered Josephine St. Pierre Ruffin, president and founder of the Woman's Era Club in Boston, to issue a call for a national meeting "in defense of Negro womanhood." In 1895, a large group of black women gathered in Boston and formed the National Federation of Afro-American Women (NFAAW), and Margaret Murray Washington, Lady Principal of Tuskegee College, was elected president. Although united in a national federation, member clubs retained their autonomy. Kindergartens, mothers' meetings, day-care centers, and home management dominated the work of many local clubs. In the South, club women continued to assist rural women in establishing homes, buying land, and promoting racial pride and consciousness by studying black history.[14]

In 1896, the NACW united hundreds of women's groups into a strong social-reform organization. Perceived as a conduit for channeling black female activism, NACW served to raise the consciousness of African Americans on the issues of race and gender politics. Margaret Washington was at the center of this new organization, formed from the merger of the Washington Colored League and the NFAAW. Mary Church Terrell, a prominent club woman from the District of Columbia, was elected the first NACW president, and Washington served as vice president. In both organizations, the assaults on black women were the main priorities. Regionally, southern black women were aggressive in their exposures of sexual exploitation of black domestics working in white households. Southern white women were held responsible because of their inability to control their men and because of their silence in the face of this persistent abuse. Female prisoners were also sexually abused, the club women revealed; and because in many prisons the women were chained and housed with male prisoners, they fell victim to rape by inmates and white guards. Southern black club women were vigilant in their struggle to overthrow not only the convict release system, but these horrible conditions for black female prisoners as well.[15]

She was no less committed to the welfare of women in African countries. At the closing session of the conference in 1910, the executive

Nellie Francis in *The Appeal,* July 27, 1912. Courtesy of the Minnesota Historical Society.

board, chaired by Margaret Washington, decided to send a petition to Congress denouncing "the atrocities committed against native Africans by Belgian colonial administrators in the Congo Free State."[16] Washington, together with Mary McLeod Bethune, Nannie Burroughs, and other members of the NACW and its southeastern regional federation, would establish the International Council of Women of the Darker Races in 1920, following the meeting of the NACW in Richmond. Women from Africa, Haiti, Ceylon, the West Indies, and leaders of black women's groups in the United States pledged their "heartiest cooperation in the new movement which has for its objective the economic, social and political welfare of the women of all the dark races." But membership in this new council would exclude white women. As the newly elected president, Washington said, "The Anglo-Saxon race [is] barred because of [its] racial antagonism to darker women—not being defamed like women of color, hence [it] would not have the interest and could add nothing to the determined purpose to ameliorate conditions for darker races throughout the world." In agreement with their president, the women declared that the many handicaps, barriers, and embarrassments "from which the women of the darker races suffer because of color prejudice can and must be overcome by a powerful organization working intensively along definite lines."[17]

Hers was a boldly nationalistic yet seemingly incongruous view for a Bookerite who believed that racial issues in the South could be resolved, if not through integration, through interracial cooperation. But the South, it seemed to her, was a world apart from the potential of black advancement in America. "As educator and reformer, Margaret felt secure in her belief that there existed a segment of white America

Margaret James Murray Washington, circa 1915.
Courtesy of the Library of Congress.

that was dedicated to fairness and racial harmony." Representing the NACW, in the 1920 speech before the Commission of Interracial Cooperation, she indicated how the two positions were not mutually exclusive when she talked about the role that white women could play in the development of the "ideal home" for the African Americans in their midst. She first described how the legacy of slavery had deprived many black women of the essential knowledge of how to build and maintain stable homes, families, and communities. Interracial work was a necessary element for ending these social deficiencies. She told the white delegates that black women should be respected, given their struggle for survival. After centuries of inadequate training in education and citizenship, it was most unfair to expect all black women to be on the same social plane as most white women. But like them, most black women sought better schools, homes, and public protection for their communities. Empowerment required education and training, and white supporters could join in the crusade for longer school terms, equal facilities, and appropriate supplies for black children. She stated: "let us make no mistake: let us realize that we are two separate races living in a country side-by-side, each equally responsible for the good citizenship of the country, and therefore each equally deserving of a fair chance and fair play in every way." However, in terms uncharacteristic of an adherent of accommodationism, she assured the women that "we are going to keep right after you until you do give us this chance, until you do recognize that we must have this chance. If we are to be the law-abiding, well-balanced, well-educated citizens the South needs . . . if we are going to take our rightful place in [the] citizenship of this country . . . we must have it."[18] This would have surely brought Nellie, had she been present at the time, to her feet.

At the heart of her work was improving the education of black children. She informed Professor Carter G. Woodson about the group's existence and "its crusade to incorporate Negro History and Negro Literature into our schools." And this initiative was not to be exclusively designed for schoolchildren but also for adults interested in Negro history, and especially the history of women of color. Washington wanted Woodson to help in this effort by recommending the titles of books on women in Africa, the Caribbean, and India. From these recommendations, the education committee—Addie Whiteman Dickerson, Mary Church Terrell, and Nannie Helen Burroughs—designed a course of study for the members and a program to be offered to public school systems. She told Woodson that the project had to be done in a definite and systematic manner for "we are going to have to deal with white superintendents."[19] Anticipating white reaction that she and her group were trying to replace the "white" curriculum, she said, "We are not trying to displace any other literature or history but trying to get all children of the country acquainted with the Negro." She said later, "I think you will be surprised to know how many schools North and South, even our own schools, where our children are taught nothing except literature of the Caucasian race. We are not fighting any race, we are simply looking [out] for our own. The first law of nature is self-preservation."[20]

As Rouse writes, "[T]he multifaceted career of Margaret Washington accepted certain premises: her moderation on interracial issues; her emphasis on home, family, social purity, morality, and racial uplift; and the importance of vocational training for many young African Americans."[21] These were all positions that her husband embraced. But despite the stern countenance he usually projected, it was Mrs. Washington who led the way. And though it was she who usually drafted his speeches on accommodation, like the one the delegates at Hampton adjourned to hear at Newport News, Virginia, when he delivered an address to the employees of the government shipyard, her most significant work came from her own passions.[22]

Her temper would rise when calling for the "struggle against evil in our communities." In these campaigns of moral uplift, Margaret Washington endorsed strategies associated with the NAACP and other integrationist groups, recommending that "first of all, we can resist the very common practice of establishing the district of segregated vice near residentials areas of black families. If need be [we must] march an army of protest to City Hall and battle for the strength and purity of our sons and daughters."[23] And on the issue of lynching, her voice once again outstripped her husband's. By 1921, her open anger at the lack of a national law against lynching was clear. No longer tolerant of southern white women's desire to wait for local and state legislation, she denounced the country's hypocrisy in having an international reputation for upholding human rights, while allowing the number of lynchings to increase. On this issue, she seemed at one with her husband's most strident rivals—Ida Wells-Barnett and W. E. B. Du Bois: "[Americans of all races] want it because it will keep the name and reputation of any community clean and above national disgrace. . . . This country boasts of enjoying the leading and commanding place among the nations of the earth. While lynchings go unpunished and without prevention, such a claim is but an empty boast! . . . flagrant hypocrisy! We are not hypocrites, we are in earnest. We want lynchings to be stopped! Let the law be passed."[24]

Ida B. Wells-Barnett in the 1890s. Courtesy of the Special Collections Research Center, University of Chicago Library.

She was very much a supporter of equality for women and agreed with Mary Talbert, a later president of the NACW, on the issue of women's suffrage. Talbert had given a speech at the NACW's biennial conference describing the importance of equality for women, emphasizing their integral role in the evolution of society. Margaret Washington wholeheartedly concurred. She secured a plank in the Alabama federation's bylaws from the early 1900s, and it became the predominant issue for the Tuskegee Women's Club, especially for southern black women, not only to limit the immorality in their communities but to ensure passage of public health and child labor legislation, to improve the working conditions and benefits of female laborers, to protect women who worked in other people's homes, and to influence decision making by racist or indifferent school boards overseeing black schools, as well as to build parks, playgrounds, better railway conditions for black passengers, reading rooms, and libraries.[25] In these many ways, Lady Principal was far more progressive than her formidable husband and she would not let his work become an obstacle to her own. Theirs was a marital arrangement that Nellie could admire.

Divided Duty

> STATE PRESIDENT RESIGNS: [The Minnesota Federation of Colored Women's Clubs] received a shock last Friday afternoon, when at the close of the Executive Board meeting at Minneapolis, Mrs. W. T. Francis, State President, [after nine months of service] tendered her resignation and announced her intention to relinquish the office. Mrs. Francis had rendered excellent service to the organization and as its President had been an indefatigable worker and lost no opportunity to place the Federation in contact with the progressive influence of the State. The Federation has sustained a severe loss in the resignation of Mrs. Francis as the head, and the members of the Executive Board showed appreciation of that fact by spending an hour in an effort to find some way through persuasion to bring pressure enough to bear upon the President to induce a withdrawal of the resignation. The reason given by Mrs. Francis was that her health would not permit her to hold the office longer.[1]

Seven months earlier, when Nellie and Billy visited Dr. and Mrs. Booker T. Washington at their home in Tuskegee, word came that St. Paul attorney Fredrick Lamar McGhee had just died. For Billy and his host, the news must have arrived to mixed reactions. To Washington, McGhee, a graduate of Tuskegee and former senior adviser and chief counsel for the Wizard's National Afro-American Council, was nonetheless an apostate who had left the Bookerite camp to help chief rival W. E. B. Du Bois form the Niagara Movement. But Billy, fully aware of this history and likely torn by divergent loyalties to his political mentor and to his friend, must have struggled to modulate the tension between how he felt and the appearance he felt compelled to exhibit in the presence of a powerful race leader not known for being generous of spirit. His shock and a sincere display of loss would come later with Nellie in the privacy of the guest room where the rawness of the news began to fully take hold. Indeed, Fredrick's death had come suddenly, stemming from an injury he had sustained from an otherwise innocuous fall, which had grown into a blood clot that dislodged from the point of an injury to his leg and traveled to his lung, where it took his life.[2] Billy would not be permitted to mourn for long. At the urging of friends, he took on Fredrick's practice, which may have seemed at the time to be a real opportunity for his own professional growth and independence. As the chief clerk in the legal department of Northern Pacific, he had both status as it existed within St. Paul's black community and the precious benefit of a steady income that afforded him and Nellie with a comfortable lifestyle. But even though his employers had been supportive of his civic, church, and political activities, he still needed to seek their permission to participate in these various engagements. Besides, there was little potential for him to move any higher within Northern Pacific's corporate structure. Now, in private practice at last, he could be his own man.

Moreover, private practice afforded him the primary position of leadership in St. Paul's black community. As Paul Nelson notes, "In some ways, Francis fit this role better than McGhee had done. McGhee never led from the center. He was a Catholic, a Democrat, and a W. E. B. Du Bois man, all minority positions, and he had an edge on him. Francis was a Baptist, Republican, a Booker T. Washington man, and a more conventional thinker than McGhee had been." On the other hand, McGhee had been a criminal defense attorney almost exclusively. "That did not suit Francis, who lacked McGhee's zest for combat." Francis's practice tended to be civil, which included divorces, real estate, probate, business law, and personal injury.[3] Just to learn the culture of criminal litigation—which entailed filings and all the necessary paperwork for motions, trial tactics, and the range of temperaments of judges, prosecutors, jurors, clerks, bailiffs, and newsmen lurking around the police court who always seemed to be looking for a racial, and therefore salacious angle to the story—had to be, at first, overwhelming.

McGhee biographer Paul Nelson described a law practice that was short on resources. It was a mixture of small cases and well-publicized murder cases, none of which paid very well. McGhee's courtroom successes never brought him, so to speak, the best class of criminals. His more noteworthy victory had been the acquittals of his two white clients, but he never again represented white people in a major case. His last murder trial, in early 1912, typified the circumstances he faced: impecunious black defendants, low pay (he was probably court-appointed), and very limited resources for mounting a defense. In this last case, one for which he mounted the insanity defense for the first time, he relied on two of his closest friends—Dr. Valdo Turner and Billy Francis. Billy's involvement was purely coincidental, helping to subdue the raging defendant after he had stabbed Mrs. Celestine Jackson to death. Turner's involvement was pivotal.

The trial dealt with one issue of fact: the defendant's condition of mind. To make the point, McGhee called his "expert" witness, Dr. Valdo Turner. As Nelson notes, "The use of Dr. Turner illustrates the potentially disastrous lack of resources available to McGhee in the case. Turner was a general practitioner and surgeon, with no special training or experience in psychiatry. What is more, he had examined the defendant only once, and thus an extremely thin foundation for an expert opinion." On cross-examination, Turner revealed the weakness of his evidence. When asked to give a more specific diagnosis, he admitted that he had not studied the case long enough to judge the form of insanity it was. Nor could he give a prognosis.[4]

"To make the trial a little stranger still, McGhee then put himself on the witness stand to testify about his own observations of [George] Parker (the defendant) in late December (1911) and early January (1912)." "Strange" though it may seem, it was par for the course for McGhee's litigation style. He was willing to do anything to get his client off. Contemporary Adina Gibbs, daughter of John Adams, observed: "He bullied, he obstructed, he belittled, he objected ad nauseum, he appealed to God, and he appealed to prejudice." These were the same characteristics that she observed in his courtroom behavior: "He was a man who would perform when he had cases in court. He just performed. He would weep . . . just cry when he needed to impress the jury. Or he would go through performances and roar and howl and all that sort of thing to impress the jury." In other words, nothing—not civil rights, not politics, not fighting racism, not even his own dignity—mattered more than his client's interest.[5] This, and attorney's fees that any pauper could afford, made him a highly desired advocate. Francis had been a performer, but a certain reserve had begun to settle into his demeanor. He would clearly have to find his own style, and somehow make a living doing it.

But McGhee's law practice had undeniably not been a moneymaker. A number of his cases came through court appointments, and compensation was very low. A Minnesota statute in effect at the time provided the court appointment of counsel for indigent defendants, with compensation of up to ten dollars a day "for the number of days he was actually employed in the court upon the trial. There appeared to be no compensation for trial preparation. He had earned enough to afford a nice home for his family and a farm in Wisconsin, and had contributed to charity and church, but not enough to accumulate real wealth in land, money, or investments. Both properties were mortgaged—his house in St. Paul had two at the time of his death—he left $375 in bank deposits and $675 in banks receivables, only $200 of which was deemed collectible, and law books worth $900. "Fred McGhee's death," Nelson reported, "had a devastating financial impact on his wife and daughter." Mattie, at age forty-three, had not worked outside of the home in more than twenty-five years, and their daughter's hopes for higher education were now dashed. It appears that they worked for their remaining years as a typist and stenographer for a downtown advertising agency.[6] McGhee's practice was far from a cash cow.

In taking on this practice, Billy was taking on a huge challenge. For now, his prospects suddenly seemed quite untenable without the safety net of a Northern Pacific salary. It would be a balancing act to hustle for work, be visible in the community and in political circles, and perform the lawyerly tasks of doing a job that largely required a monkish existence in law libraries preparing cases. It was no longer an issue of protecting property interests, but now, in addition, it was a matter of the client's freedom. If one's professional reputation was as good as the last case, the stakes for success were now wholly different. And he had to appear in control of this new venture. He would occupy the suite of offices in Union Block, Fourth and Cedar, "so long occupied by the late F. L. McGhee. Mr. Francis," reported *The Appeal,* "has faith to believe that his friends who have advised this step will give him their united support and he hopes by faithful and earnest efforts to win many more friends."[7] To cut costs, he needed the stenographic and organizational skills of his wife to run the office. Her equity would come from the survival of the legal practice that bore her husband's name.

By the new year, Billy had resumed weekly appearances as master of ceremonies at various banquets and receptions, was retained as counsel of record for a number of probate cases, flew to Philadelphia to clerk for the Supreme Court of the Odd Fellows, was elected to the board of directors of the Crispus Attucks Home, and was appointed "auxiliary chairman of the subcommittee on public comfort for the entertainment and accommodations of Afro-American visitors" who will attend the inaugural ceremonies of Democratic president-elect Woodrow Wilson in Washington, D.C., on March 4.[8] McGhee had shown that some Democrats could be friends and clients. By March, Billy had two criminal cases in which both defendants eventually pleaded guilty, which McGhee's clients almost never did. Later that month, when Booker T. Washington passed through St. Paul on a speaking tour that would take him to California, Billy met with him "for an hour's conference on matters of immediate importance to race."[9] Perhaps one of the "matters" on which he wanted to confer with the Wizard—an awkward matter, indeed—was the thousand dollars he raised for the NAACP.[10] But at this time of transition when blacks were being drawn to the Du Bois camp, it was good for his law practice to be seen lending support for that organization. These were a few of his activities throughout the first three months of the year, which reflected the high volume of paperwork that needed to be churned out. To keep up, in April, Nellie resigned her post as president of the state federation after having performed essentially two separate full-time jobs since the previous October. The decision was necessary and disappointing.

As state federation president, Nellie had worked assiduously to lobby the governor and legislators as well as to coordinate the efforts of club members, grouping them by constituency to meet with their

Margaret and Booker T. Washington with their children Ernest Davidson, Booker T. Jr., and Portia. Courtesy of Tuskegee University Archives.

representatives to persuade friendly lawmakers to incorporate federation issues into state policy. While on occasion she had to go to the capitol to meet officials or observe conference meetings, she had to conduct federation efforts in the evenings, for she was needed at the office during business hours to deal with clients, mail, court papers, invitations to speak, record keeping, and to conduct the daily business of a law practice. She was usually alone in the office to manage everything so Billy could attend to litigation matters. Her workday began very early in the morning and continued late into the evening.

During the final months of 1912, before the legislative session began, the combined workload of the federation and the office, though individually weighty, was at least manageable, particularly when Billy assured Nellie that the present circumstance was temporary; but into the new year, with no additional clerical staff (the practice could not yet afford to hire anyone), the legislative session commencing, and Billy's activities stepping up, the best time to drop either responsibility had passed. She could see that as spring approached, her federation duties would require her to travel, first in preparation for the state convention in July to be held in Duluth and then committee meetings in the eastern cities for the national organization, thus leaving the office unattended. Billy's work would soon be taking him away, as well.[11] Knowing that she could no longer do both jobs, she had to make a choice—she resigned effective a week later when the legislature adjourned.[12]

On the one hand, it was not a hard choice to make. The law practice was their only source of income and she was doing her part. On the other hand, leading the state federation in doing good work for society gave her life meaning, and the club women on the executive committee knew this. They also valued her talents, social standing, and networks that they could capitalize on, which was why they selected her to be their president in the first place; they could not fully understand or accept that there was any circumstance that would compel her to relinquish her chosen duty. Surely, Nellie and Billy were people of means, they reasoned. After all, Billy had worked all those years in the legal department of the Northern Pacific Railway. Surely, such exposure to that level of affluence had rubbed off on him. Moreover, they likely assumed that Fredrick McGhee's law practice had to have been successful, for a man of his provocative flamboyance would never have survived otherwise in the staid white-dominated legal and political community of St. Paul. And now, with Billy the successor to McGhee's status as Minnesota's most prominent black attorney and civil-rights spokesman—he now appeared almost weekly in *The Appeal,* the *Twin City Star,* and at nearly every social and civic venue—and Nellie's pristine grace in leadership and ever-present refinement, it was hard for the members of the executive committee to imagine that Billy and Nellie were in fact desperate for income. Within the proper black society that these club women embodied, coming as they did from a class influenced by the striving doctrine of Booker T. Washington, yet where "middle-class" status was more often an artifice than a reality, it remained difficult to attribute personal problems to personal finances. Poverty was a failure in character.[13] In this, to some of the grand dames on the executive board, Billy and Nellie had failed their obligations to their social class. To others, Nellie's stepping down was somehow a rejection of them. In either case, the cordial relationship between Mr. and Mrs. Francis and *The Appeal* diminished. Increasingly, St. Paul's preeminent attorney appeared in the Minneapolis *Twin City Star* while Nellie completely dropped from sight. The Minneapolis desk of *The Appeal* was managed by Jasper Gibbs, son of Ione, who seemed gratified by the misfortune of the women who had succeeded her.[14]

It was easier to just say that health was the cause. In Nellie's case, it may have been true, considering the stress she had undergone from the previous year or the delicate condition that she may have inherited from her mother and shared with her sister. But, given the strictures of proper black society, it was just as likely that "health" was the kind of explanation that tended to close off further discussion, appeal to the listeners' sense of discretion, and salvage the reputation of middle-class black men who evidently could no longer provide, and especially of community leaders, whose self-respect and social standing depended on earning enough to free their wives to perform important civic functions. She certainly seemed to drop out of sight from all church, civic, and social activities to spend time at the office and put in many weekend hours just to keep up and respond to requests for written comments on legal matters.[15] The *Twin City Star,* reporting on the state federation that was then meeting in Duluth, mentioned that "Mrs. Laura Hickman of St. Paul brought greetings to the convention from our former Pres. Mrs. Nellie Francis."[16] It was the only time she appeared in the paper. A week later, as she tended to the ever-mounting administrative duties in the office, Billy left for Philadelphia to attend the Odd Fellows Supreme Court, going on from there to conduct business in New York, Washington, Atlantic City, and Atlanta and stopping in Chicago. When he returned to St. Paul, the paper reported that "[h]e is delighted with his trip and is enjoying good health."[17]

The *Twin City Star* reported on the activities of federation chapters around the country, and that Ione Gibbs, in her capacity of vice president of the national federation, was about to go to the executive meeting in Philadelphia. Nellie, in the confines of the law office on Union Block, was churning out volumes of documents and correspondence.[18] At the time, Billy wrote a series of public letters for the newspapers advocating civil rights and raising concerns about recent congressional enactments that curtailed rights, as well as calling for a day of prayer against "bad laws."[19] Nellie typed every word in every final draft, which, once published, drew the attention of senior policy makers. In October, Governor Adolph O. Eberhart appointed Billy and, because Nellie was needed in the office, Lula to join a delegation to represent the state at the Emancipation Celebration in Chicago for 1914.[20] At the time of Billy's appointment, he was preparing for two probate hearings and two criminal trials, both sets of documents which Nellie had to organize and type.[21] When President Woodrow Wilson instituted a discrimination policy within his administration, leaders around the country—including Billy—prepared petitions protesting his action. Their friend and fellow Nashville native James Napier, register of the treasury and husband of a friend of Nellie, resigned his post rather than obey the policy to segregate his workforce. Nellie fielded inquiries into the petition that flooded into the office.[22] But in the glare of Billy's luminescent public face, she was cast in silhouette.

But in the interim since her resignation as federation president, her absence from view seemed to chill the regard that some federation members once held for her, and by November, it became even more evident when Mary Church Terrell, founder of the national organization and now leader of the NAACP, came to Minnesota for a speaking engagement. She had not been in St. Paul since the late 1890s when she was the guest of Mrs. Amanda (T. H.) Lyles, who later helped her to organize the National Federation in Washington.[23] Although her speech was not a federation event, most of the participants had that affiliation. Lyles, Ione Gibbs ("who made one of her very nice speeches"), and all of the familiar St. Paul names assembled to greet the guest of honor at Mrs. G. W. James's St. Anthony home, just doors away from the Francis home. Owing perhaps to an invitation extended by her neighbor and former state president, perhaps as a nod to good taste, Nellie was in attendance, her first appearance at such an occasion. But she was not there to speak, present, or perform but instead to be relegated to the most minor of roles: to lend her name as one of ten hostesses "assisting in receiving" and to sit in stoic dignity amid the club community that had excitedly come to see the legendary leader. Nellie was to become the compliant subject for some who looked askance at her over here resignation as president, a sign of the decline in esteem for her by the

Fredrick L. McGhee, circa 1910. Courtesy of the Minnesota Historical Society.

state's grand dames and by some whom she called friends, who, despite the invitation, felt that it was she who exhibited bad taste in coming. Her sister Lula, an officer of the state federation since its inception in 1905, did not attend the reception, nor did her husband Billy, who normally played a prominent role in such affairs, perhaps with Nellie's consent. Their family loyalty to her might have made matters worse. By the time Mrs. Terrell finally "left for the East on the late train," she showed no sign of recognition of the woman seated quietly in the corner with whom she had spent profoundly charged hours the year before—just the two of them—as they tried to save the life of seventeen-year-old Virginia Christian.[24]

Over the previous months, there had been no public exchange of unpleasant words between Nellie and the executive board members. For much of that time, Nellie had been preoccupied with the administrative duties of the law practice, so, at least for a time, it seemed likely that she was unaware that grievances among certain club members had taken root, nor did she have the time to indulge their displeasure. Her work, as banal it may have seemed to others, was crucial to giving Billy the medium through which his voice could be heard. What he had to say through the written word protected people's property interests, kept others out of jail, and enlivened the voice of protest in the name of civil rights. But none of what she did was the work of the federation, and that was the problem. Over their grand duty of good deeds and secretarial work she chose the typewriter; and with that went the newspaper coverage that came to the state federation only when Nellie was elected president, and left when she resigned. This alone had to be especially biting to the executive committee.

Ida B. Wells-Barnett would have understood this situation and sympathized with Nellie. Years earlier, when Wells-Barnett organized a demonstration in Chicago to protest the lynching of Frazier Baker, a black postmaster in South Carolina, she later went on a five-week effort to lobby Congress and President McKinley on a bill to grant compensation to his widow and children, and took her own nursing baby on the trip. While she was there, Congress declared war on Spain, which stalled the progress of the bill. But upon returning home, to support the war effort she threw her energies into helping to enlist a part of the national guard of the state: "I went to Springfield with my children and stayed with the regiment until finally it was mustered into service, and I saw them entrain for Cuba." Soon afterwards, T. Thomas Fortune, editor of the *New York Age* and reputed "dean of black journalism," urged her to help him resurrect a national movement that he had started some years before under the head of the Afro-American League. "This I very gladly did, as the second baby was just being weaned and I could safely leave him with his grandmother."[25]

Shortly afterward, she was the guest of Susan B. Anthony, and had been with her for several days before she noticed "the way she would bite out my married name in addressing me. Finally, I said to her, 'Miss Anthony, don't you believe in women getting married?' She said, 'Oh, yes, but not women like you who have a special call for special work. I too might have married but it would have meant dropping the work to which I had set my hand.' She said, 'I know of no one in this country better fitted to do the work you had in hand than yourself. Since you have gotten

Amanda Lyles, circa 1913. Courtesy of the Minnesota Historical Society.

married, agitation seems practically to have ceased. Besides, you have divided duty. You are here trying to help in the formation of this league and your eleven-month-old baby needs your attention at home. You are distracted over the thought that maybe he is not being looked after as he would be if you were there, and that makes for divided duty.'"[26]

Similar to Miss Anthony, the ladies of the executive board would not acknowledge that other responsibilities could hold more weight than club work. For Nellie, the law practice itself was not a business solely owned by Billy; it was her business, as well. And their shared ownership was an arrangement that few of the ladies experienced.

On the night of March 28, 1913, George T. Williams reported to the Union Depot in St. Paul, fifteen minutes late to work as a sleeping-car porter for the Pullman Company that ran the leg between St. Paul and Seattle. W. C. Williams, the night inspector for the Pullman Company, ordered Porter Williams off the car. When the porter refused to get off, the inspector called a police officer to have him arrested; he was charged with "drunk and disorderly conduct." Williams was confined in jail for three days before he secured the representation of Billy Francis; he was tried and acquitted. In the meantime, Williams was discharged by the Pullman Company. When he was unable to secure employment elsewhere, he directed his attorney to bring suit against the Pullman Company in the district court in St. Paul. In late February, after a three-day trial, the jury began its deliberations. After "almost 15 minutes" the jury delivered a verdict in favor of Williams for $2,999.99, "the largest verdict ever rendered in this county for malicious prosecution."[27] This had to be a sweet victory for Nellie as well, for every stroke at the typewriter to hammer out court documents was a stroke for a little more justice for her father, who had also worked for the Pullman Company; Tom Griswold would have been proud.

It also lightened Nellie's workload in the office, for with the spate of well-paying civil cases that finally began to come to the practice, in addition to the Williams victory that would surely attract more business, the practice could now hire help in the office.[28] She indulged herself with a moment of levity when she agreed to model in Madam Hart's "annual spring demonstration of ladies' head wear."[29] But a month later, when Nannie Burroughs, a nationally renowned leader of the women's club movement, visited St. Paul and Minneapolis, Nellie was effectively called back into service. Burroughs was a protégée of Anna Cooper, Mary Church Terrell, and Maggie Washington, active in the National Baptist Association, and an advocate for women's suffrage and job training for black women. But her personal history and leadership on the national stage and her very appearance spoke to many African American women who had internalized a sense that light skin was a condition for the privilege of black leadership. Burroughs's confidence flourished at an early stage. Expecting to work as a teacher in the District of Columbia Public Schools, she was told by white officials that she was "too dark"—they preferred lighter-complexioned black teachers.[30] Her skin color and working-class status had thwarted the appointment she was chosen for, but she said, "the die was cast [to]

Nannie Burroughs, circa 1913. Courtesy of the Library of Congress.

beat and ignore both until death."[31] This zeal that opened a door to the profession for low-income and social status black women led Burroughs to establish a training school for women and girls.

It was her story, under the auspices of the Minnesota Federation of Colored Women's Clubs with its new executive board, that drew people to pack the Old Senate Chamber; and Nellie—the "porcelain doll," as one of the retired executive board members called her—was given the honor of introducing her.[32] "Mrs. W. T. Francis presided and made a splendid introductory speech, presenting her to the audience." In that world one's importance was established if one had been scheduled a private meeting with the guest of honor. Accordingly, nearly a year to the day since her resignation, during which time tensions arose with members of the executive board, as recognition of past service and the future to come, Nellie escorted the distinguished visitor and later entertained her at a one-on-one lunch at her residence.[33] The visit would prove to be the first step for Nellie's return to leadership. The second step was the arrival of Juno Frankie Seay Pierce from Paris, Texas.[34]

Juno

On June 24, 1914, the Minnesota Federation of Colored Women's Clubs met for its tenth annual convention in Minneapolis's Bethesda Baptist Church. Mrs. Ida Sellers, the retiring state president who had succeeded Nellie, called the meeting to order. Miss Mattie Hicks, state secretary, read her annual report and the roll of state officers was called. The first name to be mentioned was "Mrs. Nellie Francis," who had been elected honorary president by the executive board at its last meeting. Her election would be a bone of contention. It was customary for retiring federation presidents to be elected honorary president, but Nellie had resigned from the post before her term ended, to the resentment of some of the federation members. To them, Nellie's election appeared to reflect her receiving favored treatment. Their resentment would simmer as the convention proceeded and Nellie knew, even before the convention started, that they would create problems. The report of Mrs. Mary Hatcher on the work of the year was "a remarkable record of charity and well doing." The organization had addressed the needs of indigent families, attended a young lady with tuberculosis, and placed homeless children in the Crispus Attucks Orphanage Home, which provided considerable service to the community. Mrs. Francis delivered the response, commending club members for this work and suggesting other areas that also needed attention—chiefly, women's suffrage, for which there was a round of applause. Lunch was served by the Ladies of Twin City Charity Club, the hostesses of the visiting delegates. "There was an abundance of well-cooked food, which demonstrated their knowledge of domestic science."[1]

Later that evening, Mayor Wallace Nye arrived to welcome the convention to the city; he assured the organization of his respect for their good deeds: "I am especially interested in the work of the Women's Federation." Then he referred to the fact that black people who lived in Minneapolis needed much to be done for them: "We have a great many colored people in this city in the various walks of life. Many are highly respectable. Some who are bad. Many who are good. As [mayor] I have to deal with all the people in the city. I welcome you who are interested in these people." He was not aware of the substance of Hatcher's report, but he was aware of the priorities they should adopt: "You may be interested in woman's suffrage, which is in many states beneficial; and you should be. But there is a higher purpose still. Whenever [you] can put [your] hands to, to make men and women better—[this] is the important issue."[2]

To members who understood very well the realities of urban life and the lack of social services afforded to the poor, the mayor added: "We of Minneapolis are deeply interested in our public schools, charitable work, social settlements and civic betterment. The colored people should be interested especially in themselves. They should have a place where men could have companionship under wholesome conditions." He referred to the social centers where no vices were tolerated. "I have tried to give special consideration to the claims of every citizen, regardless of station. I have not recognized race or color, creed or sex." Satisfied by his own commitment to the people whom these women represented, he concluded: "I offer to you a most cordial welcome to this city and believe that your stay will be of material benefit to all of us." The club women gave him a cordial applause.[3]

In her dignified manner, Mrs. Francis responded to the mayor's address with words of thanks for his cordial welcome and assured him that the club women of the Twin Cities, as "evidenced by their intelligence and gratitude," held him in the highest esteem and praised him for his fair consideration given to the race, "asking only for justice for her people, without apologies or favors." But here she took their purpose to an even higher plane than providing a place where men could have companionship under wholesome conditions. To the discomfort of some of the delegates who wanted a more conciliatory tone, Nellie called for "our Civil Rights . . . [Afro-Americans] were highly capable of a proper regard for their rights." Then, perhaps in a gesture to smooth corners of her statement, she said "that the Federated Women were especially honored by the mayor's address and welcome, and they would be inspired to do more after having heard him."[4]

Then a woman unfamiliar to the assembly requested the opportunity to discuss a matter that no club woman in the audience or on the podium was likely to address; but being "an active club worker" in Texas and member of a prominent black family in Nashville, the convention president gave her certain allowances that one sensed she was accustomed to claiming. At the time of the visitor's appearance, she resided with her husband in Texas, but would return to Nashville after his death in 1912. Once there, as a true force of nature, all of her skills in organizing were on display. With vision, determination, and courage, Juno Frankie Seay would establish the Tennessee Vocational School for Colored Girls. Inspired by a close friend who as a probation officer observed delinquent black girls taken to jail because the law would not permit them to enter white institutions, Pierce set out to create a foundation of support for the school. She did this by organizing the Nashville Federation of Colored Women's Clubs, the Negro Women's Reconstruction Service League, and as a founding member of the First Colored Baptist Church.[5]

By the end of the decade, her efforts would extend to the campaign for women's suffrage. In May 1920, at the invitation of suffrage leader Catherine Kenny, Pierce would address the state suffrage convention held in the House chamber of the Tennessee capitol. "What will the Negro women do with the vote?" she asked the audience. "We will stand by the white women . . . We are asking only one thing—a square deal . . . We want recognition in all forms of this government. We want a state vocational school and a child welfare department of the state, and more room in state schools."[6] After extensive lobbying, the Tennessee Vocational School for Colored Girls bill was passed by the General Assembly on April 7, 1921, and the school opened its doors on October 9, 1923. Frankie Pierce became the school's first superintendent and held the position until 1939. She would continue her activism well into the 1940s, when she would lead her club members in a march on city hall to protest racial segregation of public facilities.[7] This was the down-home force of nature who came to Minnesota to defend her more refined niece. Juno could say what Nellie could not say, and in a way that Nellie could not say it, and she acquitted herself well.

"Mrs. Pierce easily proved her ability as a speaker," even though her topic probably irked some who were annoyed by recent events; but it was her style to speak plainly about uncomfortable matters and her style to come to the defense of her niece. She talked on "the effect of unity among club-workers." She told of the many conditions which surrounded women in the "Southland" and "their many noble achievements, their contributions for the progress of the race, especially their efforts for moral uplift." In the name of those noble and heroic sisters in the South, perhaps eyeing those who were miffed that their influence within the federation had waned and that their time in leadership had passed, Juno Frankie Seay Pierce called for united spirit among club women everywhere. The Minnesota club women would stand four-square with their southern brethren. But, as Juno knew all too well, the problem for a significant few present was in accepting the legitimacy of the vote by the executive board to make Nellie Francis honorary president. The *Twin City Star* reported that "Mrs. Pierce is a most entertaining and fluent speaker, and her advice was heartily received," but the paper's conclusion was premature for Juno's remarks, to those who fully understood their intended meaning, had only lanced the boil.[8]

The board members, most of whom were new to their duties, stood firmly on their decision and the rules and procedures approved their authority to make the appointment. Mrs. Laura Hickman, who had delivered Nellie's letter of greeting to the 1913 convention after her resignation, remained a steadfast friend and proved it that afternoon when she spoke briefly "on the necessity of knowledge of parliamentary usages." She deplored the lack of information on the part of many, and advised, with a touch of sarcasm, "that some-time be given at each meeting to a study of constitution and proper procedure, which would in a great way prevent much unpleasantness." The dissenters were from Minneapolis clubs and their leader was Ione Gibbs, whom Nellie now succeeded as honorary president, just as she had succeeded Gibbs to the presidency in 1912. By the evening session, it seemed that

Juno Frankie Seay Pierce. Courtesy of the First Baptist Church Capitol Hill, Nashville.

the contentions aired during the afternoon had dissipated and a spirit of unity had enveloped the federation. This at least seemed to be the case when Mrs. Gibbs asked to speak, attempting to appear to be operating from the high ground. She encouraged the work of the women and assured them that if they did the work outlined for them they would be sure to succeed. Hers were the final remarks of the evening before the convention adjourned.[9]

The second day of the convention was uneventful, as a number of delegates presented committee reports and read papers. In the morning, Mrs. Ella Carson advocated for the right of women to participate in the affairs of the nation on equal terms with men. Lula, elected as editor of the federation, discussed the work of different clubs on behalf of black men, women, and children; and Nellie presented a "highly commended" essay titled "What of the Hour?" But it was Mrs. Dora Adams, one of the newly elected officers, who capped off any effort to upend the board's leadership when she called Juno "a blessing to the convention" who gave them "renewed inspiration and ambition."[10] It thus may not have come as a surprise to the new leaders of the federation when a number of the Minneapolis clubs withdrew their membership, "expressing their continued fealty to organized efforts in behalf of the Afro-American People, but feeling a deep regret that recent developments in the policies of the Federation made continued affiliation with the organization neither consistent nor wise." The statement was signed by Ida Sellers, the retired president. One of the six clubs that withdrew was the "Gibbs Club."[11] No longer would Ione enjoy the privilege of national exposure, for, as honorary president, she was eligible to be elected national vice president, but now that was gone too. Notably, while listing the clubs and the new officers of the federation, *The Appeal,* whose manager of its Minneapolis desk was Ione's son, did not mention that Nellie Francis was now his mother's successor—again.[12]

But none of this mattered. Following a precedent that started in 1912 in creating an honorary president who would also attend the national convention as part of the Minnesota delegation, Nellie now prepared to attend this year's convention in Wilberforce with president-elect Mattie Hicks. Meanwhile, Juno, who appeared to be a hit, stayed in Minnesota for the next few months, ostensibly to enjoy the warmth of Minnesota society, but more likely to lay groundwork for joining forces in the campaign for women's suffrage.[13] But first, Nellie honored her aunt for her invaluable support by hosting a dinner for her. A week later, she left for Wilberforce, Ohio.[14]

From Wilberforce to the House on St. Anthony

The biennial meeting of the National Association of Colored Women's Clubs opened in Wilberforce on Tuesday evening, August 4. Galloway Hall, a large and magnificent auditorium, was packed with men and women from every part of the United States and engaged in every walk of life. Among the prominent women present were Mrs. Booker T. Washington; Mrs. Nettie Napier of Washington, D.C., and Nashville; Mrs. Mary Talbert of Buffalo, chair of the executive board; Mrs. M. J. Dunbar, mother of the late poet Paul Laurence Dunbar; and, the *Twin City Star* made sure to add, Mrs. W. T. Francis of St. Paul. Also present were Miss Zona Gale, a committee chairman of the Wisconsin State Federation of Women's Clubs (a white organization) and vice president of the Wisconsin Suffrage Association; James Napier, former register of the treasury; W. E. B. Du Bois, editor of *The Crisis* magazine; and William S. Scarborough, president of Wilberforce College. The address of National Association President Mrs. Booker T. Washington "was thoughtful, forceful and well-delivered, demonstrating the wisdom of the Association in its selection of such an able executive." Executive board chair Mary Talbert "made a magnificent report covering the work of the Board."[1]

Then, "Mrs. W. T. Francis, Honorary President of the Minnesota State Federation, who is the guest of President and Mrs. Scarborough, at Wilberforce College, addressed the convention Thursday evening on 'Women's Worth in Home and Civic Life,'" a topic, considering the previous year, that oddly seemed self-disclosing.[2] With its focus on her largely ceremonial participation—facilitating the transfer of gift plates from Minnesota donors to the college's Department of Education—the

Twin City Star presented the convention as an indication of Nellie's place among the national elites of the women's movement, and all but ignoring the substantive topics that the convention addressed, including an update on the lobbying campaign against the recently enacted Jim Crow bill in Illinois and on work among children in urban slums; NACW's plea for peace in Europe; the campaign against segregation in the District of Columbia; approval of a resolution against lynching and against segregation in common carriers.[3] But it seemed that the editor's desire was to show especially to Minneapolis that Nellie had not let her prominence go to her head, that she was *still one of us*: "Mrs. Francis also called the attention of the convention to and placed upon exhibition with the Arts and Crafts Work, the excellent drawings and art cover designs the work of Virginia Kemp, of Minneapolis, the young daughter of Mrs. Jennie Kemp, founder of the Minnesota State Federation, and who dies soon after her good work was put in operation."[4]

But the first major topic of concern at the convention was women's suffrage: "The suffrage movement is apparent. The reports of the officers contain strong suffrage sentiments, and 'Votes for Women' banners are flying everywhere."[5] This was Nellie's central concern. With such a large and magnificent auditorium packed with black men and women from all over the country, it may have seemed like all of America, or at least the nation's best and brightest, shared the same sentiment, and it had to be quite an inspiring sight to behold. But for all of the stirring appearance of such a gathering, it was the scene of white women coming forth to share the dais with the national leadership of the colored women's association that suggested an even greater prospect for success in winning equal suffrage for all women, regardless of their race. Nellie looked upon this with hope that the spirit would extend to Minnesota, where the very proper grand dames of the white suffrage movement had, with only a few exceptions, discretely withheld the full embrace of their colored sisters, so she had reason to be skeptical. The history of the suffrage movement was replete with white leaders deferring to the racism of their southern white sisters or the racist sentiments of the regions from which they came.

Ida B. Wells-Barnett recounts an infamous exchange with Susan B. Anthony upon hearing that she had asked Frederick Douglass, an honorary member of the National Woman's Suffrage Association, to miss the 1894 Equal Suffrage Association convention in Atlanta, knowing the feeling of the South with regard to Negro participation with whites in the struggle for equality. "I did not want to subject him to humiliation," Wells-Barnett reported Anthony saying, "and I did not want anything to get in the way of bringing the southern white women into our suffrage association, now that their interest had been awakened." But to Wells-Barnett, Anthony's motives became even more suspect: "[W]hen a group of colored women came and asked that I come to them and aid them in forming a branch of the suffrage association among colored women, I declined to do so." To Anthony, her actions were expedient. But to Wells-Barnett, Anthony's actions had only "confirmed white women in their attitude of segregation."[6]

The truth of Wells-Barnett's observation bore out time and again in later years. Anthony dissuaded Helen Pitts, Frederick Douglass's second wife, a white woman who was a suffragist in her own right, from addressing the plight of black women in southern prison camps. However, at the same meeting, southern delegates advocated a strategy to make woman suffrage "a means to the end of securing white supremacy in the state."[7] Since the ratification campaigns of the Fourteenth and Fifteenth Amendments, many white suffragist leaders saw black male enfranchisement (characterized as the "Negro Hour") not only as a pawn to continue the subjugation of women but as a manifestation of the utter contempt white men displayed toward their own mothers, wives, and daughters by extending the franchise to an inferior class of men. The line between a political formulation and racism, always blurred, soon no longer existed. Ellen DuBois observed, "The position that Stanton and Anthony took against the Fifteenth Amendment reveals much about their political development after the Civil War and especially after their break with abolitionists. Their objections to the amendment were simultaneously feminist and racist."[8]

By 1890, with the formation of the National American Women's Suffrage Association (NAWSA), black leaders took note that white suffrage leaders, who should have been their natural allies, unapologetically resorted, as historian Paula Giddings explained, to "a strategy of expediency," if not the same virulence of southern xenophobic and race-baiting politicians.[9] In her NAWSA presidential address, Carrie Chapman Catt specified three obstacles to the achievement of suffrage—militarism, which held people "to the old ideals of force in government and headship in the family," prostitution, which revealed the way "women as a whole were regarded," and the "inertia" or "backlash" stemming from the "ill-advised" and "hasty" enfranchisement of "the foreigner, the negro, and the Indian." These influences, Catt insisted, "shaped the opinion of the opponents of women's suffrage." "The first two obstacles were self-evident," writes historian Barbara Stuhler, "but the third one—part of the prevailing prejudice of the time—reflected the resentment of suffragists that immigrant men and freedmen had the vote while that right of citizenship continued to be denied to women."[10]

But if Catt had to choose between the two classes of "inferior" men, she chose the white immigrant. "The government is menaced with great danger," she observed in 1894. "That danger lies in the votes possessed by the males in the slums of the cities, and the ignorant foreign vote." The solution, according to Catt, who led the NASWA for six years, was to "cut off the vote of the slum men (meaning black vote) and give it to the women."[11] In Minnesota, decades earlier, suffrage leader Sarah Burger Stearns told legislators considering amending the state constitution, "in harmony with advancing civilization, *placing new safeguards* around the individual rights of four million emancipated slaves, we ask that you extend the right of suffrage to women, the only remaining class of disenfranchised citizens."[12] Placing limits on the franchise of "slum men" was not the only way to "advance" civilization: the price of woman suffrage, to ensure southern congressional support during the years leading up to eventual ratification of the Nineteenth Amendment, included sacrificing the rights of black women—yet another manifestation of the strategy of expediency. After a meeting with Women's Party leader Alice Paul, NAACP president Walter White wrote to Mary Church Terrell, "[the white suffragists] are mortally afraid of the South and if they could get the suffrage amendment through without enfranchising colored women, they would do it in a moment."[13] Others would call it "separate-but-equal feminism."[14]

In 1913, the year before the Wilberforce convention, the NAWSA planned a march to take place in Washington, D.C., on the day before

President Woodrow Wilson's inauguration. Terrell would lead the Delta Sigma Theta Sorority women of Howard University and Ida Wells-Barnett would lead her Alpha Suffrage Club. But during the planning meeting, Wells-Barnett was told that she could not march with the all-white Chicago contingent of suffragists for fear of offending southern women. For the sake of "expediency," the march for political equality would be segregated: Wells-Barnett and her delegation would have to march in the rear. But when the march got under way, she was nowhere to be found until she surprised everyone by appearing from behind the crowd of onlookers as the Chicago delegation marched past her, at which point she slipped into line between two white women suffragists. The incident moved W. E. B. Du Bois to praise black women who demonstrated the courage of their convictions despite "the apparent reluctance of local suffrage committees to encourage black women to participate." The behavior of the white suffragists also undoubtedly confirmed a conviction Du Bois had expressed six years earlier: "The Negro race has suffered more from the antipathy and narrowness of women both North and South than from any other single source."[15]

To be clear, these were black club women and suffragists who faced the indignities of racism. Despite their class status, speech, dress, education, Anglo names, and often fair skin, white suffragists seemed only to see in their black counterparts the stereotype of sharecropper. It was a reason why many black women were often as reluctant as white women to join forces. The black suffragist leader Josephine St. Pierre Ruffin, when rebuffed by the Massachusetts federation, made an official statement that included the view "that colored women should confine themselves to their clubs and the large field of work open to them there."[16] This had been the story in Minnesota. At the Minneapolis Convention of Women in 1900, Mary Church Terrell addressed the group not only about the needs of black women, but also about the prejudice and lack of sympathy on the part of white women. Terrell indicted them for not extending a helping hand to African Americans whose aims were similar to their own.[17] As historian Rosalyn Terborg-Penn notes, "White women did not have the severe problems of racial discrimination and segregation that compounded black women's plight for education and employment as well as political equity. Segregation was the norm . . . and white women, either consciously or unconsciously, accepted the vicious justification for it, just as white men. As a result, black women were not only discouraged from joining the suffrage organizations of white women, they were also segregated and excluded in their attempts to demonstrate on behalf of woman suffrage and from voting in areas where they had earned the right."[18]

But Nellie, who since her high-school days had easily traversed the color line and had developed a rapport in both communities, was the only black woman in Minnesota who could forge a new alliance with the local white organization, especially when the opportunity to do so presented itself at Wilberforce when Zona Gale of the Wisconsin federation committed herself to visit the white clubs in Minneapolis in October on behalf of a suffrage effort. And Mrs. Harriet Upton, president of the Ohio Suffrage Federation, addressed the convention and asked the cooperation of Afro-American club women in obtaining equal suffrage for all women.[19] A few months after her return from a Wilberforce tour, one more crucial factor would be in place, for Clara Hampson Ueland would soon be the new president of the Minnesota Woman Suffrage Association (MWSA).

By spring 1914, throughout the suffrage community of Hennepin County, Ueland had become noted for her ability to organize communities of women to take to the streets of Minnesota towns and to attract a wide array of marchers that defied the conventional notion that suffrage marchers were "a bevy of hopeless spinsters, unhappily married women and persons who had nothing else to do." But in Minneapolis, on May 2, she organized a march that drew 1,971 marchers and included men, women, young women from the University of Minnesota, high-school students, and small children. The *Minneapolis Tribune* pronounced the great march "a fine mass meeting in the cause of suffrage" and said, in a comment that must have pleased the organizers, that the parade constituted a "a revelation and bump" to those whose ideas of suffragists came from cartoonists and humorists." Pro-suffrage state senator Ole Sageng of Otter Tail County congratulated Ueland and her coworkers on their success: "The best people of Minneapolis were in the parade . . . For the cause of suffrage, it was one of the best things that has happened in the state." Elated by this success, as well as reports that more than a thousand towns and cities in thirty-five other states had held parades or some kind of suffrage demonstration, MWSA leaders, aware of Ueland's abilities to recruit, organize, and fund-raise, looked to her as the next president of the association.[20]

On October 17, 1914, she became the thirteenth (and last) president of the organization, the last of four who had served in quick succession over the previous four years; and she was the leader they desperately needed. At her first meeting with the executive board, Ueland made her priorities clear—hire an efficient organizer, raise money to support that person, organize the association into political districts in order to magnify the association's political clout, and assign specific assignments to each board member. She also urged the board members of the Equal Suffrage Association of Minneapolis to take public speaking lessons at the University of Minnesota, and she was determined to improve the operations of the association and transform suffrage clubs throughout the state, as well as the urban-based clubs, into a highly sophisticated mechanism of persuasion and pressure. As the new president, she understood that to mobilize public opinion she would have to communicate more personally with members and prospective members to create a special kind of urgency. But just as significant to Nellie, who had probably been taking note of her effectiveness, Ueland seemed willing to depart from previous suffrage leaders who saw race as a threat to the political equality of white women, for the soon-to-become leader of the MWSA seemed interested in working with talented women regardless of ethnicity or race. Her recent successes gave Minnesota suffragists an undeniable reason to follow her. In terms of creating a white suffrage community that was receptive to working with black allies, by fall, as Ueland rose to the presidency, the stars all seemed to be in alignment.[21]

Meanwhile, inspired from a brief tour that she took with Maggie Washington and Nettie Napier to Ohio and Wisconsin, where she may have continued conversations with Upton and Gale, Francis returned to St. Paul ready to take her next course of action.[22]

First, she would create a new organization. It seemed that Nellie had determined that while she could easily join the MWSA as an individual member—she had already formed relationships with other prominent

Clara Hampson Ueland, 1915. Courtesy of the Minnesota Historical Society.

white organizations, the Women's Welfare League and the Shubert Club—an organized group of black suffragists would create a stronger impression of Negro support for woman suffrage. The problem was the state federation had never healed from the tensions of the previous months. Until she could forge a united front within the organization, it would be difficult to persuade potential white allies of the benefit of working with them. After all, MWSA was itself just then coming out of a period of organizational disarray.[23] Once home, she learned from Juno, who had spent three months getting to know the ladies of St. Paul and would soon return home, that a unified front would likely be organized by a new and smaller group of St. Paul women, who Juno had probably already identified as singularly committed to suffrage. But she was not interested in severing ties with the state organization. Accordingly, in early September, with names in hand, Nellie organized the St. Paul federation, became its president, and delivered a report on the convention at Wilberforce where calls for interracial cooperation in pursuit of women's suffrage were made.[24] The small group would serve as a precursor to the Everywoman Suffrage Club, an organization dedicated to the notion that the pursuit of suffrage in Minnesota was not only white women's work, but the work of every woman. She understood that black people could earn respect only if they were seen by the white community as leading the fight for equality.

Second, Ueland was an organizer and a pragmatist. This meant that she would more likely be impressed with a venture if it could achieve results, and as leader of the suffrage movement in Minnesota, she had to be foremost concerned with recruitment and fund-raising. To that end, preparing activities to attract potential supporters at the state fair, the "Great Minnesota Get-together," was key. Stuhler notes that the July 1914 minutes of the executive board reported that she had submitted "elaborate and comprehensive" plans. The fair gave suffragists the opportunity to entice recruits with refreshments, to have a few sing-alongs, to peddle their tracts, to present a motion-picture melodrama that promoted suffrage, and to make a case for suffrage to a larger and more diverse audience.[25] Nellie saw this as an opportunity: "Through the efforts of Mrs. W. T. Francis, President of the City Federation of St. Paul," polished Negro singers and musicians presented a novel experience to white fairgoers who had never seen black people perform. "They were listened to with rapt attention by the audience in the Hall of Fame, and heartily applauded." Proudly, the *Twin City Star* reported, "This is the first-time recognition has been given any member of our race on a program of the white State Federation."[26] The MWSA board looked at the activities that were put on in the suffrage tent—including the contribution from the St. Paul federation—and deemed the whole endeavor a success.[27]

Third, Nellie would show that she could attract national speakers to Minnesota to advocate for suffrage and could appeal to black and white audiences. Already, as Maggie Griswold's daughter she had a connection to the Eastern Star sorority, which helped her to secure the services of nationally noted speaker and fellow member of the Eastern Star Victoria Clay Haley, "one of the leading women of her race . . . who is doing so much for her people and who had been so honored and assisted by the white people because of her untiring energy and integrity."[28]

Fourth, Nellie would establish a suffrage club for black women. On Monday evening, October 12, at Zion Presbyterian Church on the

Nellie and Billy Francis's home at 606 St. Anthony Avenue in St. Paul. Photograph from *The Appeal,* October 25, 1913. Courtesy of the Minnesota Historical Society.

corner of Farrington and St. Anthony, twenty-five women met for a suffrage symposium led by Mrs. Clay Haley, who lectured earlier on "The Emancipation of the Woman." Nellie also persuaded a few white women from outstate Minnesota to share remarks on the importance of the ballot. "Mrs. W. T. Francis, president of the St. Paul Federation, presided."[29] It was at this meeting that "a suffrage club organized for the purpose of studying the question of the equal ballot" was established. Nellie was elected president of this new organization, which would be called "Everywoman Suffrage Club." On Wednesday afternoon, the group held its first meeting at the residence of Mrs. W. T. Francis, 606 St. Anthony Avenue.[30]

One of the white suffragists who attended the meeting was Nellie's friend Emily G. Noyes, who played a leading role in establishing the Women's Welfare League in 1912, served as its first president for four years, and as honorary president from then on. She committed the resources of the league to undertake the suffrage work in Ramsey County. Noyes, born Emily Hoffman Gilman in 1854, was the daughter of a businessman who, as a young man in Alton, Illinois, had risked his life during the riots in 1837 to offer shelter to the radical newspaper editor Elijah Lovejoy. "A good deal of that caring idealism rubbed off on Emily, one of thirteen children." Her marriage to Charles P. Noyes, a successful businessman, enabled her to spend a considerable amount of time doing good works in the community. And some of the key works were to establish the league as an organization to protect the interests and promote the welfare of women, encourage the study of industrial and social conditions affecting women and the family, enlarge the role of women in the business and professional world, guard them from exploitation, and provide women with the means to acquire the rights of full citizenship. The Women's Welfare League, Stuhler noted, "which Ueland considered to be the St. Paul counterpart to the Equal Suffrage Association [in Minneapolis], would prove to be a key suffrage actor in Ramsey County."[31]

But Noyes, along with Harriet Upton, Zona Gale, and others, likely told Ueland that another woman would also be a key actor and that it was time for the two women to meet. After a meeting with the Everywoman Suffrage Club, Ueland noted that the members compared favorably with what she termed "ordinary" club women—"with one or two exceptionally graceful and charming. But the leader of the club," she added approvingly, "is a star! Mrs. Frances *[sic]* is petite and what we call a 'lady,' but her spirit is a flame!"[32]

Flickering

The year 1915 began on a sad note for Nellie with the passing of Hattie Davenport, Billy's mother. With this, Nellie's spirit wavered, for she would need to take time from work to mourn. On Sunday, January 10, at her final moment, Davenport was in the house that she rented on Carroll Avenue, having succumbed to an unnamed affliction that she had endured "uncomplainingly for many years."[1] But on her last Thursday, she uncharacteristically told her son of the pain that compelled her to bed rest. By the weekend, Billy noted that her condition had changed for the worse; yet she apparently objected to having people informed of her state. Still, as word trickled out, well-wishers began to stop by to see her one last time, until late Sunday afternoon when she lapsed into unconsciousness. She died that evening. She was home at last.[2]

Two days later, on Tuesday afternoon, Billy and Nellie had a brief memorial in their home, and later a grander service at St. James AME in Minneapolis where Davenport had been a member for thirty years. Standing over her coffin draped in black broadcloth and flowers, Rev. A. H. Lealtad of St. Phillips Episcopal gave a eulogy titled "A Heroine" in which he told of the noble work done by the deceased in church and fraternal organizations, how she had "borne patiently her afflictions," and how she had been a devoted mother and a willing worker, "ever planning to do something for the betterment of humanity." He said, "I have never had the privilege of standing over one so old as she [she was sixty-four years of age], who had done so much to make our race what it is today. I realize in her death the passing, not only of an individual, but a type of which America will not see again and will regret because of [her] passing." He was followed by Rev. H. P. Jones of Pilgrim, who also spoke of her "great contributions to humanity" and of her "quiet, Christian activity, ever-willing to suffer self-denial for the benefit of others. We need such women today to make better woman-hood and such men [referring to Billy] to make better manhood." Jones was even more glowing in his tribute to his prized parishioners: "Attorney Francis, who had been a devoted son to his mother, and to his wife who had faithfully assisted him."[3]

The whole affair was a "beautiful ceremony," befitting the mother of black Minnesota's most prominent couple. But over the years it was not a status that she appeared to embrace. She had her sisterly groups (all based in Minneapolis, as if to guard against being ensnared in her children's social net), an honest livelihood of cleaning other people's laundry, houses, and offices, and disinclination to keep up appearances in order to enjoy the artifice of "proper society." Members of that class had "friends and acquaintances," many of whom they did not even know, who nonetheless seemed ready to present themselves as multitudes during times of showy displays of great public success or sorrow. She, on the other hand, did not participate in such things. Once interred in Oakland Cemetery, it likely would have pleased her to know, as *The Appeal* reported, that "Many friends and acquaintances of Mrs. Hattie Davenport and her family did not learn of her death until after the funeral."[4] She was indeed a hard woman to peg. Platitudes best provided a far better send-off for the complicated and at times prickly departed.

A few years after her birth in Louisville, Kentucky, her mother Jane Trevanne, at the first opportunity, led her across the Ohio River onto the north bank of Indiana, away from the white man whose name she kept, making their way to Indianapolis and finding sanctuary in what would become the oldest black church in the city, Bethel A.M.E., the place where she would meet her future husband. Despite the law enacted in the year of Hattie's birth designed to prevent "new" black residents from entering or settling in the state, Jane and Hattie, no doubt benefiting from their white skin, nonetheless were part of the black migration in the mid-nineteenth century that came to the state from Kentucky, Virginia, and North Carolina.[5] The family of Hattie's future husband, James Francis, would be part of that wave from North

Carolina. Hattie's mother Jane would marry William Bell, whose parents were also from North Carolina; but as a literate mulatto with a good job with the railroad company, he would have opportunities that young James, a black, illiterate laborer, would not have.[6]

It would be reasonable to conclude that Jane worried about her daughter's welfare and limited opportunity as a wife of James Francis. Just as likely was Hattie's resentment of her mother's views that were blinded, it seemed to her, by James's skin color. But the racial and political realities of the time made her mother's views and concerns understandable. Until the Civil War ended, Indiana's Black Code, which authorized the imposition of fines, imprisonment, or expulsion, dangled like the sword of Damocles over the heads of the state's residents of African descent; their African blood, not their character, would be the reason, the same drops of blood that her mother had given to her. But despite the shading of her skin and her being labeled a "mulatto" by white census takers, Hattie Francis identified as a black woman because she realized that who she was came from who she loved. The Civil War, if it was God's will, would put an end to a world where skin color was all-important. In 1864, the Twenty-eighth Regiment of the U.S. Colored Infantry organized, the only such unit in Indiana to form; and in January 1865, eighteen-year-old James enlisted, though the more respectable William Bell, who was only one year older, did not.[7] Two years later, James and Hattie had their first and only child, named William after James's father, and Trevanne after her own. But by 1880, James was dead, requiring Hattie and her young son to move into an uncomfortable arrangement with her mother and stepfather, William Bell, ten years his wife's junior, four years his stepdaughter's senior.[8] It was the kind of experience—living and working around a leering man who presumed that he had power over women, and *these* women in particular—that plainspoken Hattie would have shared with her daughter-in-law working in the male stenographer pool of West Publishing. Men wanted what they wanted, no matter how much a woman cultivated an unprovocative demeanor. Hattie taught her to be unimpressed with self-important men, for, as a laundress all of her adult life, she knew just how, where, and why their clothes were always soiled. This would be Nellie's bond to Hattie: from the older woman, Nellie heard life lessons that no one else would ever share with her. By 1885, Hattie and William—now "Billy"—had settled in St. Paul.[9]

During those first years, she struggled to make ends meet, for it was a time when the city with its swelling immigrant population had a need for cheap labor for custodial work. Being "white," as she would be labeled in both state and federal census, only increased her chances at steady employment, for white people were most guarded against black "interlopers" in the workplace.[10] Even so, she did not easily slip into gainful employment, and in the struggle to make ends meet, she had to live with her son and daughter-in-law in the then-immigrant neighborhood of Rondo.[11]

Every Sunday, it probably annoyed Hattie, perhaps even to distraction, when Billy protested her weekly trek to St. James AME in South Minneapolis instead of attending nearby Pilgrim, for he either did not fully understand, or was inclined to dismiss, the sentimental connection her Minneapolis church provided to the days with James at Bethel AME in old Indianapolis. His weekly hectoring may have even prompted her to end her time under Billy's roof, for on April 15, 1897, Hattie Francis, still a handsome woman who probably attracted her share of suitors, married Abraham Davenport. But it was an arrangement that would not last, for she soon moved into the house she rented on West Third Street, supporting herself as a janitor and living there alone, as she would in houses she later rented, while still apparently married to Davenport. By 1907, she had become a widow, and lived on her own until the day she died.[12]

For days after Hattie's passing, Nellie seemed distracted from her work. Billy's practice seemed to be thriving—he had moved his office into the third-floor suite in the First National Bank Building on the corner of Cedar and Fifth, with a steady stream of clients—but Nellie's efforts to mobilize the suffrage campaign among blacks in St. Paul had stalled.[13] Logistical matters, the oversight of which was one of her strengths, slipped by her. The next meeting was scheduled for the afternoon of January 29, in the home of Birdie High, a couple of houses from Nellie's. The time and limited setting indicated that there was little expectation of a large turnout. *The Appeal* and the *Twin City Star* published contradictory announcements for the meeting, both of which were overshadowed by more prominently placed recruiting notices to the Equal Rights League, a black national organization headed by Monroe Trotter of Boston.[14] To casual readers, the name of Trotter's organization could have sounded like the white-run Equal Suffrage Association in Minneapolis, which may have dampened any further enthusiasm. In any event, it was characteristic of a time when suffrage and civil-rights organizations proliferated on the political landscape and competed for the attention of prospective members.

On a different front, the state federation's public health committee launched an ambitious campaign against drug addiction under the leadership of Mrs. M. L. Maclay of Minneapolis, which, for the time being, may have drawn active support to yet another worthy project.[15] It is not clear whether Nellie knew that this initiative was being launched; but given the uncertain relationship that she had with federation leaders, it is plausible that she was not informed. But the fact that she did not seem prepared for what was just then happening in the legislature may indicate how distracted she still was, two months after Hattie's death. In March, a woman suffrage bill just then making its way through the legislature was defeated in the senate by one vote: Republican Ellis J. Westlake of Minneapolis cast the deciding vote. The outraged *Twin City Star* editor equated the senator's vote as a betrayal of the black voters of his district: "He was elected in the primaries by the negro vote."[16] Westlake, viewed as a friend of the race, was no fan of a woman's right to vote: "he for one did not want to see women compelled to stand in line at the polls and be contaminated by contact with politics."[17] But Nellie could not focus on this. As an officer of the state federation, she now had to prepare for the convention in June of the still-troubled organization.The Minnesota Federation of Colored Women's Clubs, reported the *Twin City Star,* "will meet this week. There is a split in the ranks, caused at the last annual convention. Every effort toward harmony should be the spirit of the session; if so, there will be a re-united Federation, worthy of its name."[18] If left unattended, surely a disunited federation of women would become fodder to the antisuffrage crowd. All had to be on their best behavior. And all, it seemed, were.

Meeting at the Old Capitol Building, the *Twin City Star* reported, "Several delegates and visitors were present and the outlook was very promising for a successful meeting."[19] Mrs. Mattie Hicks was elected president, and Nellie, elected parliamentarian and once again honorary president, installed the newly elected and appointed officers.[20] Later she led a roundtable on the importance of woman suffrage. Billy was present to give some remarks and Democratic Governor Wallace Hammond spoke to the room of Afro-American women against "hyphenated" citizens: "[T]he time is past when there is such a thing as a hyphenated citizenship. The colored citizen is no longer a part-citizen and that he should be recognized as the people of any other race as an American citizen are *[sic]* he should have full privileges and be loyal to them." He received polite applause. "The Federation Convention was very pleasant in every way."[21] No intemperate voices had been raised, and there were no challenges to rules or demonstrations of any kind. After the adjournment, the convention organizers had reason to give sighs of relief. Days later, Nellie, Billy, and Lula took a weeklong vacation at Lake City, Minnesota. And surely, never far away were thoughts of Hattie, home at last with her soldier boy Jimmy.[22]

– 12 –

Flare-up

AN INSULT TO HATTIE'S MEMORY

In a climactic scene in *The Birth of a Nation,* filmed grotesquely through a rose-tinted lens, a young white woman carrying a bucket left her home to gather water, innocently skipping to a spring in the nearby woods. She had been warned by her brother Ben against doing this, for it was dangerous with colored Union troops skulking about the landscape. These were the days of Reconstruction, when, as the viewer was led to believe, white Christian chivalry had been forced, for the time being, into the shadows, permitting black carnality to reign supreme. But the woman-child was too innocent to understand the nature of her peril: her purity of heart provided her with life-giving joy. However, as she skipped away, lurking behind a picket fence, a Negro soldier (a white actor in blackface), crouching ape-like with buggy eyes and monstrous hands, hungrily followed her.

As she frolicked with nature—marveling at the flowing water, communing with a squirrel—Gus, the "Negro," grew ever nearer to his prey. She was startled then frightened when she finally saw him, her arms flailing melodramatically, her face the mask of blanched horror, before she ran deeper into the forest until she was cornered on the precipice of a phallic-shaped cliff. Gus tried, with his grotesque countenance, white teeth bared, to reassure her that he did not want to harm her, he only wanted to marry her; but she won't have any of it. When he approached her, she turned and leaped to her death. Her brother who found her dying at the base of the cliff, knowing that Gus drove her to this, carried her home where she died, and he vowed that there would be justice. Summoning his friends, they found Gus, and, donning their spiked Klan hoods and white robes, they tried, convicted, and lynched him.

Later, the Klansmen dumped Gus's body at the doorsill of the corrupt, Negro lieutenant governor Silas Lynch, who just then tried forcing through a new law that would legalize interracial marriage.

At the end of the movie, in a tribute to the end of Reconstruction, the white race was fortified by the marital union of two prominent white families, one from the North, the other from the South. The final scene showed a giant warlike figure who gradually faded away to the scene of another group finding peace under the image of Jesus Christ, then returning once again to the two blissful newlyweds. The end of Reconstruction meant that the white nation could finally, blessedly, reunite. The epilogue reads: "Liberty and union, one and inseparable, now and forever!" And with this, began the birth of a new nation.[1]

The Birth of a Nation premiered in Los Angeles in early 1915. Considered a landmark in American cinema, it was lauded for its innovative techniques and storytelling power, winning so much acclaim that it was the first motion picture to be screened inside the White House, where it was viewed by an approving, southern-born President Woodrow Wilson. Widely credited as being one of the key factors that inspired the re-formation of the Ku Klux Klan, the film depicted the Klan as a heroic force that waged war against carpetbagging Republicans and freedmen, whom the film characterized as unintelligent louts and sexual aggressors against white women. When the film came to Boston, home of the first local chapter of the NAACP in the nation, the moment was primed for conflict. Together with William Monroe Trotter, a former ally of Du Bois, and Ida B. Wells-Barnett, the NAACP spearheaded a vigorous campaign to ban the film.[2]

On April 17, the film first appeared at the Tremont Theatre, attracting thousands of curious and excited white Bostonians. Trotter and a number of blacks attempted to purchase tickets and were refused. But when they protested, police arrested them for disturbance. The following day, a huge demonstration gathered at Faneuil Hall. Protests only intensified afterward. On April 19, more than two thousand black Bostonians assembled at the State House to protest the film. A delegation met with Governor David Walsh, who shortly thereafter introduced the Sullivan Bill that would greatly increase the mayor's power to impose censorship. When the bill was enacted by the legislature, the mayor established a censorship board to judge *The Birth of a Nation*; the board ruled that the film was not at all objectionable.[3]

Again, whites filled the movie house.

On April 25, about eight hundred black women gathered at the Twelfth Baptist Church in Roxbury to hear speakers denounce the film. In anticipation of white violence that many felt would surely erupt because of the film, Mrs. Olivia Ward Bush-Banks, organizer of the meeting, purposed to form a "protecting league of all colored women of Greater Boston for the maintenance and protection of their civil rights." Another speaker, Dr. Alice W. McKane, was more pointed: "We want *Birth of a Nation* removed from the city of Boston and we women of Boston propose to see that it goes. If we can't get rid of it by fair means, it will be by foul means." She declared, "If there are men here who are afraid to die, there are women who are not afraid. This [movie] would not be tolerated if it affected any other race or people . . . They think us a poor helpless set of black people, but if this thing is humiliating to us it should be doubly humiliating to the white people."[4] Instead, it seemed to embolden them, precisely what black people feared more.

Two days later, five hundred blacks appeared when the Judiciary Committee held hearings on the Sullivan Bill. On May 2, rallies were held at Tremont Temple and later on Boston Common. Three weeks later, the bill was passed; but when the censor board met to consider the film, it ruled that *The Birth of a Nation* was "not at all objectionable." The film that Chicago writer John M. Lynch would describe as "painted from a diseased and prejudiced imagination, with a false and deceptive background," was shown in Boston 360 times over a period of six and a half months. It showed for as long a time in other cities and was hugely profitable. By the end of 1915, in New York, alone, gross receipts were $3,750,000.[5] The profits to theater owners engendered by such a reprehensible film were irresistible.

In Minnesota, as early as May, community leaders braced for the inevitable. In Minneapolis, *Twin City Star* editor Charles Sumner Smith expressed his confidence that city authorities would respect the sensibilities of the leadership of the black community on matters of censorship. "*The Birth of a Nation* has been warned not to book in this city," Smith wrote confidently, inferring that he had been following events in Boston. "Mr. Gleason has several clippings to show the feelings in other localities." Officer Thomas P. Gleason, the official censor of the police department, had authority from Mayor Nye to suppress pictures if recommended by the citizens' committee, comprised of the editor and two black attorneys, William R. Morris of Minneapolis and Brown S. Smith of St. Paul. "Mr. Gleason," Sumner Smith wrote, "is a big hearted, broad-minded, unprejudiced American. He would have nothing shown to cause ill-feeling among the races. His record is too well-known for comment." The editor insisted that Gleason was nothing like the late county attorney Al Smith, who censored a film of Jack Johnson defeating Jim Jeffries in a heavyweight prize fight because the film showed, the county attorney said, "a nigger beating a white man." With Nye and Gleason now in charge, the present censorship process in Minneapolis was in reliable hands.[6]

To further bolster awareness that the campaign was a national movement, Sumner Smith sponsored Trotter's Equal Rights League in a program on May 23 at St. Peter AME "to eulogize the many friends of the race who have done extensive work to suppress the appearance of *The Birth of a Nation.*"[7] All seemed to be in place, even when they heard that the film had entered the state on its northern flank—Bemidji. Even so, they had reason to feel emboldened when they learned that the film had been removed from the town's public library at the insistence of Mrs. Charles Scrutchin, one of "the oldest and most respected white settlers of Bemidji and a leading church and civic worker who was also the wife of the local [black] attorney."[8] Later in the summer, the *Twin City Star* echoed its own praise for Officer Gleason's determination "to suppress any moving picture that tend to degrade any nationality, or bring friction between the races." In this instance, Sumner Smith referred to a different film that detailed the murder of Mary Phagan, the fourteen-year-old factory worker in Atlanta, Georgia, and the arrest and conviction of Leo M. Frank for the murder. Gleason banned the film "because of reflections cast upon police methods, the jury system, and the courts." The film, "not strictly in accordance with the facts of the case," left no doubt that Frank had committed the crime when it was supposedly evident that Conley, the Negro, was the actual murderer.[9] In the logic of "broad-minded" censorship, Gleason's decision to ban the film was deemed, in the editor's view, correct.

To be sure, it was a peculiar logic, but no more so than the combustible nature of American racism, always present and subject to ignite at any time, under any circumstance, from the slightest provocation. The riots at Brownsville (1906), Atlanta (1906), and Springfield (1908) were still fresh in the minds of black America, and the lynching of black men with impunity had been commonplace in virtually every section of the nation since the second half of the nineteenth century: the absence of white violence that promoters constantly referenced as proof that *The Birth of a Nation* was harmless entertainment, willfully missed the point. Lynchings were an evil form of entertainment for the mob and it piqued the morbid fascination of normally decent white spectators. The absence of the rope was merely the calm before the storm, a calm that was a thin veneer of the fury below. *The Birth of a Nation* granted viewers the license to kill shrouded under the ghoulish anonymity of a hood and robe. In a city and state where racism was just beneath the surface, and where the black population, being so small, was especially vulnerable, the movie provoked frustrated white men and women to unleash their baser instincts. Duluth, for example, would witness Klan cross burnings in the next couple of years.[10] Even Mayor Nye and St. Paul's Commissioner Henry McColl, who was acting mayor of St. Paul, could see that it was not an issue of taste but of survival. For black people who remembered the truth of Reconstruction, northern white complaisance to southern white terror—fathers and fathers-in-law who served in the deadly struggle for black freedom and national unity, and mothers and wives who loved them—it was not just a matter of sentiment but of honor.

The lie of *The Birth of a Nation* was that it portrayed the redemption of America by waging a never-ending war between white nobility and black villainy, and as such it lulled white men with foreign accents into believing that they were somehow free of the *danse macabre.* But when so-called patriots had no blacks to lynch, especially during a time of war, much like the conflict then raging in Europe, a conflict in which the United States would soon be engaged, and the question of loyalty to the home front spiked the fury of paranoia, there was always the immigrant to blame. In October 1917, a German-American family in Lester Prairie in northern Minnesota whose loyalty was wrongly suspect would be attacked by a group of men identified as Klansmen because they wore "white cloth masks over their heads."[11] More such reprisals would follow against other immigrants in other parts of the state.[12] Foreigners, many of whom had escaped the turmoil in Europe and now only sought a peaceful life for themselves, should have been allies, but there had been no plan to reach out to them.[13] In turn, would-be allies concluded that it was better to avoid confronting the nightmare of Klan violence. Others took another tack: becoming an American required that they embrace the prejudices of white nativists, a practice that survived from the nineteenth century. When Frederick Douglass toured Ireland to raise funds for the abolition campaign, Daniel O'Connell, the Great Liberator, gave his friend a note of support to deliver to the Irish immigrant population in New York. But after Archbishop John Hughes, the titular head of the Irish community, rebuffed the communiqué, O'Connell famously said, "There's something in the atmosphere in America that bleaches green to white."[14] By the summer of 1915, it seemed that those furies would sleep a little longer.

When Nellie, Billy, and Lula returned to St. Paul from their vacation in Lake City, it seemed that all that could be done was done to keep the noxious film out of Minnesota theaters. In late August, Nellie led a delegation to receive Mary Talbert, vice president of the national federation, who came to Minneapolis to lecture, and entertain her in their home.[15] In early September, in gratitude for the leadership that Nellie and Billy had shown the community, their friends threw a surprise celebration to commemorate their twenty-second wedding anniversary.[16] In October, Victoria Haley, scheduled to represent the national federation at the International Congress of Women in California in November, returned for a second speaking engagement, this time before one of the more prominent white congregations in Minnesota, the Hennepin Avenue Methodist Church, on the topic "The Club Work of Negro Woman." She made an urgent appeal for cooperation between the races along all lines of progress and reform.[17] One "line of progress" was opposition to the promoters of *The Birth of a Nation.*

In late October, the owner of the Shubert Theater in Minneapolis announced that the film would be shown beginning on the thirty-first of the month, triggering a number of complaints to flood Mayor Nye's office. Having seen the film in Los Angeles, he ordered Gleason to ban the showing because it "contained objectionable features." "That order," said Nye, "still stands." Despite the mayor's order, the Shubert planned to show the film, challenging his authority, as if daring him to act. Upon hearing this, Nye said that "if the promoters could get the people to withdraw their objections to the picture," he would allow it to show. "But unless this is done I shall be compelled to bar the film in Minneapolis."[18] Dr. F. E. Spaulding, superintendent of Minneapolis public schools, led the way in praising the film: "I most heartily approve of *The Birth of a Nation,* and its wonderful educational value cannot be over-estimated. It is the most wonderful and instructive pictorial lesson in the history of the nation I have ever seen . . . It should be seen by all." Nye permitted the film to be shown to foster more discussion.[19] This was becoming a demonstration of morality by referendum.

The incident had become a political issue. As long as there was no widespread interest in a film being considered for censorship, the mayor treated his own decision (of course, on the recommendation of his panel) as final. But *The Birth of a Nation* was different. People wanted to see it. The controversy only made it as alluring as forbidden fruit. On October 27, the film was shown at the Shubert Theater to one thousand invited guests, including a jury of fifty appointed by Mayor Nye. Unlike the first panel that included black attorneys, this new jury had neither black people nor women on it. "On [the committee's] recommendation, the mayor will rest his decision."[20] Meanwhile, the order remained in place. A. G. Bainbridge, manager of the Shubert, issued a statement that "if it were legally possible he would get an injunction restraining Mayor Nye from preventing the showing of the picture." In response, Nye threatened to revoke operating licenses of any theater showing the film. The mayor was digging in his heels, at least until his panel made its recommendation.[21] On Saturday, October 30, Judge W. C. Leary issued an injunction restraining Nye from interfering with the showing of the movie. That afternoon and evening, *The Birth of a Nation* appeared before "packed houses." On Monday, November 1, Judge Steele deliberated on whether to reverse Leary's ruling, thereby putting Nye's ban back in place. "More than 100 colored men and women waited in Judge John H. Steele's court room yesterday prepared to protest against further exhibition of the picture."[22]

In mid-November, Judge Steele decided in Nye's favor, even though it was a partial victory "owing to the technicalities of the law, which worked to the benefit of the producers."[23]

Although Nye had stated that he would impose a ban, he now followed the recommendation of his panel. Politics, it seems, won out over the mayor's prerogative. "*The Birth of a Nation,*" reported the *Twin City Star,* "will be shown in this city." The promoters had apparently trimmed some scenes "and that [was] the extent of their efforts." The "damnable photo-play" would appear in a Minneapolis theater.[24]

Sumner Smith counseled his readers to protest peacefully and to refrain from mob violence, and if protest is not enough, direct their attention to enacting a city ordinance that prohibited "demonstrations that incite riot and race hatred in the community." There was a cost to letting emotions get the better of self-restraint, as was illustrated in Boston, and later in Chicago and Philadelphia. The explosive Trotter's action had led to his own arrest. "Threats amount to nothing," wrote the editor. "We cannot demand anything." He reminded readers that the black population in Minnesota, when compared to those of Boston, Chicago, and Philadelphia, had minimal political influence: "[W]e represent so little." This was rich considering how brash the editor had been in threatening reprisals against the state senator from Minneapolis who had voted against the woman suffrage bill earlier that year, and the mayor on the issue of banning the film—"We hold Mr. Nye to his campaign pledges and believe he will not give us cause to regret his action." But that was a different forum. Now, the editor tried to lower the stakes: "We have no record anywhere that the [film] of itself has done such great harm to negroes." Although he hoped the film would not be shown, he counseled: "let us as Negroes make the best of it."[25]

The Appeal was more hopeful about events in St. Paul and Nellie was in the thick of it. At its November meeting that convened at Pilgrim, the NAACP, of which she was an officer, directed Billy to draft an ordinance for the city council that would ban *The Birth of a Nation* from St. Paul.[26] Doubtless, Nellie assisted him in this effort, researching the law and editing drafts. The council approved the bill thus starting the process toward enactment. Commissioner Henry McColl assumed the responsibility for it.[27] To keep up the pressure, Nellie used her contacts with a small group of women who many in the know, such as Clara Ueland, considered the power behind the throne, the Women's Welfare League, whose spouses and family ties effectively ran much of the business, civic, and political affairs of the city. By now, Nellie was a member of the group, and it was before them that she made the case that they should join the colored people of St. Paul to suppress this film. Col. John X. Davidson, former owner and editor of the St. Paul *Pioneer Press,* and former president of the St. Paul chapter of the NAACP, was joined by Mrs. W. J. Kenyon and made strong pleas for the suppression of the entire film. The league voted without a dissent to send resolutions to the city council.[28] Encouraged by the partial victory from Judge Steele in Minneapolis, which provided a road map for Billy's draft that the St. Paul city council later received and McColl committed to shepherd through the process, black St. Paul had reason to be "truly grateful."[29]

St. Paul residents who wanted to see the film would have to cross the river to do so and they could thank Billy, Nellie, and Henry McColl for the inconvenience.[30] This too was a partial victory, "partial" because white men and women, by going to the Shubert in Minneapolis, could still find entertainment in the cruel images of *The Birth of Nation,* "partial" because in doing so they felt none of the pain or judgment of their fellow black citizens, "partial" because the rules that white society lived by blinded its people to the truth that lay before them. Billy would soon explain why this was so before an assembly of prominent white men, displaying how far he had evolved from being a fervent Bookerite.

> As the Negro gains in culture, in efficiency, in his struggle for a competence, he withdraws into a world of his own, a world which lies all about the white man, yet whose existence you rarely expect. The inefficients *[sic]* of the race, the handicapped, the unambitious, the physically and morally degenerate—all these remain in that economic morass which you regard as purely racial: and from that class is drawn the notorious

> Negro and the jail bird. This kind of Negro attracts your attention, but as fast as a Negro rises out of that class he disappears from your field of vision, for as the Negro rises higher to intellectual and industrial levels in most of the sections of this country he is by segregation pushed out of your lives and denied the right to compete with the white man.[31]

It was quite a statement and it was the first time Billy, before white men of privilege, had spoken so boldly and unequivocally against racism. The movie that celebrated what likely was the final moment of his father's life, and the white crowds that enthusiastically crammed into the theater to soak in the macabre images, had brought it out of him. And such callousness by venal—as well as well-intended—whites existed when God-fearing, industrious black people were forced out of sight. Earlier, when Nellie showed him the final draft of his remarks—she had researched the data he would use to illustrate the progress of black Minnesota in property and home ownership, education and employment of the burgeoning middle class, edited the speech, and helped him prepare for his presentation, just as she had directed him in their youth when he performed in plays that she had written—as Lula later wrote to Juno, "It was as if their minds had once again become one."[32]

Mrs. Grey and the Spirit of Detroit

Two weeks after Billy's speech to the Men's Club, in late January, and with little public notice, a bit of racial and gender history in the person of Mrs. Emily Grey passed away in Minneapolis, at age ninety-two. Noted simply as "one of the pioneer settlers" of the city, her story, now forgotten, told of acts of immense courage and sacrifice in the pursuit of freedom.[1] In 1857, she arrived in St. Anthony, that part of Minneapolis that nestled along the east bank of the Mississippi River, where she joined her husband Ralph, a barber. She soon started a seamstress shop on Main Street, at the foot of the Winslow House, a favorite destination of southern tourists, who, on occasion, brought their slaves in tow.[2]

In August 1860, a slave woman named Eliza Winston entered Grey's shop on an errand for her mistress and asked Grey to help her leave her master, which Grey agreed to do. Learning of the plan, Winston's master relocated his family and Eliza to lodgings on the shore of Lake Harriet. But Grey knew where they were and led a posse of armed men through the streets of Minneapolis to rescue Eliza Winston. It had to have been a curious sight for whites to see a black woman ride at the front; even more so for disquieted white laborers who knew that Grey was about to threaten their jobs in the tourism trade that primarily catered to Southerners who had sailed up the Mississippi River. When they arrived at the lodgings, Grey told the mistress that they were there to take Eliza Winston to court where a judge would set her free.

They later arrived with Winston at the Minneapolis courthouse, already crowded with hostile men determined to return the slave to her master. They rioted when the judge ruled that she should go free. That night, gangs of men roamed the streets of St Anthony and Minneapolis looking for abolitionists and destroying their property, including Grey's shop. For months, the residents of both towns roamed the streets with loaded weapons, poised to open fire on neighbors over the issue of slavery, on the free soil of Minnesota. Only Lincoln's call to arms after the bombardment and surrender of Fort Sumter in Charleston Harbor diverted their attention. But for the sake of freedom, Emily Grey's action nearly led Minnesota into its own form of "Bleeding Kansas," while placing her own life in the line of fire.[3]

Fifty-six years later, the Minneapolis city council, either unaware of this history or incredulous that nineteenth-century mob rule might be akin to a crowd's attraction to the images of mob rule, declined to do what its counterpart in St. Paul did—ban the showing of *The Birth of a Nation.* There simply were not enough elected officials in Minneapolis to do the right thing. For Nellie, the lesson was clear: only voters could make them do the right thing, and this is why women getting the franchise was so important. As Mrs. Walter H. Thorp, chair of the State Press Committee of the Minnesota Woman Suffrage Association, wrote, "The franchise for women cannot correct all evils, but its influence, like that of the church, will be on the side of good."[4] There were just fifteen states in the Union in which no women voted for anything whatever. Eleven provided full suffrage to women. Only one state permitted women to vote only for the president, and in twenty-one other states women had partial suffrage to vote—generally for members of school boards. The last category included Minnesota. The time was long overdue for the broader franchise. As the black-owned *Twin Cities Star* noted, quoting the pro-suffrage *Independent,* "Since women may vote on child education, why not on child labor [and all matters of public concern]?"[5]

It had been a busy time for Nellie. Since November, when she and Billy worked on the ordinance and led a campaign to get it approved by the city council, she had moved from one assignment to another. In January, when Billy received the honor of delivering the speech on the race problem to the prestigious Men's Club of the German Methodist Church, she put in many hours helping him to prepare for his presentation. Immediately afterwards she worked on the semiannual meeting of the state federation that belied *Twin City Star* editor Smith's expectations that it would be a failure. The success of Billy's "race" speech was compounded with two verdicts in his favor—a divorce settlement and a large award for personal injury. His associate was Governor J. A. A. Burnquist, "but owing to [the governor's] pressing duties of late, he did not appear in court." Billy won a huge award for his clients. The press called it "quite a victory for Lawyer Francis." By April, Lula had taken ill again and went to Mayo Sanitarium for her blood and nerves and Nellie stayed with her, returning the following week. Upon her return, Nellie, as chair of the press committee for the national association, planned for the fall convention.[6]

In an announcement titled "On to Baltimore," she wrote: "Easily the greatest forward race movement of the age is the National Association of Colored Women's Clubs."[7] Even as she wrote, she had already become a dedicated member of the NAACP, whose national affiliate, though ascending in prominence, was not yet equal to the NACWC in budget and membership. The national association, where she served as an executive officer, was established in 1896 and had a longer history of activism in behalf of woman's rights, welfare of the children and the poor, adequate education, housing conditions, desegregation, and antilynching and a stellar legacy of national leadership; many of its leaders had launched notable civil-rights organizations, including the NAACP. And now, its indominable leader Maggie Washington was back to finish her term in office as president after a year of mourning the death of her husband. "Emerging from the gloom which has recently enveloped her," wrote Nellie about her friend in an official notice, "she had apparently re-consecrated her life to the uplift of the race, and by her helpful messages of encouragement to club leaders all over the country is inspiring officers, department heads, and members to the greater activity that even before been evinced in the work."[8] Nellie placed herself in that number of protégés. By 1916, there were more than three hundred newly registered clubs with a membership of nearly a hundred thousand, up from one regional and six state federations in 1901. The national headquarters in Washington, D.C., alone illustrated the vitality of the organization as well as its significance in the national dialogue on matters dealing with gender, race, and class. During World War I, the national association would raise more than five million dollars in war bonds, and additional sums for kindergartens, libraries, orphanages, and homes for the elderly. Nellie officially announced that the next biennial would be held at Baltimore, in August, with "Mrs. Washington presiding."[9]

The meeting promised to be "the most interesting in the history of the Association." The Hampton convention in 1912, when Nellie accompanied Mary Church Terrell to Richmond in a failed attempt to save the life of young Virginia Christian, "was immensely interesting and inspiring." The Wilberforce convention in 1914 that provided Nellie with the springboard to establish a coalition among black and white suffragists in Minnesota, "was wonderful and far reaching in its effects." Nellie wrote: "'On to Baltimore' is the slogan of every race organization of women, and where the women (and the men) will likewise be found."[10]

The hopeful themes of the state federation were overshadowed in May when Carrie Chapman Catt, president of the white-dominated NAWSA, published an inspirational call for state suffrage associations to send delegations to Chicago to participate in a march of solidarity, even though another march was scheduled for St. Louis. The *Twin City Star* published Catt's invitation clearly indicating the president's interest in having black suffragists participate.[11] But the black suffragists of Everywoman had reason to be skeptical, considering the racialized history of NAWSA leaders who vacillated between conciliating the whites in the South and courting the blacks in the North. In 1911, former NAWSA president Anna Howard Shaw had endorsed black suffrage, whereas Carrie Catt, who served as president from 1916 to 1920, felt the South had to be placated, because, she reasoned, a strong national organization—even if splintered along racial lines—was essential to the success of the national movement. Catt believed in conciliation by any means, including urging southern white women not to attend the 1916 national convention in Chicago because the Chicago delegates would be largely black.[12] Using the same reasoning, the Chicago march was expected to be racially diverse while the southern march in St. Louis would be all-white. Everywoman, Nellie's organization, elected not to participate, avoiding any semblance of being co-opted into any scheme of segregation, even if it was in the name of promoting women's suffrage.

Their commitment to this notion would soon reappear with news of the actions of the federation members in Michigan. The all-white Detroit Federation of Women's Clubs was informed that its admission to the white national association would be denied because it had included a colored woman's club in its membership. In response, the Detroit members threatened to relinquish their membership in the all-white group if it insisted on the discriminatory stance.[13] Nellie knew that this might be an opening for other white federations that regretted their discriminatory policies to feel emboldened in welcoming their black sisters into the fold, and in doing so apply more pressure on the national organization to change its racialized strategies. It would have been better for the "sisterhood" of her own state federation to speak up, but, as *Twin City Star* editor Charles Sumner Smith had noted, deep fissures remained within the organization. She could anticipate that personal grievances held by certain members, especially against herself, might frustrate any effort to expeditiously move forward on the matter. She knew that other members felt the same way that she did. One reportedly said, possibly in connection to this matter, "Club women should throw out the jealousies which kept the work of the [state] federation from being where it ought to be." Another expressed "a hope to see the day when the state federation would carry on their work by united effort."[14] But these were not the commonly held views of the state organization. However, Nellie knew that she could rely on Everywoman, an organization whose very name reflected a belief in inclusion. In its edition of May 13, *The Appeal* published a resolution that Nellie drafted to praise Detroit's action to stand by its colored members:

> Whereas, the Detroit Federation of Women's Clubs, an organization composed of white women's clubs of the city of Detroit, Mich., has decided to a rule of its members that it will not affiliate with the national federation (white) [unless] the Detroit Study Club, composed of colored women of the city of Detroit, is permitted to affiliate.
>
> Therefore, be it resolved that the Everywoman Suffrage Club of St. Paul, Minn., Mrs. W. T. Francis, president, does hereby heartily

> commend the action of this magnanimous body of women, engaged as they are in an effort to uplift ALL women without respect to race or color, and to wish them success in this effort.

She emphasized the word *ALL* here. She then called on the president of each of the state federations comprising the National Association of Colored Women's Clubs to request each club in her federation to send a resolution in support of the Detroit federation and the Study Club, and to publish the "Everywoman" resolution in the "National Notes" and send copies to the two Detroit groups and to prominent race newspapers, which should "make public the generous attitude of the [white federation] toward this colored club of their city."[15]

The resolution would appear in subsequent issues of *The Appeal* and the *Twin City Star,* but not before the state federation convened on the evening of June 28. It was the tenth annual convention, held at Zion Baptist Church in Minneapolis. It opened with singing and prayer by Rev. Franklin Withers, who also welcomed the federation on behalf of the church, to which Mrs. L. A. Henderson-Porter gave an appropriate response. Rufus Skinner delivered the welcome on behalf of the citizens of the city and, speaking in praise of the Crispus Attucks Home, he said that it met the needs required. He also asked the men to pledge themselves to help the women in their work. Mrs. L. Vance sang a solo accompanied by Mrs. Marguerite Fields Lee, which received tremendous applause. Mrs. Mamie Donovan spoke on behalf of the Twin City Charity and Majestic Clubs, which was the host of the delegates and assured them that every arrangement had been made for their comfort. Mrs. Jennie Wilkinson read a paper, "Mother as a Friend," that appealed for better relationships between mothers and children. The annual message of Mrs. Hicks was an epitome of the work and history of the federation, a recommendation for juvenile clubs and for a juvenile court officer for Minneapolis and Duluth, and an expression of hope to see the day when the state federation could carry on its work in a united effort. It was all quite sedate up to then. But what happened next raised eyebrows.

Lowell E. Jepson, Republican nominee for Congress, had come to the convention to ask the delegates for their support even though they had not yet won the right to vote. Nellie had invited him. Afterwards, she responded to his remarks and urged that he be elected to Congress. In a surprising departure from decorum, it was editor Smith who took exception to Jepson's speaking before the delegation as an opponent "to our present Congressman, Thomas D. Schall, the blind orator, who was doing his best for our race at Washington, [and] a personal friend of Attorney W. T. Francis." He informed the delegates that Francis and Schall "graduated in law together and that Mr. Francis did much to elect Mr. Schall and he would be ready to advocate his re-election." Smith, a Schall supporter who had never given space in the newspaper to Jepson, was incensed and wrote: "We left feeling that we had attended a political meeting. It was a gross intrusion on the part of Mr. Jepson to take advantage of a privilege granted to address these ladies. He was very indiscrete *[sic]* to make a campaign speech in a Federated Club meeting."[16] In fact, it was a jab at the women who ran the meeting and at Nellie in particular, however veiled, deferring to her status as a federation leader and wife of Billy Francis, who had just become the candidate to represent the Thirty-eighth District.[17] Just the same, the editor, self-assured of his own progressive views on women's equality, felt it appropriate to scold women for what he deemed to be their poor choices.

Despite Smith's dustup, the convention was a "harmonious and successful meeting." "Mrs. Nellie Francis and Mrs. M. R. Hicks of St. Paul and Mrs. Mamie Donovan of Minneapolis, will represent the Colored Women's Club of Minnesota at the National Convention in Baltimore, Md. Mrs. Francis is the chairman of the Press and Publicity Committee of the National [Association]. Mrs. Hicks of St. Paul is honorary president; and Mamie Donovan is the newly-elected president of the State Federation."[18]

Even while preparing for the national convention in August, Nellie kept busy on Billy's campaign and organizing suffrage activities for Everywoman, which included a lecture by Mrs. Robert Seymour of the St. Paul Art Institute. When the world-renowned Fisk Jubilee Singers under the leadership of John W. Work came to Minnesota, Nellie introduced them at Pilgrim and at the Women's Welfare League and offered to help them in fund-raising for their university in Nashville. Protests in

Minneapolis resumed with the return engagement at the Shubert Theater of *The Birth of a Nation.*[19]

But none of these events prepared her for the major disappointment that would soon befall her. It seemed to begin two weeks later with the otherwise benign visit from her friend and mentor Maggie Washington, who as national association president was making her rounds to various state federations. Having arrived in Minnesota, she requested—to the likely consternation of the other state officers—that it be Nellie who would escort her to speaking engagements around the city. Later that evening, the two women met in private "to discuss various matters of concern to the National Association that were likely to arise," a broad topic that presumably would have included the state's president and honorary president. Whether it was at the request of Maggie or Nellie, it is evident that both women wanted this quiet time. They left no record of what was discussed, but Nellie's Detroit resolution was probably mentioned, as well as the resistance it seemed to be facing from the membership. In this instance, more than disappointed, Nellie must have felt frustrated, for the resolution posed no threat to the association or its federation affiliates. Indeed, it provided a road map to gaining more political momentum in solving the big issues facing all women, black and white. But as it stood now, with the potential alliance already fractured along lines of race, women were no better than the men they hoped to redeem with their newly acquired ballot. With a heavy heart, Nellie made plans to make her case directly to her fellow members.

Meanwhile, Lula had been ill for several months and was transferred to the university hospital, where she underwent a blood transfusion from her husband Richard, which "greatly strengthened her." She would now spend a few weeks at Camp Wills, at Chisago Lake. In early August, meeting with key delegates in New York, Philadelphia, Cape May (New Jersey), Atlantic City, and Washington, Nellie went on to Baltimore.[20]

At the convention, delegates endorsed Charles Evans Hughes, a respected progressive and supporter of women's suffrage, for president of the United States. Members were urged to acquaint themselves with laws of states and communities that governed elections, and they emphasized the importance of sanitation and improvement of health conditions. The association approved a child labor bill then pending in Congress, urged the submission of the so-called Susan B Anthony equal suffrage amendment to the U.S. Constitution, and recommended the enactment of a uniform divorce law. The convention denounced all forms of discrimination in transportation, calling such laws "a wrong, a disgrace and an indignity up on a tenth of the most loyal citizens of this country," and approved resolutions proposing that the National Memorial Association erect a monument in Washington, D.C., in honor of colored soldiers and sailors who had fought in all of the wars of the United States; it urged all clubs in the association to support the monument. About the time of the convention, a photograph appeared in newspapers that captured the most recent outrage of a black man tortured and hanged before a cheering mob of white men in Waco, Texas. A petition to protest lynching and demand justice for colored men as well as for whites was agreed to. The resolutions concluded with an expression of regret and acknowledgment of loss in the death of the president's husband, Booker T. Washington. The uncontroversial proceedings went so smoothly that the convention adjourned ahead of schedule. There was no mention of Nellie's Detroit resolution.[21]

When Nellie returned to St. Paul, *The Birth of a Nation* was being shown in Minneapolis to sold-out audiences. The Lost Cause of the Confederacy had been found and placed on full display on Hennepin Avenue for the morbid entertainment of the good citizens of the Twin Cities. The photograph of the recent lynching of the black man in Waco, depicting a white man in the background gleefully looking on, was chilling enough. Meanwhile, in recent editions of the *Twin City Star,* United States Steel Corporation had placed advertisements that encouraged black laborers to relocate to Duluth for work, which at the time, had been occupied by white striking miners.[22] It seemed that the elements were in alignment for another Waco-type tragedy, but this time in Minnesota's northland. Soon, downriver in East St. Louis, white workers would riot against black migrants who had been brought in to break their strike. The film seemed to predict that blood would flow in the streets. In November, Billy's loss at the polls, though disappointing, should not have been a surprise considering the rise of racial tension, though his concession remarks were, as expected, magnanimous.

Then, Mamie Donovan, president of the state federation, "tendered her resignation to take effect immediately."[23] On top of that, Nellie's resolution, far from inspiring interracial unity, instead led to her leaving the association. On nearly all fronts it seemed that clouds of foreboding were rolling in; and with the war raging in Europe for more than two years, it seemed just a matter of time before the United States would enter the conflict.[24]

There was, however, one hopeful event that allowed for a ray of light. On December 4 and 5, Nellie and delegates from Everywoman attended the thirty-fourth annual convention of the Minnesota Woman Suffrage Association in Minneapolis, where they "received a warm welcome at the hands of the president and the convention." Nellie and four others remained for a reception. The proud John Adams, editor of *The Appeal,* reminded readers of the significance of the occasion: "Every Woman Suffrage Club of St. Paul is the only woman's suffrage club in the state composed entirely of Negro women."[25] It had to gratify Nellie to know that her white sisters in Minnesota had at least taken the spirit of her Detroit resolution to heart.

About the early days, Mrs. Grey wrote: "The lack of women's companionship began to be felt. The want was not long endured. First one neighbor called and then another, until we became acquainted and our visiting relations were easy and smooth. Fashionable and formal visits were not much in vogue, but the good old-time neighborly calls . . . were generally indulged in."[26] After Eliza had been freed and the rioting and destruction had run its course, these same women came around to help Emily Grey rebuild. "Oh! The good neighborly fellowship, you can never forget."[27]

After Baltimore

In January 1917, the National Association of Colored Women Clubs launched an ambitious campaign to raise five thousand dollars, the sum necessary to pay off the mortgage on the home of the late Frederick Douglass in the village of Anacostia, in the District of Columbia, to be personally led by Mrs. Mary B. Talbert of Buffalo, incoming president of the association. In her efforts to bring the matter before the public for action, Mrs. Talbert received "the full co-operation of the general officers of the organization, the executive committee and the various state federations of women's clubs." The Douglass initiative, approved at the last biennial meeting of the association held at Baltimore, would require a special act of Congress. The purpose of the venture would be to seek first, to preserve the memory of the life and character of Frederick Douglass; second, to collect, collate, and preserve a historical record of the inception, progress, and culmination of the antislavery movement in the United States; and third, to assemble into the homestead all such suitable exhibits of records that commemorated the antislavery movement.[1]

"The project was of great symbolic importance to the women," notes historian Paula Giddings, a matter of race loyalty that the association felt was more greatly developed among the women than the men. Redeeming Douglass's home represented a tribute to the ancestors. Giddings wrote: "[D]espite all the evidence of their successful acculturation into American society, these clubwomen continued to gauge themselves against the achievements of their forebears who had not been free."[2] The time was right. As Talbert stated, "After careful consideration of all the facts, the committee concludes that this is

A circular for the Douglass Initiative featuring Mary B. Talbert, circa 1920. Collection of the Smithsonian National Museum of African American History and Culture.

the psychological moment for the association to show its true worth and prove that the women of the race can measure up to those sainted women of the race like Sojourner Truth, Harriet Tubman, Amanda Smith, Frances Ellen Watkins Harper and others who passed through the fire of a slavery and stood the test. We believe that the attainment of the goal depends upon the enlistment of every man, woman, boy and girl of the colored race in America." She added: "We seriously realize that it will require us to mobilize all the resources of our association and show that we are not afraid to put ourselves on record being able to save the house by one day's cooperative effort."[3]

The women who were asked to serve on the governing committees included Nettie Napier, treasurer for the project; Nannie Burroughs, Hallie Q. Brown, and Victoria Clay Haley of St. Louis; Maggie Washington; Meta Pelham of Detroit; Mary Church Terrell; Mary McLeod Bethune; and, from St. Paul, Mrs. Clara B. Hardy, sister of the national association president.[4] Nellie, who was chairman of the Press and Publicity Committee of the national association—the logical officer to be included whose job was to inform both the organization members and a nationwide audience of the work of the association, a responsibility that logically should have included the progress of this monumental effort—was no longer a member of the leadership of the association. Indeed, mobilizing "all the resources of our association" did not include employing Nellie's prodigious organizing skills because Nellie, as would soon be clear, was no longer a member—out of sight and, for the time being, without a voice.

Her life could not have been more different six months earlier, when she was energized by a sense of purpose, a sense that her work was gaining traction. Black opinion makers throughout the Twin Cities spoke with approval of the Detroit resolution, noting the positive effect it appeared to have had in cementing an accord between Minnesota's black and white suffragists. Nellie hoped that her resolution similarly might lead to calming the interracial tensions between national women's groups at a time when a unified front was most needed to advance both woman suffrage and an antilynching campaign, and she looked forward to conferring in late July on these matters with Maggie Washington, her friend, mentor, and, until August, national association president. In town to speak before the Sunday schools of the Twin Cities, and ostensibly to lay the groundwork for the announcement of the Douglass initiative, Washington was a guest at the Francis home, where the two women could talk.

By then, the resolution had appeared twice in the local newspapers, which allowed Nellie to show Maggie how well it was being received. However, it was likely at this time when Maggie delivered disappointing news: the association would not be endorsing the resolution. Furthermore, there was grumbling over the manner in which it had been brought forward and it came as a direct rebuke. The resolution appeared in the papers under the heading "National Association of Colored Women's Clubs," connoting that was an official statement of the organization. Even though she had mentioned that it came from Everywoman Suffrage Club under the authorship of "Mrs. W. T. Francis . . . president [of the club]," the resolution was clearly signed by Nellie as "Chairman, Press Committee, National Association of Colored Women Clubs." She had made a mistake. Whether in the way she drafted the statement or in failing to proofread the copy before publication, these were blunders she should have avoided as the national chair of the press committee. She had been known as one with keen political and tactical skills, and not known for misrepresentation, which was a reason she had been elevated to the chairmanship post. Yet, if she approved the copy without foreseeing that it would upset the association, her error in judgment was an unforgivable miscalculation that stemmed from not really knowing or supporting the organization she was elected to represent. Whatever the case, it must have been conveyed that the association would decidedly not be in the business of undercutting its white counterpart, even if it was in the spirit of promoting black–white unity.

Indeed, many felt that the unity of black and white club women was both premature and suspect, for white women, because of their race and class, not only enjoyed a privilege that black women could not share, but, if required to choose between the interests of all women and only white women, white women would choose the latter. The club movement had come about from that recognition. It was not to be minimized, but celebrated; and the time for that celebration of black womanhood was now. "To be a woman of the race, and to be able to grasp the possibilities . . . was a heritage . . . unique in the ages," Anna Julia Cooper wrote. "That uniqueness made them the 'most interesting women in the country' . . . To be alive at such an epoch is a privilege, to be a woman, sublime."[5]

The colored women's club movement had a unique purpose, as Fannie Barrier Williams pointed out: "I believe that it is possible for us to work out, define, and pursue a kind of club work that will be original, peculiarly suitable to our peculiar needs and that will distinguish our work essentially from white women's clubs." These needs, combined with the beliefs that had molded black women's thinking, made the mission of black clubs quite different. The issues confronting black women were rooted in the problems of the race rather than those of a particular class. Although they were middle class, they understood that their fate was bound up with that of the black masses. As Mary Church Terrell, one of the wealthiest and best educated black women of the time, declared: "Self-preservation demands that black women go among the lowly, illiterate and even vicious, to whom they are bound by ties of race and sex . . . to reclaim them." One reason "progress" meant that much more to black women was that all black women were perceived in the light of those who had the fewest resources and the least opportunity. In commenting on the NACW motto, "Lifting as We Climb," Terrell wrote that the club members "have determined to come into the closest possible touch with the masses of the women, through whom the womanhood of our people is always judged."[6]

Nellie agreed with all of it and she supported all of the items to be addressed at the convention in Baltimore. But she was now facing an impenetrable wall that had been erected between herself and a large portion of Minnesota's community of black club women, whose antipathy, she would soon learn, had spread to national leaders. Nellie had apparently overstepped her bounds, and Maggie Washington, who had come to the Midwest on a speaking tour, probably told her so during her July 19 visit to St. Paul. Washington had just called on local prominent white club women, among them Sophie Kenyon and Kitt Chun, president of the Four District of City Federation of Women's Clubs, and friends of Nellie.[7] Although there is no record of the conversations, it is likely that these were cordial visits that nonetheless allowed her hosts to share rumors of displeasure from white club women over Nellie's resolution that intruded on what essentially was the business of white federations. This was compounded by the opportunity her black critics now saw in Nellie's misstep when she signed the resolution as an officer of the national association, without the association's approval. One imagines that the quiet moment between the two friends, mentor and protégée, was sobering, painful even, for the resolution—and indeed, Nellie's rise in the association—was allowed to die on the vine.

That evening in July, after Maggie left St. Paul for Chicago—it was the last time the two women would see each other—a stung Nellie stoically joined Alberta Bell as a delegate from the Everywoman's Suffrage Club to march in the grand street parade of the Prohibitionists. *The Appeal* referred to them as "[black St. Paul's] representatives with the suffrage people."

Then, on August 1, Nellie and Miss Bell left for an extended trip to eastern cities to prepare delegates for the convention, and possibly, one imagines, for Nellie to get for herself a sense of her standing among the membership. She found them to be friendly enough—some swore that they knew nothing of the issues that Maggie had mentioned to Nellie in St. Paul, and that, at any rate, she should not worry about anything. But at the end of the day, she realized that she and the club members were on separate paths and that her friends would no longer be her allies.[8]

By November, a very tense month owing in part to Lula's uncertain health, Nellie determined to keep a closer eye on her sister when she invited Lula and husband Richard to move in with them at their modest St. Anthony residence. Even for the normally outgoing Billy who understood that the Griswold family had typically taken in family members, friends, and even students for periods of time, it could not have been an easy decision. And this time it had to be even more trying, for his practice was quite busy, his church and civic obligations remained multiple; and even though he graciously bore his recently failed bid for a seat in the legislature, it must have been quite difficult for him to share his home at a time when he probably most wanted privacy. Now, with a full house of in-laws, his home was no longer his sanctuary; but he did not complain. On Tuesday, November 7, Lula's condition became such that she was forced to return to the university hospital; Nellie stayed close by, leaving Billy to deal with Richard and his social life. The Friday after Lula entered the hospital, Richard hosted a dinner entertainment for his club. And on the evening of the following Tuesday, Billy's Sunday school class surprised him by arriving at the house to express, through song and recitation and the sumptuous refreshments that they had brought, their admiration for the manner in which he ran his campaign. This was the price of being a very public couple. Their private time was never really their own. Nearly every occasion they participated in was recorded in the newspapers. In this instance, the friendly editor included a list of all of the good sisters who had crowded into the Francis home that evening. One name missing, however, the name of the person who presumably chose not to be present, was "Mrs. W. T. Francis," who, though it was not reported in the article, was likely absent from the festivity because she was tending to her sister at the hospital.[9]

All of it—including the multitude of circumstances in which one was easily misunderstood and when "petty jealousies" diffused the focus needed to address the more pressing issues at hand—seemed to contribute to Nellie's slipping into a depressed state that appeared to haunt her periodically throughout much of her adult life. Billy had seen it before, had come to understood it all too well, and had learned to support her need to be relieved of the demands of the call to duty in a world driven by duplicity. In March, the national association, showing that it was after all willing to coalesce with white women, proudly announced the newfound interracial accord in the Douglass initiative.[10]

On April 6, 1917, the United States entered World War I. President Woodrow Wilson declared that it was a struggle to make the world safe for democracy. But at the end of May, in East St. Louis, Illinois, three thousand white men, initially marching to protest wages at the Aluminum Ore Company and the American Steel Company, began attacking and murdering black men, women, and children in a six-week rampage before the compliant eyes of the police and the National Guard, and the president. A political cartoon appeared in the press that read, "Mr. President, why not make America safe for democracy?" The caption referred to Wilson's catchphrase, depicted on the document he was pictured holding while looking sternly upon a black mother kneeling before him as her two children clutched her under smoke arising from the massacre in East St. Louis. After Brownsville, Atlanta, Springfield, and Waco, what more could be said? The NAACP held a mass march in New York City and the national association launched a demonstration of prayer.[11] In July, as death and destruction continued unimpeded in East St. Louis, the thirteenth annual state federation met in Duluth, seemingly oblivious to that tragedy and to brewing racial tensions in the city where they were meeting. Rather, *The Appeal* reported that the meeting was "well-attended" and "a decided success in every way." Delegates heard such papers as "The Social Class Harmless," "Pitfalls of Club Work," "Some Things We Should Know of Noted Men," "The Unfolding Mental and Spiritual Life," and "A Plea for Informed Mothers." But Nellie did not attend. Instead, she and Lula, and on weekends Billy and Richard, spent much of the summer out of town, convalescing at the cabin on Chisago Lake.[12] Nellie would not be moved to publicly speak on a more substantive topic until the spring of 1918.

On the afternoon of April 25, the women's clubs of Pilgrim Baptist Church, which included Everywoman, assembled at the esteemed all-white First Baptist Church of St. Paul, whose members in 1864 were instrumental in helping the fugitive slave leader and Pilgrim founder Robert Hickman establish his church.[13] The club members came as guests of the Women's Missionary Societies of the Baptist Churches and the subject of the day was "The American Negro: Wrong Conditions in America Affecting Him as a Citizen and the Remedy for the Same." The host group had requested that Nellie Francis deliver an address and, as if to use the setting as a megaphone to reach a much larger audience, she made a very strong plea for the civil and political rights of Afro-Americans. In her dispassionate manner, she decried what happened in East St. Louis and the authorities who enabled the violence and destruction, and elevated her plea to an unavoidable conclusion: the moral inventory of a nation was based on how it treated the least of its citizens. In that spirit, she called for the enactment of laws for the suppression of lynching, better educational facilities for colored children in the public schools in the South, and for the elimination of discrimination and segregation in the nation's army. "Surely, the very men who show loyalty to the nation during this urgent moment, deserve loyalty from the nation they serve."[14]

This was the first and last public statement on anything related to the war effort that she would make, and even here it was only about the welfare and honor of black soldiers whom the government initially rejected. Indeed, the question that many Minnesota blacks, like their kin nationwide, debated was whether they, as historian Peter DeCarlo writes, "[s]hould blindly support a government they saw as duplicitous? Or might they be able to prove their loyalty while framing their demands for democracy and equality, thereby turning the war into an opportunity?"[15] Du Bois addressed the question in his famous "Close Ranks" editorial in the July 1918 issue of *The Crisis* magazine, acknowledging why black people would turn their backs on the war effort; but he insisted ultimately that the year 1918 was "the Great Day of Decision," and beseeched the members of his race "to forget our special grievances and close our ranks shoulder to shoulder with our fellow citizens."[16] Even her friend Clara Ueland came to endorse the war, though she was an ambivalent supporter.[17] It would be wrong to conclude that Nellie was any less conflicted, even though Billy's stance was definitively more pronounced.

His friend and political ally, Governor J. A. A. Burnquist, appointed him a Ramsey County representative of the notorious Minnesota

Commission of Public Safety assembled to root out all dissenters for prosecution. Billy's assignment was to observe the draft board in St. Paul's Eighth Ward, which included the majority of the Rondo district where many young black men lived, report any "irregularities," and, as an appointee of the adjutant general, to represent the government in appeals from decisions of local boards granting discharges. He would later be "selected by the War Department as one of the speakers to present the war aims of the government to the colored people of the country."[18] Billy's support of the war effort was unambiguous and aggressive.

Given Nellie's speech earlier that year at the First Baptist Church, his appointment may have been the most recent source of tension between the two that they kept out of sight, as all couples of high culture and sensibilities did, reserving the airing of their differences, as Lula later remarked, not even within the parlor that showcased their public sides, but rather within the privacy of their upstairs bedroom, behind a door that they kept securely shut, not by a lock and key but by the sheer volume of their busyness, good deeds, charm, discretion, and self-restraint.[19] If she could not wholeheartedly support the war, she would support the warriors, as illustrated by her work organizing a group of community women in wrapping bandages for the Red Cross.

It was not the first time that Nellie and Billy held different positions. Until recently, when he joined her in the leadership of the NAACP, he had been a strident Bookerite while she had sympathized with the Du Bois camp; and during the recent congressional election they had endorsed opposing candidates. Still, it was to be expected that thoughtful people intimately engaged in the issues of the day would occasionally choose conflicting sides. But it is equally fair to say that they had gone through more than their share of rocky moments in their marriage, especially during the early years that launched Billy's professional and political career. To be sure, Billy's ambition had endeared Nellie to him from the start, reminding her of her father as a young man as she understood him to be from family lore, and it was the same ambition that propelled her husband to work virtually around the clock, taking every opportunity to advance his, and by extension their, security and public standing. But his unchecked ambition had come at a high

The Rachel E. Harris Red Cross Unit of St. Paul. Nellie Francis is seated in the front row, fourth from the left. Photograph from *The Appeal,* August 31, 1918. Courtesy of the Minnesota Historical Society.

price—her feeling both abandoned and alienated. Contrary to their commitment to always communicate with each other over both large and small matters, Billy had left her unawares when he decided, while holding down a full-time job in the legal department of Northern Pacific, to concurrently attend law school, facilitate the NAAC conference, then run for elective office, focusing finally on election returns as Nellie watched her mother pass away.

There were other instances that must have made her question the value he placed on her and her work. In the interest of holding the national focus on the NAAC conference, which he felt required the presence of a notable black leader who would remain until the final session, Billy had sought to exploit the reserved charm of his wife to entertain Du Bois for the afternoon, knowing that the young race leader had a predilection for women who were "comely, cosmopolitan, and café-au-lait." A decade later, Nellie would sacrifice her work as president of the state federation at a crucial moment during the legislative calendar for the sake of Billy's opportunity to take over the criminal practice of his deceased friend Fredrick McGhee, though Billy was then a law clerk at Northern Pacific with no experience in trial work, criminal law, or running a law office. To be sure, she had acquiesced to Billy as befitting the social custom according to which a higher purpose was always associated with men's work. Nevertheless, her consent came grudgingly, cloaked in the stoic resolve to forgive, or at least to exhibit indefatigable patience. Not coincidentally, it seems that at this time she found solace in Negro spirituals.[20] By the same token, the consent that always came was founded, as Lula later noted, on a love that began thirty-one years earlier, during which time he had supported her in many ways. He had cut short a business trip in the East in order to sit beside her in symbolic support during the inaugural meeting of Everywoman, the only man to do so at a meeting that was open to both men and women; and on several occasions he argued on behalf of women's suffrage and stood by her when she was at war with the sisterhood. For the sake of their marriage, Billy was learning to listen to her. Despite and—just as likely—because of all the moments, both good and really bad, they continued to find in each other a marvel, which enabled them to weather together the ever-present cloud hovering over their household: their childlessness.

Theirs was a complicated marriage because it was also a partnership as well as a public enterprise. They recognized their responsibility to the community to appear united, and that was not always easy. They were becoming different kinds of personalities. As Billy luxuriated in the public's eye, Nellie, even while filling her role as a public person, seemed to grapple more with opposing impulses—what Du Bois might also have termed "two unreconciled strivings"—in this case, the duty to serve and desire for privacy.[21] As Billy relished the limelight, Nellie seemed disposed only to endure it. They were companions in song and performance for each other and before an adoring audience that needed the performance. And for all the rest who were motivated by guile, the golden couple would sing and dance almost in defiance of them.

A Glorious Performance in the Parlor

The parlor in the handsome home at 606 St. Anthony was elaborately decorated with the national colors and flags of America's wartime allies Britain and France. Across one end of the parlor on a ribbon, the figures 1893–1918, twelve inches long, in silver gilt with gold dots, were suspended. On the walls were pictures of the bride and groom from six months of age to the present and photographs of relatives and old friends that made a very attractive display. The decorating scheme was the creation of "the fertile brain" of Mr. Charles H. Miller. When the hour for the festivities arrived, Mr. Francis began to sing the popular upbeat ditty "Mandy, (There's a Minister Handy),"[1] walking grandly in tempo from the parlor to take his place at the foot of the stairway, where, from the top landing, his bride of twenty-five years began to sing in harmony, as she, keeping tempo, descended the stairs, interlocked her arm in his, and together they strolled to the far side of the parlor where the "handy minister," Mr. Miller in formal dress, awaited. "Dearly beloved . . . ," he intoned with exaggerated solemnity.[2]

After the exchange of vows, the bride and groom kissed each other, sparking another round of applause. The "newlyweds" began to serenade each other and then turned to their friends to lead them in songs, swaying together in the tempo they had set, encouraging their friends to join in the chorus, which in turn drew an even heartier applause from all their well-wishers. To those who knew them intimately, such as Lula, who for the evening was Nellie's "maid of honor" just as she had been twenty-five years earlier, it had to have been wonderful to see lightheartedness return to these two people who in recent years had come to display the weight of the times in their eyes, and to Nellie's sister in particular, whose mien seemed to have transformed into a countenance on which not even a song left a hint of a lingering smile. But to many of the people in the parlor, it seemed to be a blessing to just be present to revel in their elegance and charm and celebrity and their commitment to the advancement of their people, this couple, black Minnesota's best and brightest. The sound of merriment filled the parlor, where other notable events had been held.[3] Most recently, in the same room that housed a more serious gathering, Nellie hosted an important meeting for the Everywoman Suffrage Club with suffrage leaders from Indianapolis, Kansas City, and Chicago. Clara Ueland, president of the Minnesota Woman Suffrage Association, and Miss M. J. Newson, Nellie's English teacher at Central High School and likely facilitator for the scholarship offers Nellie received from the University of Minnesota and the Minnesota School for Dramatic Arts, and mentor of classmate and now Harvard professor Walter Bradford Cannon, were guests of honor and the main speakers.[4]

Now, Nellie "the bride" was focused on a lighter moment, wearing the same gown "that enhanced her beauty 25 years before," with the same veil and lace handkerchief and fan. Instead of orange blossoms, however, she wore a wreath of little sunflowers. Billy was not able to wear his wedding suit, as time, war, and moths had robbed him if it, but *The Appeal* reported that he "looked all right just the same." Nellie and Billy had not sent out invitations, leaving the event open to anyone who wanted to come. They let it be known that they did not want presents and that the occasion was to be informal. In both ways, they broke from the custom of proper society. As *The Appeal* observed, "There have been numerous wedding anniversaries in St Paul but none was quite so original and unique as that of 'Billie' and 'Nellie.'"

The guests—"many of them elegantly attired"— came bearing gifts nonetheless. Their names frequently appeared in the columns of *The Appeal* and the *Twin City Star* and included visiting dignitary Hallie Q. Brown, a friend and colleague of Nellie, who was in town for a speaking engagement. A daughter of former slaves, she grew up in Chatham, Ontario, Canada, and in 1870 entered Wilberforce University. After her graduation in 1873, she taught in Mississippi and South Carolina, where she was dean of Allen University in Columbia, in 1886. In

The Folk-Song Coterie of St. Paul. Nellie is seated in the front row, second from left. Photograph from *The Crisis* magazine, 1920.

1892–93, she served as principal at Tuskegee Institute under Booker T. Washington, and later helped in founding the Colored Women's League of Washington. Teaching and lecturing throughout Europe, appearing twice before Queen Victoria, Brown was later a speaker at the 1895 Woman's Christian Temperance Union in London and she represented the United States at the International Congress of Women there in 1899. From 1920 until 1924, she served as president of the national association.[5] But more than the civic pedigree that Brown held, and far more meaningful to the "bride," was that she had stood by Nellie during the Detroit resolution imbroglio two years earlier. While she was in town, she agreed to give a reading for her friend before the Welfare League, and in return Nellie took her as her guest to the open-air performance of *As You Like It* at Como Park.[6] At the "wedding," Brown demonstrated her admiration for her friend who worked to advance the interests of her gender and race in saying a few very kind words.[7]

Everyone who was present had been touched in some way by Nellie or Billy through activities they were engaged in, either as a couple or as individuals. In Nellie's case, in addition to being president of the Everywoman Suffrage Club, director of St. Paul's Folk-Song Coterie, and various leadership roles of the colored women's club movement on

Hallie Q. Brown, circa 1885. Courtesy of the Library of Congress.

the city, state, and national levels that frequently had her on the road, her many roles included president of the Church Aid Society, superintendent of the Primary Department, and teacher for twenty-seven years; officer in Household of Ruth 553 Masonic Order; and member of Booklover's Club, the Social and Literary Society, and the Committee on Bettering Industrial Relations Relative to Colored Girls and Women. She was also a member of the Women's Welfare League and was a leader of its Red Cross Suffrage Group, a member of the Committee on Distribution of Bread Board, a member of the Hospitality Committee of Soldiers and Sailors, and chairman of the membership committee for the local branch of the NAACP.[8]

It all kept her very busy, as busy as Billy, whose activities, in addition to frequently traveling for his law practice and for political purposes, included an equally dizzying array of responsibilities, ranging from being a Republican candidate for the city assembly and for the state legislature, chairman of the Finance and Trustee Fund of Pilgrim Baptist Church, Sunday school teacher, a popular toastmaster, and national officer of the Fraternal Order of Odd Fellows, to being a member of the

Mayor's Advisory Board, the Republican State Central Committee, the Selective Service Regulations and War Orator, and the Ramsey County Public Safety Commission.[9] The wedding was one more act of community service.

After rounds of singing, *The Appeal* editor John Q. Adams stepped forward as master of ceremonies and read a description of the wedding a quarter of a century earlier as published in his newspaper. He was followed by a series of well-wishers who wanted to extend their own blessings. After the last speaker—Rev. A. H. Lealtad, who had eulogized Billy's mother, Hattie Davenport—"elegant refreshments were served in abundance," *The Appeal* reported, "and a general spirit of jollity prevailed."[10] Even the prickly editor of the *Twin City Star,* never one to allow readers to forget the envious ladies in their community who viewed Nellie as undeserving of her favored social and civic status, nevertheless reported in his own over-the top way, "In spite of jealousy and criticism [from others], [Nellie and Billy] can look into the mirror of memory and see a pleasant past—a record of service to church, state, and society—the happy heritage worthy of a king's ransom."[11]

It had been a grand production, worthy of any of those that Nellie directed in her youth, but now, more than a quarter century later, the mock ceremony, the festivity in the cramped parlor, and the role she played for the occasion had left her exhausted. Within days, she began her weeklong break at the Bumble Bee Cottage on Chisago Lake as the guest of Mrs. G. W. Wells. When she returned rejuvenated and ready to resume her social duties, she entertained Dr. and Mrs. Ray Walter of Albert Lea. Billy missed both occasions, for he spent much of the month of September out east where he visited Emmett Scott, former secretary to Booker T. Washington and now special assistant to the secretary of war, "on war work," venturing up to New York City for the Odd Fellows convention, where he was elected deputy grand master, then on to Chicago where he visited friends, before returning to St. Paul on September 21. Except for a few days, he spent the remainder of August and most of September away from his "bride."[12] But during that time, he modified his public stance on the war to now reflect some of Nellie's views:

> We are living in an age and an epoch which is characterized by a growing and insistent demand for justice and democracy. The United States is sending men, money and munitions to the battlefields of Europe in its demands for justice, freedom and equality for opportunity for all peoples, and it would be well for the Americans at this time to remember that here in our own country for the past fifty years since the abolition of slavery, is a race of loyal, patriotic people *who are not enjoying at the hands of this government here at home the principles of that democracy for which we are fighting to make the world safe,* and in which fight God helping us, we will be victorious.[13]

This was the life and marriage that they had chosen for themselves. It was also time for Nellie to go back to the real work at hand. With this, she forever stepped away from all federation activity and brought Everywoman even closer to the Minnesota Woman Suffrage Association and formally became an affiliate of the organization.[14]

– 16 –

This Broad United Stand

In October, Nellie published the following letter to the editor of the St. Paul *Pioneer Press,* reprinted in *The Appeal,* which flatly declared—in the spirit of her erstwhile Detroit resolution—her support for the white suffragists who stood with their black sisters in the national campaign for suffrage:

> To the editor of the [St. Paul] *Pioneer Press:*
>
> The southern senators offered the suffragists the tempting compromise that the passage of the Anthony Amendment would be assured if the suffragists would consent to the provision that Negro women would not be permitted to exercise the privilege of the ballot as granted to the white women of the country. *To the honor and credit of the suffragists be it written in the annals of history that the infamous proposal was promptly turned down.* Personally, I am not surprised at the high ground taken by the suffragists. It is exactly what I would have expected of suffragists, as I know them and keen would have been my disappointment if they had failed to make this sacrifice.
>
> It is in this broad stand, the actual practice of the principles for which they contend, that has inspired me to add my humble effort to the struggle for equal suffrage. Suffragists are the broadest group of white women it has been my privilege to know by observation or to be associated with: and I have given this phase of our problem no little study and consideration.

Reinforcing the notion that suffrage was the final step to freedom, as a granddaughter of slaves she sought to pay suffragists the highest compliment:

> They are the modern abolitionists, and fortunate indeed is the Negro woman to have in the suffragist a champion who is willing to sacrifice all that is dear (and next to winning the war the triumph of equal suffrage is dearest to the heart of the suffragist) rather than accept a victory that is tainted with dishonor
>
> *This broad united stand of the suffrage body for the principles of democracy which must include black women as well as white will win for the cause of suffrage many sympathizers who would otherwise have been indifferent to its success.* The cause of suffrage will triumph, for it is just.
>
> Mrs. W. T. Francis, President,
> Everywoman Suffrage Club[1]

The interracial accord to which she referred was in clear view within the suffrage community in St. Paul and Minneapolis, which Nellie and her colleagues had cultivated through the influential Women's Welfare League, the MWSA, its leadership, and especially its president, Clara Ueland, whom she had hosted earlier in the year at 606 St. Anthony. For the remainder of the year, Nellie was often seen about the Twin Cities in the company of suffrage leaders. She lunched at the exclusive Minneapolis Athletic Club with Mrs. George (Sophie) Kenyon, first vice president of the MWSA, who would succeed Ueland after her second term ended, and who had also served as promoter of *The Suffragist,* the official publication of the Congressional Union, which was created specifically to facilitate strategies to lobby Congress for passage of the Susan B. Anthony Amendment.[2] And in December, Nellie, "the pioneer suffragette among our women and [holder of] a high place in state affairs," led a delegation from Everywoman to attend the MWSA convention in the Gold Room of the Radisson Hotel in Minneapolis.[3] Minnesota was on firm footing in terms of pushing for woman's suffrage without the threat of excluding the state's black women in order to appease bigots. With its small black population, which had an able, refined, and at least outwardly racially ambiguous leader in Nellie Francis, equally at ease in the presence of white power brokers as with her own people, the race issue that afflicted the national movement seemed irrelevant in Minnesota. Governor Joseph A. A. Burnquist, president of the St. Paul chapter of the NAACP, a friend both of the race and of women's suffrage, as well as a significant number of legislators, were on board. This was not the case on the national front.

As Congress debated the Anthony Amendment by the end of 1918, black women and men throughout the North looked on warily.[4] Would their right-thinking representatives continue to do as they had promised—pass a women's suffrage bill that would include all women—or would they capitulate to their southern colleagues who sought to amend the bill to empower states to exclude black women? Their concerns were justified, for since the beginning of the decade they had seen white suffragists seek to avoid offending southern support for the bill by flirting with the notion that they would support the caucus for partial suffrage. NAWSA leaders were even more direct, starting with the organization's president, Carrie Chapman Catt, who was still very much committed to her strategy of appeasement. Writing to Democratic Representative Edwin V. Webb of North Carolina in 1917, she said:

> The women of New York are not the political equal of men in New York, but the white women of the South are the political inferiors of the negroes who can qualify to vote. Upon the theory that every voter is a sovereign, the present condition in the South makes sovereigns of some Negro men, while all white women are their subjects.[5]

By November 1918, black suffragists saw that the dynamic had deepened. A black correspondent declared in a Philadelphia newspaper that southern legislators had begun to formally initiate antiblack legislation:

> Recently Mississippi's senior senator, John Sharpe Williams, proposed an amendment to the Anthony suffrage bill to the effect that only white women should be permitted to vote . . . It is certainly out of place, just

> now, when so-called Democrats are shouting the loudest about making the world safe for democracy.[6]

The Senate vote for the southern-oriented provision was laid on the table. However, in 1919, Mississippi Senator Pat Harrison attempted unsuccessfully to have the word *white* placed in the original amendment, while Louisiana Senator Edward J. Gay called for an amendment providing the states, instead of Congress, the power to enforce it. Both efforts failed, but racism proved to be a persistent force in this debate.[7]

The closer the women's suffrage bill came to passage, the more white supremacists in the South resorted to tactics designed to sabotage it. In 1918, James Callaway, a Georgia politician, wrote an article in which he attempted to discredit Susan B. Anthony. In an effort to subvert women's suffrage as a whole, he recounted the "strange history" of the late suffrage hero by publishing photographs of "three immediate women friends of the Anthony family." Two were prominent white suffragists, Carrie Catt and Anna Howard Shaw. The third was Mrs. R. Jerome Jeffrey, a black women's club leader from Rochester who was pictured with the caption "negro" printed below her name.[8] He then indicted Anthony for betraying the white women of the South by quoting excerpts from her biography that revealed her relationship with black suffragists. He ended his article with a plea to the Senate to reject woman suffrage. For months, the article was posted in public places throughout Georgia and Virginia. In 1919, likely in response to the sentiment sparked by the article, the Equal Suffrage League in Virginia joined the NAWSA state chapter in rejecting a membership application from the Northeastern Federation of Women's Clubs, explaining that this decision was good for the state suffrage effort.[9]

This bears closer examination. Although Republicans prevented the vote on the antiblack amendment, black suffragists were concerned about NAWSA duplicity, and they began taking steps to thwart Catt's group by taking a deceptively simple but effective step: using a modified tactic of Nellie Francis, they sought to join the organizations of the white suffragists whom they knew were wooing the Southerners.[10] In 1919, the leaders of the Northeastern Federation of Women's

Clubs, representing six thousand African American women, showed their tactical acuity when they submitted their organization for membership in the NAWSA. The white suffragists, as Giddings noted, "were dumbstruck." They begged the colored federation to withdraw its application, at least until the suffrage amendment was passed.[11]

To press the case, Catt dispatched Ida Husted Harper to plead NAWSA's case with Mary Terrell and the national association president Elizabeth C. Carter. Harper began the letter by establishing her "liberal" bona fides. Her parents had been abolitionists, she said, and their "doors were always opened to colored people." She also informed them that Susan B. Anthony had authorized her to write her biography because of her sympathy with "all that she stood for," presumably referring to her own history of promoting freedom.[12] And while drafting the manuscript, she and Anthony entertained several "colored" guests including Booker T. Washington and Ida B. Wells-Barnett. Now that she felt that her credentials were fully stated, she got down to the business at hand. It was a critical time for the Anthony Amendment, and if the moment was lost, "there will not be universal suffrage in your lifetime." Her usage of the word *your* instead of *our* seemed pointedly judgmental and caused reason to reinforce Terrell's suspicion of Harper's, and by extension Catt's, sense of unity.

Harper continued: "Every Southern State Suffrage Association now supports the Federal amendment." Democratic votes from a number of the industrial northern states were needed, and eight congressmen from six states represented by the Northeastern Federation of Women's Clubs were opposed to the amendment. Finally, as Giddings noted, "the specter of black enfranchisement was the greatest potential monkey wrench in any bill that needed Southern support." Harper continued: "Many of the Southern members are now willing to surrender their beloved States rights and their only obstacle is fear of the colored woman's vote, in the states where it is likely to be equal or exceed the white women's vote." Insisting that the NAWSA had always been committed to the enfranchisement of black women, she concluded that if the black women proceeded in their application, their entire struggle would be defeated. She then asked whether they would "sacrifice" the "immediate gratification" by applying at a later time.[13]

Carter's response was direct: "I would be willing to recommend to our Federation that they withhold their application . . . provided, and provided only, that [NAWSA] or any other organization into which it has merged shall stand unequivocally for the Susan B. Anthony Amendment as originally drawn." In other words, as the amendment stated, the enforcement of the amendment shall be given to Congress and not to the states, either directly or by concurrent jurisdiction.[14]

This, Carrie Chapman Catt and the NAWSA were not willing to do. But at this stage of the campaign, it was moot. At the next session of Sixty-fifth Congress, the House of Representatives repassed the bill, and it passed in the Senate in June 1919. Now the real struggle of getting the amendment ratified by three-fourths of the states was upon them.[15]

In Minnesota, the suffragists prepared for the new legislative sessions in St. Paul and Washington to commence. On January 2, Ueland wrote to state legislators requesting support for a resolution urging the U.S. Senate to pass the federal suffrage amendment. Four days later, she asked Governor Burnquist to speak in favor of woman suffrage in his forthcoming address to the legislature. In his commitment to do so, he sent her a copy of his message that included a resolution requesting that Congress submit the suffrage amendment to the states, and its ratification by the state legislature. Just weeks later, the legislature acted on his request. At the next regular meeting of the Everywoman Suffrage Club, members were briefed on the status of the resolution as well as the Anthony Amendment in Congress and they discussed the importance of keeping up the pressure through the petition.[16]

The MWSA was also pushing for one more bill that would immediately extend to women the right to vote in presidential elections, which could be done by a majority of votes in the legislature. However, their effort was frustrated when another suffrage group—the Minnesota Equal Suffrage Constitutional Amendment League (ESCAL)—persuaded legislators to introduce a suffrage amendment to the state constitution that would only be approved with a majority of all votes cast in the election. In the short time the MWSA had to educate and lobby legislators, it felt the two bills would only confuse matters and surely gum up the works. Ueland felt that the amendment proposal, coming at a time when increasing numbers of legislators were prepared to "pass almost any kind of suffrage measure," would fritter away their hard-won momentum.[17] It seemed that Ueland was right, for immediately after passing the resolution calling on the U.S. Senate to take action in support of the federal amendment, the state house passed the ESCAL state amendment bill. Ueland and the MWSA saw that vote as "a near catastrophe" for Minnesota suffragists. Legislators defended themselves by saying that they would have been viewed as inconsistent had they voted for the federal suffrage amendment and against a state suffrage amendment, and they had a point. But legislators nonetheless seemed befuddled by the bills, as one MWSA staff member observed:

> The poor dear men are in a confused state of mind, because three distinct and separate groups of women are besieging them in the interest of suffrage.—Mrs. Bertha Moller for the National [Woman's] party working for a resolution, Mrs. Angie Kingsley (ESCAL) the female arch-fiend who persists in bringing up the State amendment and always gets some fool men to stand behind her, and one group working for the National Association's policy (MWSA)—I do not wonder that the poor old dears look confused and bored when all or sundry of us appear.[18]

It was time to rally the troops. The MWSA urged suffrage leaders throughout the state to write their senators urging them to vote against the state amendment as "unwise and inexpedient." Every day, Ueland and her colleagues made their views known in the legislative halls. On February 28, the state senate did indeed vote down the motion to pass the state amendment bill. With it out of the way, the legislature at last acknowledged the right of women to vote for presidential electors, with house members voting to approve the measure by 103 to 24 and the senate 49 to 11. This was, the St. Paul *Dispatch* reported, "a good beginning." Stuhler, noting that "[t]he vote was a testimony to the strategies of the MWSA," reported that four of the MWSA workers had organized every legislative district and had increased the number of working committees in cities and towns outside of Minneapolis, St. Paul, and Duluth from 450 to 480. A poll of both houses had been carefully planned and executed by Ueland before the vote, which was made even more challenging considering that a number of newly elected legislators now sat in both chambers. "[I]t was no easy task and required Ueland's infinite tact and diplomacy," not to mention a degree of tactical agility. On March 24, Governor Burnquist, surrounded by suffragists, signed the bill "with his native grace, great decision and stout stub pen."[19]

Nellie must have taken many notes on the way to effectively move the Minnesota legislation forward, and it would all come in handy over the next two years. There was also the added benefit that came from her "war" work. Despite her persistent reservations about the "war to end all wars," she found that she could hold to her principles and still do her part for the welfare of the men in uniform, and in doing so wrap herself and her twin concerns of gender and racial equality in the garb of national loyalty. For many of the men, supporting woman suffrage had become the patriotic thing to do.

The unanimous affirmative vote of the Minnesota delegation in both the Sixty-fifth and Sixty-sixth Congresses attested to the ability of the suffragists to effectively mobilize a persuasive campaign. In mid-August, Governor Burnquist issued a call for a special session on September 8, 1919. MWSA members were invited to sit on the senate floor on the day the legislature convened. The house vote for ratification was 120 to 6, and the senate voted 60 to 5. The whole process was completed in thirty minutes. At this time, one observer reported, "The moment the Senate vote was polled the corridors, floors and galleries of both houses were in an uproar, hundreds of women cheered and laughed and waved the suffrage colors while in the rotunda a band swung into the strains of the Battle Hymn of the Republic." After signing the ratification certificate on September 11, the governor presented the pen to Clara Ueland.[20]

Throughout the early part of 1920, thirty-five states ratified the amendment. Only one more state was needed, but by June it seemed that the momentum had died. Delaware had defeated the bill, the only state north of the Mason–Dixon line to do so. Of the five remaining states, Florida and North Carolina were expected to oppose ratification, and the antisuffrage governors of Vermont and Connecticut refused to call special sessions. There was only one last hope: Tennessee.[21] Governor Albert H. Roberts, a supporter of the amendment, scheduled the session to begin on August 9. Soon suffragists and antisuffragists converged on Nashville. It was about to be a donnybrook. Because of Tennessee's large black population, race was a major factor in the contest, but vested interests against Prohibition, which had just become federal law, and factory owners who exploited women laborers in southern mills, and of course antisuffrage male and female proponents all set their sights on defeating the amendment. "Bargains were struck, deals made, trade-offs negotiated," resulting in an impasse. It was very unlike the comparatively gentle nature of Minnesota campaign.[22]

Partisans descended on Nashville throughout the sweltering hot summer in what became one of the dirtiest political fights in American history. In newspapers and behind the scenes, the finest women of the South were waging a volatile war on each other. There was bribery, illegal alcohol, public slandering, spying, and wiretapping because the southern way of life was at stake. Plus, southern aristocracy and power, and white male domination, would have no leg left to stand on if black women could vote. Though baited by the leader of the "antis" to play a visible role of leadership in the suffrage campaign, thereby conveying the sense that it was nothing more than another northern invasion, Carrie Catt, who had just arrived from New York City, understood that success would be attained if southern women took the lead. Two of the state's most effective spokespersons were Anne Dallas Dudley and Abby Crawford Milton, and they would be formidable proponents indeed—educated, wealthy, and beautiful mothers who effectively advocated with their charm. The "antis" called them the "suffrage sirens." Stymied from moving forward, NASWA leaders, trying to continue their efforts from just out of sight, recognized that they needed more help. Astonishingly, as Giddings wrote, "none other than Alice Paul appealed to none other than the NAACP for help."[23]

"You cannot find a more impossible time to appeal to anyone interested in the Negro to help women in their fight for suffrage in Tennessee," replied Mary Ovington to Paul's request. Ovington, a confidante of Du Bois and a white leader of the national association, explained at the recent Republican National Convention. Robert

Church—a major political figure in his own right and half brother to Mary Church Terrell who served on the NAACP's executive council—had been unseated as a delegate. The action against Church, Ovington charged, was precipitated by the Tennessee women who did not want to sit "with a negro from their state." The behavior of white women "has ruined any chance for their receiving support from the colored people in the suffrage fight. I know it has been the determined policy of the suffragists to ignore the colored question in the South."[24] Neither national figure—Paul or Ovington—was thinking about the diversity of women's leadership within Tennessee, the leadership that Juno Frankie Seay Pierce provided, and the people she represented.

But this was not a white woman's campaign, even though many continued to see it that way. At the invitation of suffrage leader Catherine Kenny, Juno Pierce, a leading black voice in Nashville, addressed the May 1920 state suffrage convention held in the house chamber of the Tennessee capitol. "What will the Negro women do with the vote?" she asked her audience. "We will stand by the white women . . . We are asking only one thing—a square deal . . . We want recognition in all forms of this government." Indeed, throughout the summer, both sides—"antis" and "suffs"—struggled against each other in a standoff until one junior legislator switched his vote in favor of ratification. On August 26, with Tennessee now in the ratification column, the Nineteenth Amendment to the U.S. Constitution became the law of the land. As important as suffrage was, Pierce, the aunt of Nellie Francis, understood what winning the vote meant: "We want a state vocational school and a child welfare department of the state and more room in state schools." She would leverage the suffrage victory, and the creation of a statewide vocational school for girls was added to the legislative agenda of the newly formed Tennessee League of Women Voters, led by Abby Milton. Only eight months after Tennessee ratified the Nineteenth Amendment, the general assembly passed a bill creating the Tennessee Vocational School for Colored Girls.[25]

Yet, with women's right to vote, the fact sadly remained that race still mattered in the South, and in Tennessee in particular, which, in a sense, was Ovington's point. The passage of the Nineteenth Amendment was not a universal victory for black women, and a black female poet under the pen name of Anise explained how that was so. On the first day that black women went to the polls, the poem said, they were humiliated and kept in lines for hours, "but still the colored women kept on coming." On the second day, they were given tests and disqualified on technicalities, "but the colored women kept on coming." And on the third day, the sheriff threatened physical violence, "but the colored women kept on coming." The poem ends with the rumor that the judge is going to throw the women's ballots out:

> For fear those colored women
> Might really come
> To believe
> That representative government
> Exists
> In America.[26]

Segregation and Jim Crow laws, which remained on the books with the support of white women voters, still kept many black women from voting. It would take another long series of battles, fought behind the scenes and in the streets and led predominantly by black women such as Juno Pierce, before full suffrage could be realized through the Voting Rights Act of 1965.[27]

The racial dynamic that played out in Tennessee throughout the spring and summer of 1920 was in stark contrast to the Minnesota campaigns waged by both pro- and antisuffrage leaders, and Nellie never experienced the humiliation that Juno faced leading up to the vote and afterwards. Indeed, Nellie's affiliation with the MWSA and such prominent organizations of white women as the Women's Welfare League seemed to always be cordial and supportive. Indeed, many of these women may have been drawn to her because of her novelty—the first black woman they had ever seen or worked with, the only black woman they knew who looked and sounded as she did, a Negro woman who could easily pass for white who nonetheless identified herself as black. In the eyes of women who had little if any contact with black women, all this undoubtedly left an impression. On the other hand, her very presence in a room of white women, when seated not at the dais or with her delegation of black women from Everywoman—but seated alone among audience members—obscured her racial designation. During the celebration of Minnesota's ratification, Anna Dickie Olesen, who would become the first female major-party nominee for the U.S. Senate, said what many of her comrades probably felt: "millions of American women forgetting differences in social conditions . . . religion . . . nationality—we stand united."[28] Race was not a significant difference in the diverse unity. In Minnesota, given the small numbers of black people in the general population and the minuscule number of black women engaged in the state's suffrage movement, the movement—at least in terms of race, certainly as it was perceived by many black people who did not make distinctions between ethnic groups but saw only the color of the skin, and were not yet aware of the work of Everywoman—remained largely a white affair. There appeared to be no women and men of color listed in the letterhead.[29]

This was what Carrie Catt and others in the leadership of the NAWSA had long been saying, though in their case it was about betraying the interests of black women in order to appease southern racists whose support was critical to ratification. In Minnesota, the suffrage of black women no more threatened the balance of power than did black male voters in the late nineteenth century. As an active member of the NAACP, Nellie had to be aware of the tense interaction between the national leaders of the association and NASWA, but, as ensconced as the state was in the northernmost region of the nation, the sort of racism that played out on a national scale was not Minnesota's drama. It was not Carrie Catt who dispensed orders on how to proceed, but Clara Ueland, who was the face and voice of the suffrage movement in Minnesota, and she knew and deeply respected Nellie as a colleague—the exceptional one of her race and, perhaps in Ueland's scrutinizing eyes, the only acceptable one. Describing to her husband her first meeting at Nellie's home, Ueland noted with the air of a matriarch:

> I went to a meeting of Negro women the other day that was very interesting. It was a suffrage club called "Every Woman's Club." They were a nice lot of women comparing favorably with the ordinary club women—with one or two exceptionally graceful and charming. But the leader of

> the club is a star! Mrs. Francis is petit and what we call "a lady," but her spirit is a flame. To help her race is her ruling motive . . . Her husband is just as interesting. He is a lawyer—lean and eager, public-spirited like Mrs. Francis, and devoted to her. They brought me [to their] home in their car.[30]

Here, Ueland, looking at the home of two very busy people living on a modest income, portrayed the domestic privilege that she enjoyed and could take for granted owing to, as Mary Firmin wrote, "[t]he presence of two hired girls [who] enabled Clara to spend time on educational and community activities as well as manage a household for nine people."[31] Clara Ueland continued:

> Extraordinary for such intelligent people to have such an unattractive house: the walls covered with cheap pictures while here and there would be *Mona Lisa* or *The Ruins of Parthenon,* but chiefly the photographs of people (they probably were very interesting people). The furniture was ugly and things were cluttered and disorderly.[32]

She concluded: "She is on the Board of some national society for the improvement of the Negro situation. She is interested in Negro music and sings the spirituals with a group of Negro women."[33] Ueland was familiar with some of these "Negro folk songs," for the young Norwegian-American who courted her daughter Anne used to sing them to her along with, among others, Shubert's "Serenade."[34] She may have learned about Nellie's interest from her own associates in the Shubert Club who attended a concert that Nellie sponsored when the Fisk Jubilee Singers came to St. Paul to raise funds for their university or from a journal that had published a feature on Nellie's Coterie.[35]

Clara's nominal familiarity with this musical genre may have been one more reason why she could relate to Nellie. But, unmindful of all that Nellie had endured with the dustup surrounding the Detroit resolution, the fallout with many of the colored club women and their leaders, and the exile that followed, all of which frustrated her long-held desire to unify black and white suffragists, Clara, at their first meeting, was impressed with Nellie's passion, but also amused—perhaps,

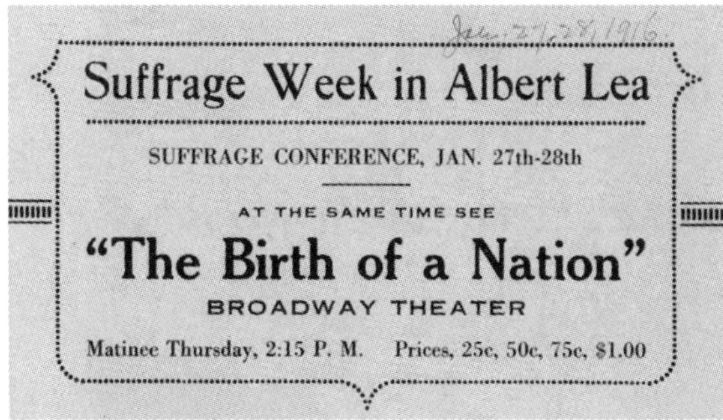

Suffrage movement invitation to view *The Birth of a Nation,* 1916. Courtesy of the Minnesota Historical Society.

condescendingly—by the younger woman's enthusiasm: "She talks well in an emotional, eloquent way, indeed talks constantly if she has a sympathetic listener."[36] And Ueland was indeed sympathetic, if not quite a sister. Nellie presided over a group with very few members. In 1919, the roster included only four women. Compared to most other club membership lists, Everywoman was barely noticeable, much like Minnesota's black population itself. Yet, befitting the racial consciousness of the time, the central office of the MWSA prominently labeled Everywoman "colored," to make the barely noticeable club noticeable.[37] It was as if the organization, led by people of goodwill, needed the racialized paradox. Yet, no name of a woman of their "noticeable" race would be added to the letterhead.[38] The good intentions of the women's suffrage movement would see to all of the problems that black women faced even though racism was not mentioned in its agenda. To the drafters, race did not matter and they did not need to be reminded of the people who were easy to overlook. The Nineteenth Amendment had the power to transform all citizens into people of goodwill, even presumably the suffragists of Albert Lea who believed that the good way to attract audiences to Suffrage Week in 1916 was to offer free viewings of *The Birth of a Nation.*[39]

With the ratification of the Nineteenth Amendment on August 26, 1920, the culmination of Ueland's work was completed. But for Nellie, a new chapter had already begun when news struck two months earlier that three black men had been hanged from a lamppost just outside the police station in Duluth.[40]

Under the Shadow of the Bright North Star

Black men in uniform returning home from war expected that they would find a different America waiting for them, one that respected their service to the nation, their demonstration of loyalty and patriotism, their continued commitment to believing that the legal and political institutions of government could be used to secure equality and opportunity when neither had ever before been secured. Between 1900 and 1915, more than one thousand African Americans were lynched.[1] Now, following the armistice, what they found instead was a society that granted even more license to white men to act with impunity against the Negro because of any grievance—real or imagined—than it might have. Adding to the extent of the 1917 citywide riot in East St. Louis, Illinois, when six thousand African Americans were driven from their homes, their neighborhoods destroyed, and forty-eight people killed, the summer of 1919—the "Red Summer"—saw no fewer than twenty-five race riots around the country in which hundreds of people died, were injured, or were displaced from their homes.[2]

In Chicago, thirty-eight people died, twenty-three of whom were black, fifteen were white, and 537 were injured.[3] Between 1918 and 1927, 456 men and women, of whom 416 were black, were lynched, by being hung, shot, burned, dismembered, or beaten to death. In the summer of 1919 alone, more than seventy black people were lynched in the United States.[4] Black soldiers still in uniform were among the victims.[5] As John Hope Franklin observed, "Few Negro Americans could have anticipated the wholesale rejection they experienced at the conclusion of World War I."[6]

Even fewer would have imagined this horrible expression in the North Star State, even though race relations in its cities provided enough kindling. Duluth's black community in 1920 numbered only 495. A few blacks held prominent positions in the city, but most found jobs as porters, waiters, janitors, and factory workers. The United States Steel Corporation actively recruited black laborers from southern states and northern cities, as the company had done in East St. Louis, so that by 1920 a significant portion of the city's blacks were employed at the U.S. Steel plant. Despite its presumed tolerance, blacks in Duluth endured similar treatment to those in the rest of the country. Certain restaurants did not serve blacks. A downtown movie theater forced blacks to sit in the balcony. Blacks working for U.S. Steel were paid less and excluded from living in Morgan Park, an idyllic "model city" specifically built for U.S. Steel workers. Many settled in nearby Gary, a poor neighborhood with substandard housing.[7] The Negroes most white Duluthians knew were easily cast in stereotype.

On June 14, 1920, the J. A. Robinson Circus came to the working-class neighborhood of West Duluth for a one-night stay. Later that night, as the tents and equipment were being taken down and packed away for an early-morning departure, a white couple—Irene Tusken and James Sullivan—stopped by to watch. They were allegedly surprised and held at gunpoint by six of the black laborers. According to the couple, Tusken was gang-raped while Sullivan was assaulted and forced to watch. The next day, the two reported the incident to the police. Within hours, six workers were taken into custody and held at the police station in Duluth as the circus left for Virginia, Minnesota. Later that day the county sheriff, police chief, and a contingent of police officers went to Virginia to take more circus laborers into custody, leaving Sergeant Oscar Olson in charge. While they were away, on the evening of June 15, a mob formed in West Duluth and headed to the police station, being urged on by men in a green truck to "join the necktie party." At approximately 7 p.m., as the crowd that by now had grown to thousands looked on, a mob stormed the station, overwhelming the police, who used only fire hoses to defend the building, took the three prisoners to be "convicted" in a mock trial, and then outside to be hanged. By midnight it was over, as the bodies of Isaac McGhie, Elias Clayton, and Elmer Jackson remained hanging from a nearby lamppost.[8]

The next morning, the police contingent returned to Duluth with more suspects, but by then the state had three more crimes to prosecute besides rape. It now had to charge white men for the crimes of instigating to riot, rioting, and murder. Lynching was not yet statutorily designated as a crime. As a total of thirteen black men now sat in jail, the St. Louis County Attorney Warren E. Greene decided to set aside the prosecution of the alleged rape, to allow for the investigation to identify and prosecute the ringleaders of the lynching. This would be no simple task. Thousands of people had clogged the streets as hundreds filled the halls of the police station amid a din of shouting voices. Property was destroyed, holes were punched through thick cell walls that allowed the mob to surge through to take the prisoners, and murderous chaos became the rule of the moment. In response to the threat of more violence, thousands of Duluthians volunteered to be deputized until Governor Burnquist could deploy 130 heavily armed National Guardsmen, further securing order in the city. No single man could be identified as the leader.[9] Only those who were plainly visible were brought into custody—the men in the truck who called for a "necktie party"; the young man who scaled the lamppost in order to position the rope and kicked the face of Elias Clayton as he died hanging; one of the men who pounded in the doors of the police station; the two men who handed prisoners to the mob; and the man who threatened the police lieutenant with a sledgehammer. After three weeks of investigations, thirty-seven indictments were returned—twelve for murder in the first degree and twenty-five for rioting or instigating to riot. Meanwhile, the neighbors in West Duluth were raising a defense fund.[10]

In a stinging rebuke, a report criticized Commissioner William Murnian, Sgt. Olson, and the police department for their incompetence in light of their knowing that "[t]here is a mob from West Duluth coming down to the station tonight to take the niggers out and kill them."[11] The state's report, which was sent to the governor in early August, concurred about Murnian, accusing him of "malfeasance for forbidding police from using their weapons and taking no steps to quell the riot . . . Their inaction," it concluded, "had emboldened the rioters."[12]

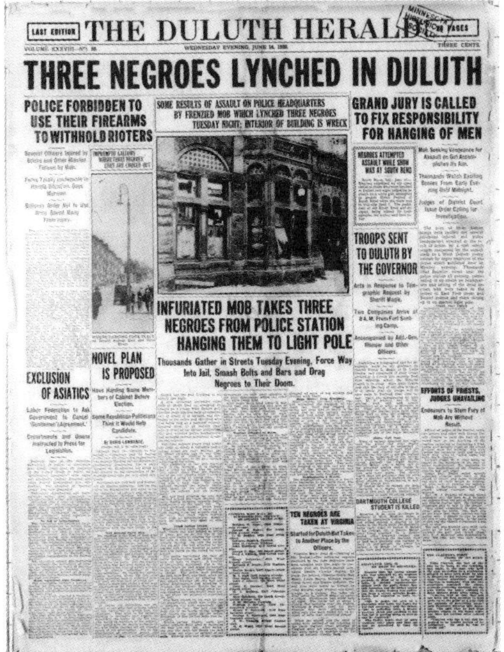

LAST EDITION THE DULUTH HERALD

THREE NEGROES LYNCHED IN DULUTH

POLICE FORBIDDEN TO USE THEIR FIREARMS TO WITHHOLD RIOTERS

SOME RESULTS OF ASSAULT ON POLICE HEADQUARTERS BY FRENZIED MOB WHICH LYNCHED THREE NEGROES TUESDAY NIGHT; INTERIOR OF BUILDING IS WRECK

GRAND JURY IS CALLED TO FIX RESPONSIBILITY FOR HANGING OF MEN

TROOPS SENT TO DULUTH BY THE GOVERNOR

INFURIATED MOB TAKES THREE NEGROES FROM POLICE STATION HANGING THEM TO LIGHT POLE

Thousands Gather in Streets Tuesday Evening, Force Way Into Jail, Smash Bolts and Bars and Drag Negroes to Their Doom.

NOVEL PLAN IS PROPOSED

EXCLUSION OF ASIATICS

DARTMOUTH COLLEGE STUDENT IS KILLED

TEN NEGROES ARE TAKEN AT VIRGINIA

The front page of the *Duluth Herald,* June 16, 1920. Courtesy of the Minnesota Historical Society.

The local branch of the NAACP sent Charles Sumner Smith to Duluth to investigate.[13]

As if the report was not enough to shake the public's regard for the pitiable department, on July 6 police chief John Murphy and deputy U.S. marshal Frank L. Bradley were arrested for smuggling into Duluth a large quantity of Canadian liquor. They were indicted two weeks later by a federal grand jury, which fueled a steady stream of rumors alleging corruption of the entire police force. Even though Prohibition had become federal law, the city seemed wide open to the illicit trade.[14] Meanwhile, as the *Duluth Herald* published stories of lynching, riots, and radical activities occurring throughout the country, Duluth's streetcar operators went on strike. The police were also demanding better pay. On August 27, Mayor C. R. Magney, who had been out of town on the night of the lynching, resigned his office to prepare to run in November as a district court judge. Incoming mayor T. W. Hugo insisted that "Mr. Magney has left me very little to do . . . His work was cleaned up today and there is no unfinished business to complete."[15]

In this context, the first of the trials of the ringleaders began. "Dame Justice," proclaimed the *Duluth Herald,* "is ringmaster for a three-ring circus."[16] In St. Paul, the local branch of the NAACP "confidently expected" that they would all be convicted.[17] Before three packed courtrooms, the first accused instigators were tried on the charge of rioting and instigating to riot, after the county attorney determined that the lesser charge would be easier to successfully prosecute. After three days of testimony, the jury pronounced a guilty verdict against Henry Stephenson, who had been identified as one of the men who had turned the fire hose against the police, stormed the jail, broke into the cell, wielded the sledgehammer at Officer Carl Sundberg, shouting, "We are going to lynch those niggers," and presiding with others over the kangaroo court that ordered the black men to be hanged.[18] But the verdict would prove to be pyrrhic, for although the defense's case—Stephenson's action was the result of police incompetence—did not persuade the jury, the argument would gain traction in the other trials.[19]

In the second trial for rioting, police credibility replaced the actions of alleged ringleader of the lynching, William Rozon. After thirty-two hours of deliberation, the jury reported that it was "hopelessly divided" and the judge ruled a mistrial.[20] And so it went. Leonard Hedman, identified as the man riding in the truck exhorting pedestrians to "join the necktie party," was acquitted on the basis that the police, knowing that a mob was forming to storm the jail, did nothing to quell it. Byer Olson, whose trial occurred right after Hedman's and in the same courtroom, was also acquitted that day. After four trials, the state could point to only one conviction.[21]

With all eyes on Duluth, a northern city not noted for racial bigotry that had somehow descended to the moral depths of Springfield and southern cities like Brownsville, Atlanta, Waco, and East St. Louis where mob violence against black men had been allowed to run riot, the successful application of law was the only way that the stain could be removed from the city's name; and so far, the challenge was not being met. At a time when the city's class tensions roiled just beneath the surface, the so-called jury of the defendant's peers—ordinary men—were using the verdicts as means to strike back against the privileged class: more acquittals would surely incite more lawlessness. Judge Bert Fesler, who served Duluth as a district court judge for thirty-one years, seated four jurors from the Stephenson trial, which had delivered a guilty verdict, and the Rozon trial, which had been deadlocked. When challenged by the defense, Fesler reversed himself by seating "men of substance and position and of a decidedly conservative bent" who resembled those who had served on the grand jury.[22] In fifty-five minutes of deliberation, the jury found Louis Dondino guilty as charged for inciting pedestrians to riot.[23] But the tide changed with the next trial, as John Burr, accused of presiding over the kangaroo court and pushing Isaac McGhie to the mob outside, was acquitted because as "judge" he had been selective in finding guilt with other prisoners, allegedly having said that "We don't want to do anything to innocent men." But the working-class grievance became evident when the defense attorney said during summation, "If the defendant had not been a working man . . . wearing poor clothes he would not have been placed under arrest." Evidence from all the trials indicated that laboring men and businessmen were part of the crowd, but only working-class men had been indicted, a fact that showed that the legal system was biased. The jurors had set out to rectify this fact. When the verdict was read, the gallery erupted in a thunderous applause.[24] Across the hall in Judge H. A. Dancer's court, Carl J. Miller, identified as battering down the doors of the police station, was likewise acquitted of rioting. It took the jury twenty-four minutes to reach its verdict.[25] The state had lost five of seven cases.

"The sounds of cheering spectators must have sharpened the state's resolve that justice be done in Judge William A. Cant's court."[26] This would be done with the successful prosecution of Carl John Alfred Hammerberg, an eighteen-year-old Swedish immigrant of marginal intelligence, poor, and the youngest defendant to be tried. Identified as a ringleader, evidence showed that he merely watched the actions of the mob, at times being carried along by the chaotic current, entranced by the curiously horrific and almost hypnotic scenes of the evening. He never signed his statement, nor was he informed that he had the right to counsel. Nevertheless, over the objections of defense counsel, Judge

Cant admitted the statement as evidence.[27] The die was cast, for the trial was no longer of Hammerberg but, oddly, of the jury system in Duluth. "It is the lack of faith in the jury that causes lynchings. Is the jury system a failure?" the prosecutor edgily asked the jurors. "If it is, you men are going to know your share of responsibility for it."[28] The judge instructed the jury to determine that the very act of riding in the truck that carried those who had incited the mob action, as Hammerberg admitted doing, constituted "substantial character" of guilt.[29] But in a more fundamental sense, a guilty verdict would acquit the jury system, as well as the city of Duluth. On September 15, after six hours of deliberation, the jury found John Hammerberg guilty as charged.[30]

Faced with the mood of the community that displayed widespread contempt for the police, whose officers testified for the state, and a prevailing sense that the legal system was corrupt, the county attorney faced a dilemma. In November the *Duluth Herald* reported that an insufficient number of men subpoenaed for grand jury duty had shown up to serve. Many Duluthians now criticized a system where countless immigrant and working-class residents of West Duluth filled the jails for petty offenses. Others, as author Michael Fedo noted, made uneasy comparisons between the court's role in convicting Hammerberg and acquitting Hedman, who had condemned the black prisoners to the noose. The crimes that a Chicago newspaper had called "as black and ugly as any that has brought the South into disrepute" went unpunished.

Three men were convicted for the acts of many, and each would serve one year of a five-year sentence.[31] By November, the state as well as the white community as a whole moved on to the rape trials, for which thirteen black defendants had waited in jail for five months. There was no more talk of removing the stain on Duluth's good name, for the stain was indelible. At best, most hoped that the sight and sounds of the nightmare of June 16 would fade in time as memories dimmed.

Not even the Minnesota Federation of Colored Women's Clubs, which had held its annual meeting in Duluth one week after the riot, seemed willing to draw attention to the lynchings, no doubt out of fear of reprisal: "The convention was one of the most successful and pleasant held in years."[32] But for black Minnesotans, the image and proximity of the event could not be erased, even though for many restraint seemed to be the prudent response to two unanswerable questions that must have been asked, albeit furtively: How much of "Duluth" was hidden within the souls of Minneapolis and St. Paul? And, more importantly, Where had all the right-thinking white folks gone? Black Minnesotans wondered why so many of their white friends could not believe that the permission to show the images depicted in *The Birth of a Nation* had effectively provided the license to kill. It must have given them pause to consider just how flimsy the legal process could be, even when black men were on trial. The beast during these dangerous times nationally needed only the slightest provocation, for it had already tasted blood, as blacks who had seen Duluth as a safe harbor now left town forever. From 1920 to 1930, as the city grew by two thousand persons, its black population dropped by 16 percent.[33]

By mid-September, a number of troubling circumstances took a toll on the resolve to try the lynchers. The court system of the Eleventh Judicial District was burdened with cases arising from the devastating fire that had swept through the region, requiring the attention of all five judges presiding over the lynching trials. Then, on September 16, a bomb exploded in New York City that leveled the J. P. Morgan building, injuring and killing scores of people. That reminded Duluthians of their own tentative security in the face of recent "radical" activities. Then it was learned, in late October, that most of the confiscated whiskey that had been stored in the police vault was stolen. Making matters worse, the county sheriff's department was rocked by allegations of vice at the jail, including sexual abuse of female prisoners. Any pretense of lawful propriety had gone up in smoke. Mindful that the salacious and potentially explosive display of trials of the accused black prisoners might provoke more violence, in November the prosecutor was ready to dispense with most of the pending rape trials. Thirteen men had stood accused, but seven were released for lack of evidence, leaving six to stand trial. Max Mason, against whom the evidence seemed the most overwhelming, was the first of these to be tried and convicted, even though the presiding judge, several jurors, and prosecuting attorney Mason Forbes later admitted that they doubted Mason's guilt.[34]

The evidence was further weakened on the questionable identification by Tusken and Sullivan, which was the issue that brought Mason's conviction on appeal to the Minnesota Supreme Court, which ultimately was upheld. Justice Homer B. Dibell, in his lone dissenting opinion, outlined a credible argument pointing to the flimsy nature of the state's case, but then concluded that Mason's identification had to be questionable because Negroes from outside the state "look much alike to the northerner."[35] Nonetheless, Mason, as the scapegoat, was sentenced to serve seven to thirty years. However, after five years he was released on parole provided he agreed to leave the state.[36] William Miller, the second and last defendant to be tried, was acquitted.[37] The charges for the remaining four prisoners were dropped. With that, the work of forgetting the whole chapter could commence for the people of Duluth.

But in St. Paul that would not be the case for Nellie Francis.

Shun the Snares of Petty Discord

As gut-wrenching as the previous months were, not just for Nellie but for all right-thinking Minnesotans—black and white—it remained unclear whether the body politic would want to draw more attention to what many wishfully hoped was an anomaly. There were segments of society comprised of vile white men for whom violence and racial epithets were common forms of expression, and an uncomfortably larger number of ordinary white citizens who had demonstrated a prurient interest in the images depicted in *The Birth of a Nation,* seeing the spectacle of a black man being lynched as harmless entertainment. And for all the outrage expressed from black pulpits and in the black press, it remained to be seen whether blacks who came to the state for the jobs would choose to remain in the state and agitate for a change in the law, or, closer to Nellie's own community, whether proper black society would choose to potentially disrupt the placid waters on which they sailed in their social, business, and political affairs, much of which required benevolent relationships with white people who might feel the law was somehow a slight against them and therefore unnecessary. Indeed, was the state capable of committing one more progressive act, one that chiefly benefited its already grateful colored citizens? All of this would have to be figured out in due course, but Nellie had to busy herself with a more pressing matter—preparing women to participate in their first election.

As the November elections approached, white suffragists fanned out across their communities with a new sense of empowerment to register women to vote; and Nellie did the same in the black neighborhoods of the Twin Cities. But her challenge was unique, for in the wake of the

Nellie Francis, 1920. Courtesy of the Minnesota Historical Society.

Duluth lynchings, she—a person perceived by some of her own people as someone who enjoyed obvious privilege, but who nonetheless, in three years' time, would face a howling white mob in front of her St. Paul home—had to motivate her sisters to push beyond long memories of abandonment by white allies during race riots and unchecked terror that had erupted every decade since ratification of the last voting amendment fifty years earlier, and who now must have wondered whether this new franchise and the recent tragedy up north foreshadowed the backlash to a new failed Reconstruction.[1] About this, Nellie could give no guarantees. For them all, caution continued to be the order of the day, for race still mattered.

Appointed by the national Republican party to chair the Minnesota (black) Women's Department, she presided over a mass meeting to inform women about how to participate in the electoral process and led a massive effort to get women registered. She would also act as a ballot judge on election day. She understood that many black women remained reluctant to do what they had never before done, so she held special classes for the colored women of Minneapolis on registering to vote. In November, she was invited to address the Hennepin County League of Women Voters in Minneapolis.[2] After the election, reviewing the final tally and seeing her candidate's name in the winner's column as a result of her efforts, Nellie showed a side of herself that had been rarely seen. She appeared happy for the first time in a long while. Her grandmother had just come to town. At the home of Fogg, an old family friend from the Nashville days, Nellie enjoyed a veritable family reunion, surrounded by all of the people who meant so much to her—Billy, of course, her grandmother, Alice West (Nellie's aunt and Juno's sister), Nellie's sister Lula, and Lula's husband Richard Chapman. They reminisced about the old times, for the Fogg family had housed the Griswolds when they first arrived in St. Paul, thirty-seven years earlier.[3]

Nellie Seay—"Gramma" to the family—had always inspired her youngest daughter Juno and granddaughter to political action, imbuing them with a determination to pursue their senses of purpose, if need be in the lonely pursuit of leadership. She conveyed to them that the world would not always understand or support them and that their special gifts to serve, lead, and move their agenda forward could just as likely alienate potential allies and presumed friends. But the struggle for a higher purpose always tested the mettle of relationships and usually required sacrifices. Her wisdom came from 114 years of experience on this earth and she was a force of nature. She circulated petitions that resulted in the establishment of Nashville's first high school for black children, and she organized a variety of political organizations to promote black progress in the city and state. "Her daughter, Frankie Pierce," reported journalist Delois Wilkinson, "continued in her footsteps."[4]

She had seen her girls through all of their ups and downs and had sadly watched Maggie, her oldest, pass over before her, five years before Gramma buried her husband Frank. She had also assisted Juno in getting her college degree, Alice her nursing certificate, and two grandsons (Alice's boys) through medical school. Lightfoot, the oldest son, would become chief surgeon of Mercy Hospital in Memphis, and T. G. was a staff member at Hubbard Hospital and an instructor at Meharry Medical College in Nashville.[5] She could afford to do this because of the landholdings she had acquired and sold off over the years, starting with the land she received from her husband Frank and son-in-law Thomas in 1877 and 1895.[6] Now she was needed for another task—to assess the resolve of Nellie's many communities to mount yet another campaign—and to do this she needed to see Nellie's multifaceted world. Throughout the winter of 1920–21, they attended a variety of meetings with black and white liberals of St. Paul society, including sessions of the Everywoman Progressive Council—the name was changed after the ratification of the women's suffrage amendment.[7] At one session they unveiled the John Singleton Copley print of the famous St. Gauguin's bronze relief of the Fifty-fourth Massachusetts Regulars, which the council purchased and intended to present to

Nellie Seay, circa 1918. Photograph from the *Nashville Globe*. Courtesy of the University of Tennessee.

the Frederick Douglass Home at Washington, D.C.[8]

During their evenings alone at home, the two Nellies talked about the campaign to come and the need for a bill that would fend off the creeping sense of helplessness that would surely result if black Minnesotans did not force their state into taking a stand against the threat of future atrocities.[9] The state federation had made it clear that this was not a priority for it. But in the long-run it did not matter. Nellie was already laying groundwork for what would be one of her most important achievements; and Gramma Seay was raring to play an important role in that campaign, for she had long realized the impact on an audience that saw a woman, aged but animated, making her case for justice. Juno, who could not come to St. Paul at the time, had done similar work years before when her niece sought to preside over the state federation, but now, in Nashville, in the wake of the successful Tennessee suffrage campaign, she was in the midst of her own campaign with the newly formed League of Women Voters of Tennessee to lobby the general assembly for a bill to create a vocational school for African American girls.[10] Gramma Seay was ready to step in and lend a hand.

Nellie escorted her grandmother to a luncheon at the Women's Welfare League, and later they attended Billy's Sunday school class.[11] While Nellie hosted a planning luncheon for the League of Women Voters at the Curtiss Hotel in Minneapolis and later in St. Paul, her grandmother visited two white Baptist churches—Woodland Park and Merriam Park Baptist—and later, on January 29, she spoke at the Adelphai Club.[12] Meanwhile, at the formal meeting of the league, Nellie's friend and now collaborator Clara Ueland, as the presiding officer, vigorously denounced the lynching of colored citizens and made a strong appeal for support to the NAACP. Nellie was then given the floor to explain at length the object and scope of the association and what it was doing to combat lynching.[13]

What happened the next day illustrates just how far apart Nellie Francis and key members of the state's colored club women had grown. Mrs. W. R. Hardy, who had replaced Nellie as Minnesota's representative to the Douglass Initiative, demanded at the urging of her sister, NACWC president Mary Talbert, that the convention demonstrate its "sympathy and public opinion" to support the antilynching bill that had just been presented in Congress by Sen. Charles Curtis of Kansas and Representative Leonidas C. Dyer of Missouri. Mrs. Hardy sought to approach any delegate who would listen to her. The first woman she met told her she was sorry that nothing could be done to place it on the agenda. Mrs. Hardy replied: "Surely nothing can be more important than human life, and I will not consider your answer."[14]

She waited until the executive committee came out of its meeting and confronted Clara Ueland, who was presiding at the afternoon session. She made such a strong appeal that Mrs. Ueland, who had spoken on the matter the day before, told Hardy that she would nevertheless bring the matter before the women. But because the bill was a federal matter, Ueland added, the convention could not take any action beyond urging the national organization to take up the matter; she said she would bring that recommendation to the convention. Unsatisfied with this, Mrs. Hardy arose during the general assembly and stated that as she had presented this matter to Mrs. Ueland, she would like to tell the women the reason why: "Woman, when the unborn have been lynched in Georgia, is it not time that we should begin to be interested? Let me tell you a story." She then related the story of Mary Turner.

In Brooks County, Georgia, in 1918 a brutal white plantation owner named Hampton Smith was known for beating his workers, including Mary Turner. Her husband, Hazel "Hayes" Turner, who tried defending her against Smith's abuse, was arrested, convicted by an all-white jury, and sentenced to a chain gang. When another laborer killed Smith and wounded his wife, a large manhunt ensued that resulted in the killing of thirteen black people over a period of two weeks. Among them was Mary Turner's husband, who was later lynched by a mob during a transfer to another prison. His body was left hanging from a tree over the weekend. Thirty-three-year-old Mary Turner, eight months pregnant, threatened to have the mob arrested. On May 18, 1918, in reprisal, a mob of more than a hundred white people took her to a tree near the Okapiloo River. Walter White, who investigated the incident for the NAACP, later reported:

> Mary Turner was tied and hung upside down by her ankles, her clothes soaked with gasoline, and burned from her body. Her belly was slit open with a knife like those used in slitting hogs. Her unborn babe fell to the ground and gave two feeble cries. Its head was crushed by a member of the mob with his heel, and the crowd shot hundreds of bullets into Turner's body.

Mary Turner was later cut down and buried with her child near the tree where she was hanged. A whiskey bottle was used to mark her grave. The NAACP would use the incident in its campaign for a federal anti-lynching law.[15]

When Hardy finished, *The Appeal* reported, "there was not a dry eye in the room." Several women came over and shook her hand and said they would do all they could to help the cause. They asked her to send them "colored" literature, as they intended to be interested in the colored people from then on.[16]

As if to slight Nellie, who had known nothing of the club women's plans, Hardy, reflecting the simmering resentment of favored news coverage that Nellie had enjoyed, said that while she had "no newspaper notoriety," she—Hardy, flailing for relevance—knew that she had "helped some." Then, speaking for Mrs. George Gooden and Mrs. A. S. Foster, the other two black delegates, and in deference to a Jim Crow policy that she presumed to be in effect at the Curtiss Hotel, Mrs. Hardy "loudly" praised the courtesy shown them by the managers of the hotel, "and in the dining room especially."[17] As gracious as the gesture was, Hardy would have known that the hotel had discontinued its discrimination policy had she simply consulted Nellie, who had often been there for meetings. Rather, they were intent on showing that the colored club movement of Minnesota did not need Nellie Francis. But the same did not hold for the sisterhood on the national level.

In late February, Nellie was invited to Washington to attend a meeting called by Lethia Cousins Fleming of Cleveland, Ohio, a high official in the national association. As one who was active in politics on the local and national levels, she chaired the executive board of the National Association of Colored Women's Clubs and was president of the Ohio federation, as well as serving on the executive boards for the National Association of Colored Women and the National Council of Negro Women, in addition to serving as president of the National Association of Republican Women, as executive director of the Republican Colored Women's organization, and as a charter member of the Urban League of Greater Cleveland, the Traveler's Aid Society, and the NAACP (Cleveland branch). As *The Appeal* reported, the purpose of the meeting was "to form a permanent organization that would be launched on March 3."[18] Nothing more was reported as to what the new "permanent organization" might be. In any event, a different agenda seemed to be in play.

While in the city, the NACWC committee that managed the Douglass Memorial Home invited Nellie to attend a business meeting. It was her first time with the group since her ouster in 1917. Since then, she had had no official contact with the national organizations and minimal contact with the federation. Now, she, not the existing president of the Minnesota federation—not even President Talbert's sister—was about to be asked to weigh in on a matter of crucial importance. The Douglass home had been cleared of all debt through the efforts of the NACWC campaign, but six thousand dollars was needed to make the changes and improvements necessary to have it what they desired it to be. Already, four thousand dollars had been raised for that purpose, but two thousand more was needed. This was where they thought Nellie might be helpful. Committee chair Mrs. J. C. Napier, also a friend from Nashville and wife of James Napier, an associate of Nellie's father in the old days, asked Nellie to appeal to the Minnesota federation to contribute its share "so that the Home could be put in proper shape by summertime."[19]

Apparently, the Minnesota Federation of Colored Woman's Clubs, at its last convention in Duluth held eight days after the lynchings and deemed by *The Appeal* to be "one of the most successful and pleasant held in years," did not see fit to address its responsibility in this matter. It must have seemed rich to Nellie, whose Everywoman Progressive Council was the only colored woman's organization in Minnesota to donate to the home.[20] It also may have been rich to Aunt Juno as she wanted her niece to enjoy the overture from an organization that had treated her poorly. Juno, after all, was in a position to influence the committee's decision considering that she had recently been elected the fifth vice president of the NACWC, as witnessed by her mother, Mrs. Nellie Seay.[21] In any event, Nellie Francis apparently felt it inappropriate to insinuate herself—now, an outsider—into association–federation business.

On March 3, Nellie was back in Washington to attend her first meeting of directors and state leaders of the Republican National Committee in charge of work among colored women. She presided as chairman of the program committee of that meeting and as the newly elected chairman of the Press Committee of the Western Division. In the evening, she attended the meeting of the executive board of the NACWC at the Frederick Douglass Home when it formally came under the stewardship of the national association. It was during this meeting that Nellie, on behalf of her organization, officially presented the Copley print. Mrs. Elizabeth Carter, honorary president of NACWC, accepted it and said that nothing more appropriate could have been selected as a gift to the home. The picture would be hung "as soon as certain repairs and alterations had been made in the premises."[22] Nellie, whose higher priority was to gain support for placing an antilynching law on the books, seemed contented to leave the responsibility of "repairs and alterations" to be hammered out between the Minnesota federation and the national association.

The next day, Nellie attended President-elect Warren G. Harding's inauguration and the grand reception at the White House. As a person of newly acquired standing the Republican Party, she had played an important role for the party during the Minnesota campaign, and now, as a result of that work, she enjoyed recognition from the new administration. At the inaugural reception, she was approached by Charles A. Cottrell, a confidant and former classmate of President Harding, who introduced her to various dignitaries and escorted her and other prominent women to meet the new president and his wife. For the remainder of her time in Washington, she made the rounds, no doubt garnering support for the work ahead and staying at the home of Henry Lincoln Johnson of Georgia, the only colored member of the Republican National Committee.[23] Of all the people she encountered during her Washington trip, Johnson, one of the founders (along with Robert Church, brother of Mary Church Terrell) of the Lincoln League formed to force the Republican Party to take a firm stance against lynching, Jim Crow laws, and voter disenfranchisement, may have provided her with the most sobering information.[24]

Coming from a state with such a troubled history on race and lynching, Johnson no doubt gave Nellie all of the support he could to advance her campaign to come in Minnesota. But what he had to share was quite sobering. Between 1880 and 1930, Georgia had the highest rates of lynching in the nation. The NAACP reported that 92.8 percent of the lynching victims in the state were black, and this was of those that had been reported.[25] But Johnson must have told her that a new law alone would not likely be enough to change what one historian referred to as "a new national pastime," for despite the horrific numbers, lynchings in Georgia rose even though the legislature had enacted a law to prevent mob violence. Passed unanimously in 1893, this legislation made it the duty of law-enforcement officials, when they learned of mob activity, "to prevent such mob violence" and to "use every means in their power to prevent such mob violence." The law required the sheriff to arrest those participating in mob activity and "place them in the common jail of the county."[26] But, as historian Christopher Meyers notes, "[c]ounty sheriffs in Georgia were not powerless to stop lynching; most simply chose not to intervene and many, in fact, assisted."[27] Brooks County, in particular—the site of the horrific lynchings of Mary Turner, her husband, and several other black men, and named after Congressman Preston Brooks of South Carolina, who nearly bludgeoned to death Charles Sumner in 1859 as he sat unawares in the chamber of the U.S. Senate—had the dubious reputation for mob violence that occurred on a regular basis and on an unprecedented scale.[28]

The lesson was clear: men could enact and swear on an oath to uphold a law and later, at the moment of truth, undermine the same law instead of standing with family, friends, and constituents. Duluth gave Nellie reasons for pause about the resolve of Minnesota's lawmen. But the bill that she and Billy were about to draft required a leap of faith in the character of their white friends and in the soul of the state. After Nellie's return to St. Paul, at the first meeting of the Everywoman Progressive Council, she reported on the Washington trip and the impressive amount of political endorsements to add to an already growing list she had compiled for the soon-to-be-drafted bill. Then she formally announced that the time was right to advance "a weighty political matter which, if adopted, will be of great benefit to the race," and she prepared her group for the campaign to come. The campaign for Minnesota's antilynching law was about to begin. In early April, before Gramma returned to Nashville, she told Nellie of events around the Twin Cities that had helped to lay the groundwork for the campaign.[29]

Since December, William Miller, one of the black defendants acquitted of raping Irene Tuskin in Duluth, had been making the rounds in the company of various black leaders in an effort to keep the memory of the lynchings alive. At a mass meeting in December sponsored by the local branch of the NAACP, Miller was given a hero's welcome.[30] Meanwhile, *The Appeal* was making its case for an antilynching law, arguing that the time was right for such a measure: Since white men who lynched white men were prosecuted and convicted, reasoned the editor, then soon black victims will have the same justice with convictions of white men who lynch black men: "We now predict that white men who lynch colored ones will eventually be apprehended, arrested, tried, and convicted for this horrific crime, in the South, as they recently have been in Duluth, Minn."[31] Although his facts were wrong and his logic was flawed, the editor was striving to make a more fundamental point: Minnesota needed to do something to place value on the lives and welfare of its colored citizens, that indeed black lives mattered.

A similar belief seemed to be spreading across the country, as reflected by the prevailing sentiment in the House of Representatives. In 1920, a Republican representative from Missouri, Leonidas C. Dyer, a white legislator who represented a majority African American district, sponsored an antilynching bill in the wake of the race riots in St. Louis and East St. Louis that received support from President Harding, as well as a large majority in the House. Then the bill stalled and was ultimately prevented from coming to a vote in the Senate in 1922, 1923, and 1924, owing to filibusters by the southern Democratic bloc. It would all be a part of the disappointing legacy of such efforts that would stretch far into the future. From 1882 to 1968, nearly two hundred antilynching bills were introduced in Congress, with only three passing the House. The Dyer bill would be one of them. Seven presidents between 1890 and 1952 asked Congress to pass a federal law. But not one bill was approved by the Senate because of the obstreperously powerful southern Democratic bloc.[32] The nation's upper chamber would remain resolute in preserving the villainous privilege to murder men and women with impunity. But with no southern Democratic bloc at work in Minnesota, Nellie Francis saw a clearer path to establishing a state antilynching law.[33]

Billy, as an executive officer of the local NAACP, requested information about lynching from the national office. He immediately received a packet of material, including a copy of Kentucky's antilynching law, which formed the basis of the Minnesota bill that he and Nellie drafted. Now it fell to Nellie to coordinate the lobbying effort to persuade legislators to support the bill, viewed as the harder stage of any campaign. But because of her vast network of experienced workers from the suffrage campaign and her widening contacts with prominent state and national Republican leaders, she came to the task well positioned to have the bill taken seriously. A mass meeting held at St. James AME on April 17 attracted hundreds of "race-loving colored citizens," as well as a number of elected state legislators, all intending to show support for both the state and the federal bills then making their way through Congress.[34] But unlike the federal bill, Nellie's easily cleared the Minnesota legislature and it was signed into law on April 18. Governor J. A. O. Preus had said before the bill's passage that he would be pleased to sign it. The vote in the house was 81–1, and in the senate the vote was 41–0.[35]

"The colored people of Minnesota," *The Appeal* proudly reported, "are much elated over the passage of what is known as the 'Anti Lynching Law,' this week." With this law, $7,500 could be recovered by the kin of a person lynched by a mob, and the sheriff of any county in which a lynching occurred could be suspended from office if he did not protect prisoners from mobs. With the law, Minnesota joined Alabama,

Louisiana, Kentucky, South Carolina, Kansas, New York, Ohio, Pennsylvania, California, Maine, New Hampshire, Illinois, New Jersey, and Wisconsin, whose laws included all or part of the provisions of the Minnesota law. "Mrs. W. T. Francis of St. Paul is the author of the law; and, to her indefatigable labors, in its behalf, with the members of the legislature is its successful passage due."[36] At an enthusiastic mass meeting of celebration held under the auspices of the Everywoman Progressive Council that included pastors who had canceled their church services for the day, Nellie spoke of the great achievement black Minnesota had just won and she thanked those who had been instrumental in getting the bill passed. D. W. Lawler, the former mayor of St. Paul, joined several legislators in speaking to how the new law also solidly placed all Minnesotans on the path to spiritual healing, and they praised Nellie Francis for her indomitable leadership.[37] Later it was decided that a fund be established citywide to purchase a silver loving cup to later be presented to her at a public testimonial.[38] It would be a St. Paul celebration.

On Sunday afternoon, May 1, hundreds assembled at Pilgrim Baptist Church to join in a mass tribute. "The citizens of St. Paul were indeed proud of Mrs. W. T. Francis, and justly so," reported *The Appeal* about a person who for years had been one of its favorite and most admired subjects, "for ever since girlhood and her graduation she has devoted the principal activities of her life to the uplift of our race . . . This public testimonial and this beautiful loving cup is evidence of the fact that we appreciate all that Mrs. Francis has done for the race, not only with regard to the Anti-Lynching Bill but through all of her years of service, and all good citizens of St. Paul stand ready to support her at all times in all her efforts in our behalf." It was all as much to celebrate her good deeds as to vindicate her leadership—indeed, all of her personal traits that had served her well to advance the interests of her community—which over the past few years had just as often seeded envy and created rivals. The handsome seventeen-inch, silver gold-lined loving cup stood as a tribute to her self-enfranchising determination to chart a better path to uplift her race, rejecting the edicts of leaders who seemed more interested in the trappings of office and protracted procedures that stymied genuine progress rather than achieving ambitious and potentially threatening goals.[39]

Charles Miller, one of the organizers and the preacher at Nellie and Billy's mock wedding anniversary, observed:

> Failure was in your path; but you met it face to face, you were not afraid, but with clear-minded will, faith, courage, perseverance you grasped the opportunity to protect the race; and, with the help of God you compelled failure to work to your advantage. Plunging into the tide of politics at its flood you were swept to victory. The anti-lynching bill passed, you were its initiative, to you belongs the reward of efficiency.[40]

He noted a less grand, though no less important, achievement:

> I am reminded of another of your achievements as I listen to the melodious noted pealing from the organ. I become reminiscent. With dynamic power charged with the vibrations of living force you met the financial king of the world, Andrew Carnegie, and succeeded in securing a gift of $1100.[41]

And, notably, because there had been no sentiments, no warm regards, and no congratulations from Minneapolis, or, even more remarkably, from Duluth, nor even the NACWC or the Minnesota Federation of Colored Women's Clubs, an organization that Nellie had once led, he pointed to the temperament that spawned pettiness and envy, not from racists but from the very people who once called her "sister." Miller wanted this beloved sister to know what he knew, and he wanted everyone present to know as well just what Nellie had to contend with over the past several years:

> You have been charged with self-aggrandizement but bless your soul, every time you have advanced by your own will power and brain up the ladder of fame. Unlike many others of the race with equal advantage who have dodged behind pillar and post to get away from the race, you have brought the race up with you. *So mind not what others say or think in these matters concerning you and the race. Live so as to make the most of the life God had given you, and let the tongues wag as they may. It is a sad mistake to say there are only seven deadly sins, there are eight and ingratitude is the first.*[42]

His remarks must have aroused the admiring crowd, who themselves had experienced the haughty and paternalistic disapproval of Minnesota's sisterhood of colored dowagers. Applause filled the sanctuary. After songs were sung, Nellie rose, "visibly affected," and responded to entreat and admonish her people to work together for mutual benefit:

> Your children will reap the harvest of our solidarity—of our determination to stand together, to fight together, and, if need be, to die together; for they are dying, every day, the men and women of our race, martyrs to lynch-law, the fiery stake and the awful savagery of peonage; that these, your children, may know full liberty and an equal chance in life. Or they must reap in the bitterness of sorrow, the fruits of our passivity and indifference; the frittering of our strength by suffering, petty strife and narrow jealousies to becloud the larger vision of our responsibility to coming generations.[43]

And then, echoing a sentiment that described her life's story, she said:

> [We must] frown with all the strength of our minds upon the destructive and selfish agencies and efforts to hinder earnest and altruistic service which imperil our efforts to enlist the cooperation of those who would sponsor our cause and be of service could we but present a united front. Listen to the plea of the black poet:
>
> O, black people, cease your sleeping,
> Get you off the road to folly;
> For your children's sake awaken!
> Shun the snares of petty discord
> Which dishearten and divide you,
> For division is our weakness—
> And the cause of your condition.[44]

With this, she ended what would be her last campaign of public service.

– 19 –

Hold On

It was indeed her last campaign and she seemed to know it at the time, for in publicly expressing for the first and only time her irritation with irksome allies, as she seemed to do in her elliptical manner, Nellie was retiring from public leadership and its turmoil; she was closing the door on an impressive chapter in her life. But she came to realize that the new chapter would not include residing in the same house and neighborhood, or in time even the state that had been her home since childhood. There had simply been too many trials.

Over the next few years, Lula, in her declining state, and her husband Richard continued to live with Nellie and Billy in the cramped 606 St. Anthony residence. By the fall of 1924, the Francises had begun to look for a new home and they thought they found it at 2092 Sargent Avenue in the modest all-white Macalester–Groveland neighborhood of St. Paul. They had no reason to know that in occupying the new house they would be stepping into the crosshairs of racial bigotry. In early October, the Cretin Improvement Association organized to discourage the Francises from moving in, and when they did not heed the veiled threat, the harassment began.[1]

On October 4, a cross was burned on their lawn after the association had requested police protection for the cross burners. On November 1, two hundred people marched through the neighborhood "[a]rmed with horns and noise-making devices." Even George Olson, who had sold 2092 Sargent to Billy and Nellie, was subject to harassment when flares were lit in front of his home; and after Oscar Arneson, president of the association, offered the Francises a thousand dollars to give up their house, an offer that would expire at 11 a.m. on December 6. The night before, a second cross was burned in front of the Francis home to underscore the determination of the Arneson group. He was quoted as saying, "[T]he Ku Klux Klan never burns more than two of these warning crosses." The NAACP lodged protests, but it had to be adding insult to injury when none of the Francises' powerful friends in the government and civic arena, or even from their old community, came to their assistance. As Paul Nelson wrote, "[T]he Francis' decades of public service, leadership, Republican politics, and middle-class respectability counted for nothing."[2]

What also seemed to count for nothing was the influence (or rather the reluctance to use influence) that progressive political leaders had over their constituents, especially in the matter of equal racial opportunity. Their poses as friends of the race, and their well-publicized support of the universal women's suffrage amendment, the antilynching law, and bans on *The Birth of a Nation,* amplified by a friendly press seemingly intent on fostering the illusion of the progressive image of the state (notwithstanding Duluth), all conveyed the sense that they were committed to extending the principle of racial justice for their constituents to follow. But what the leaders did not understand—or perhaps understood all too well—was that for the voters, principle and practice as they related to the Negro were miles apart. To the white voter, principle ruled as long as the Negro was a mere abstraction, which was easy in a state whose black residents numbered fewer than 1 percent of the total population. But when a member of that minuscule class moved into a white neighborhood, the residents treated it as an invasion to be repulsed.

Nellie and Billy's experience in St. Paul's Macalester–Groveland neighborhood was not unprecedented, nor was it limited to St. Paul. In 1909, the Minneapolis home of Amy and Madison Jackson located in Prospect Park was visited by a white mob that demanded that they vacate their property. The first known restrictive covenant, as the courts would later call them, in Minneapolis came just months after the encounter at the Jacksons' home when a Swedish baker on Thirty-sixth Avenue South stipulated in the deed to his property that the "premises shall not at any time be conveyed, mortgaged, or leased to any person or persons of Chinese, Japanese, Moorish, Turkish, Negro, Mongolian, or African blood or descent." The practice would only expand throughout the city, not just by individual property owners, but by real-estate developers like Edmund Walton whose properties, by 1914, all incorporated the same language.[3]

The largest and most widely publicized racially motivated demonstrations in Minnesota's history were against the postal worker Arthur Lee and his wife Edith in July 1931. The young couple was African American and they chose a house in the Field neighborhood in South Minneapolis, considered to be "white" and established as such in 1927 when the Eugene Field Neighborhood Association had all of the neighbors sign a contract stating that they would only sell their properties to white people. After the Lees moved into their newly acquired home on 4800 Columbus Avenue South, association members tried to force them to leave, offering five thousand dollars to purchase the house. When the Lees refused to leave, the racial taunts and small demonstrations escalated, culminating on the evening of July 16, 1931, with an unruly gathering of four thousand people who packed the lawn and spilled into the street in front of the house, splattered it with black paint, threw garbage and human excrement on the property, and posted on the front lawn signs proclaiming "We don't want niggers here!" and "No niggers allowed in this neighborhood. This means you!" Until then, the *Minneapolis Tribune* acceded to the request of association leaders to avoid reporting on the situation at the Lee house; but the mob action on July 16, by now too large to ignore, became a front-page story under the headline "HOME STONED IN RACE ROW!"[4]

Still, the Lees remained at 4800 Columbus Avenue South, even after the neighborhood association went through the same paces followed by other groups in similar housing conflicts—offering to purchase the property back from a black family, throwing things at homes owned by blacks, and appearing as a mob to demand that the family move out of the neighborhood. Although they received support from individuals and organizations such as attorney Lena Smith and the NAACP, as well as police protection until September 1932 and an escort to kindergarten for the entire year for their six-year-old daughter, the family, anxious for its safety, slept in the basement of the house for the entire time it lived on Columbus Avenue South. Eventually, in late 1933, the

A mob assembled outside Arthur and Edith Lee's home in South Minneapolis, where they lived with their six-year-old daughter, Mary, in July 1931. Photograph from *The Crisis* magazine, 1931.

Lees moved to a nearby neighborhood with a higher black population.[5] Forced by restrictive covenants and enforced by coercion, the black ghetto in South Minneapolis increased by one family.

What made the Lee episode noteworthy was that it received any attention at all. More often than not, such events went unreported. Whether because newspapers shied away to avoid sullying the good name of the city or avoided publishing stories that would only draw to the site more troublemakers or curiosity seekers—in the mosh pit of the crowd, they tended to all look alike—such stories made life for public officials quite uncomfortable, showcasing the impotence of public officials. There were no good ways to put an end to the embarrassing episode. Doing anything was sure to cause more problems. For those with ambition, their role in it would leave an indelible mark next to their name. It was one thing for politicians to feel compelled to respect the constitutional rights of bigoted property owners who had the right to assemble and speak. Less than a year later, the U.S. Supreme Court would rule in *Corrigan v. Buckley* that restrictive covenants were constitutional.[6] But it was quite another thing for politicians to defer to mob violence. Granting the Macalester–Groveland Association a permit to burn a cross at 2092 Sargent Avenue came close to the line. But declining to decry the torment only gave license for more violence. It must have roiled Nellie and Billy that none of their political friends spoke out against the threats that they received daily, not just in their own interest, but for the advancement of black opportunity. The silence of political leaders only perpetuated segregation and the stereotype of the Negro spreading his wretchedness to everything he touched. As Billy had said, showing uncharacteristic candor, "[A]s fast as a Negro rises out of that class [of poverty] he disappears from your field of vision, for as the Negro rises higher to intellectual and industrial levels in most of the sections of this country he is by segregation pushed out of your lives and denied the right to compete with the white man."[7]

As if this adversity was not enough, while enduring further harassment that included mysterious phone calls, vandalism, and occasional taunts from passing cars, in January Nellie suffered an even harder blow with the death of her sister. Lula, the one person who had been in her life since she was born, her confidante and protector, who preferred being in the wings of Nellie's dramatic life, was now forever gone. Although the couple, with great heartache, continued to live with so many bad memories at the Sargent address until 1927, what bonds they had with the city had thinned to a mere thread. Billy's diplomatic appointment by President Calvin Coolidge as U.S. consul and minister to the Republic of Liberia came on July 12, 1927. It was the culmination of his ambition. It was also their way out.[8]

On the other side of the globe, Monrovia, the capital of Liberia, their home for the next two years, had a commercial center consisting of nine streets, none of which was paved. The largest substantial building was the president's official residence. It was humid when it was not raining. The town had no sewer or water system or indoor plumbing, and it was considered, wrote Nelson, "one of the least healthy places in the world for newcomers."[9] Just miles from the coast, there were no roads, no good footpaths, no permanent bridges, no telegraphs, no postal system, no agricultural effort, no medical or educational facilities, no public works. The country, founded by the descendants of African American slaves, was "tiny, poor and corrupt" and the government traded in forced labor. Billy was immediately given a secret assignment from Secretary of State Henry L. Stimson to investigate the matter and report back to Washington without tipping off the Liberian government. In fact, the State Department had directed Billy to address an issue that it had known about for ten years. Over the previous ten or more years there had been many public reports of forced labor and mistreatment of Liberians. In 1912, members of the Kru tribe had appealed to the State Department for help against Samuel Ross, one of President C. D. B. King's henchmen, and author Henry Reeves documented the practice in his 1923 book *The Black Republic*; and yet the United States had done very little of significance until Billy submitted his report.[10] Nellie performed her role by keeping up the appearances of a proper diplomat's wife.[11]

Because there was no way that he could go into the countryside to investigate the charge without catching the unwanted eye of some Liberian official, Billy culled through all the documents he could assemble. Finally, on March 22, 1929, he drafted a report that concluded that the Liberian government had knowledge of, was engaged in, and was making large sums of money from the exportation of forced labor that resembled slavery. The U.S. government decided to take action and directed Billy to present an ultimatum to the Liberian president: submit to a rigorous investigation or risk grave consequences to Liberia's relations with the United States. President King consented, requesting as one condition that one of the three members of the investigative commission be Liberian. The commissioners—Cuthbert Christie, an Englishmen; Dr. Charles S. Johnson, future president of Fisk University in Nashville; and former Liberian president Edwin Barclay—conducted an extensive investigation starting in the fall of 1929. Their findings confirmed Billy's preliminary report and went further, documenting in detail the illegal fines, the floggings, the kidnappings, the payoffs, and the involvement of Liberian officials, including President King and his vice president. Both men resigned after the report came out. But Billy would not get the satisfaction of witnessing this outcome.[12]

Months earlier, in mid-June, he began complaining of headaches that progressively grew unbearable. Nellie watched helplessly as her life partner of thirty-six years, whom she had never seen suffer from anything more than a cold, lapse into fevers, then chills, until he developed trouble breathing brought on by pulmonary edema. Although he seemed to rally, his condition turned worse when, on July 11, his stomach was so distended that a tube had to be inserted to relieve the pressure. On July 13, Nellie dictated a brief note to various people, including friends in St. Paul, describing Billy's "pain, weariness and exhaustion," and his being "in a VERY weakened state," yet she noted bravely, as much for her own benefit, that he was "still managing to hold on with some of marvelous old rallying strength."[13] But two days later, on July 15, at 5 a.m., William T. Francis—"Billy," Nellie's partner in a distinguished life—died from yellow fever. "My deepest sympathy goes out to you in your great sorrow," Stimson telegraphed her. "The tragic death of Mr. Francis deprives the United States of one of its most able and trusted public servants." It would prove to be a tribute in word only.[14]

In August, Nellie brought Billy's body to New York, where the national office of the NAACP organized a reception. Then, by train, they returned to St. Paul for a memorial service at Pilgrim with former secretary of state and 1929 Nobel laureate Frank Kellogg representing the State Department. Soon after the services, they left for Nashville, Nellie's hometown, where Gramma still lived. St. Paul was no longer their home, nor would it be Billy's place of final rest. She had long ago decided to make this move.[15] The State Department would not ship Billy's body from St. Paul to Nashville, so it was left to Nellie to cover the cost. It was money she could not afford to spend. Despite their station, their contacts, their accomplishments and notoriety, they were broke. After interring Billy—civic and civil-rights leader, attorney, and diplomat—in Greenwood Cemetery, Nashville's traditional African American burial ground, Nellie had only the remainder of her husband's last check, $412. Nellie went to Washington to meet with Assistant Secretary of State William Castle seeking financial benefits for a surviving spouse of a diplomat who died while in service to the nation, but the secretary told her that the department could only pay what was authorized by statute.[16] Her only option, he said, was an act of Congress, for which he held out little hope. In 1930, the U.S. House of Representatives rejected a bill to award her five thousand dollars, equivalent to her late husband's annual salary, on the grounds that she had not shown herself to be "dependent" on him.[17]

The congressmen had probably concluded that she was employed; if so, this was likely because Aunt Juno, as superintendent of the Tennessee Vocational School for Colored Girls, had likely created a position for her favorite niece. But as the Great Depression began to smother the Tennessee economy, the legislature stopped paying its employees at the school, promising to compensate them once the economy turned around. In 1966, Nellie, at age eighty-eight, would receive ten thousand dollars for her work.[18] But that remuneration would come in the distant future. In 1930, as the Depression deepened with spreading unemployment, the annuity for the "nondependent" Republican Nellie Francis was hard to sell to a Democratic congressional majority.[19]

Months after Nellie received the disappointing news from Washington, nearly two years after the death of her husband, Gramma, 117 years of age and reputedly "the oldest negro in Tennessee," died at her home. Nellie was at her bedside.[20] The legacy that Gramma Seay left behind was in the character and deeds of all of her girls and in the recognition of her church, the predominately white First Baptist, that would last long after her passing, and she was immortalized by naming the Bible club after her.[21] But for Nellie, the tribute did little to mitigate the losses of Billy and Gramma and Lula, who had passed nearly a decade earlier but yet was still painful. It was all now compounded by her financial uncertainty. She busied herself with church and civic activities, but living in Gramma's home, with the matriarch's things still there, with her scent, the memories, her spirit seemingly everywhere, somehow the simple purging act of mourning so much loss was stifled. "My girl," Juno recorded simply, "needed some time."[22] Nellie took an extended tour of the West Coast, a region of the country she had never seen, arriving in Los Angeles, where a number of her old St. Paul friends now lived in retirement. In time, she witnessed what for her was a special adventure—the Olympic Games. It was the first athletic event she ever saw and would ever see. She spent a California winter in Long Beach.[23] But after a few months, she knew it was time to go home. "The sunshine out here heals my soul but I cannot hide behind it forever," she wrote to Juno in one of her few letters to survive. "It is time to come home."[24]

Meanwhile, in Washington, the effort to convince Congress to appropriate an annuity to Nellie was renewed in the spring of 1934 when Minnesota Republican Representative Melvin Maas of St. Paul reintroduced his bill. He had just been reelected after being swept out of office by the Democratic landslide that had brought Franklin Roosevelt and his New Deal congressional majorities to power. But even though St. Paul was a Democratic city, voters sent Maas back to his seat by a slim margin, and he did not forget about Nellie. This time, he pulled together the votes he needed, no doubt with the tacit bipartisan support from President Roosevelt, to honor the couple who had done so much for the advancement of colored people.[25] In 1935, Congress passed the bill, which directed the U.S. treasurer to pay "to Nellie T. *[sic]* Francis, widow of William T. Francis, the late minister resident and consul general at Monrovia, Liberia, the sum of $5,000, equal to one year's salary of her deceased husband."[26]

The sum gave her some relief, but she still needed to work, both to earn an income and out of her strong compulsion to serve. For a time, she apparently continued to work at the vocational school without compensation, but, as the *Tennessean* reported, she also "was instrumental in founding schools for Negro children both in Nashville and in Minnesota."[27] Remarkably, to earn money during the desperate years of the Depression, she was not above hiring herself out to do housework, but as the new decade began, now in her mid-seventies and still active in her church and civic duties, she took a secretarial post at nearby Tennessee State A & I University, living together with Juno in Gramma's house just as the matriarch would have wanted, with her two favorite girls looking out for each other.[28]

This familial union ended when Juno died at age eighty on March 28, 1954. She had spent more than forty years working in the state and community "to further the interest of Negroes," serving as president of the Tennessee State Federation of Colored Women's Clubs from 1924 to 1953, and named Woman of the Year for 1953 by the local chapter of the Links, Inc. She died just short of seeing the legal death of Jim Crow when the U.S. Supreme Court unanimously ruled that the doctrine of "separate but equal" in public education was unconstitutional.[29] In recognizing Juno when they did, it was almost as if her community of friends and associates, sensing that her end was near, wanted to recognize her before her time finally came. "Her only survivor," reported the *Tennessean,* "is Mrs. William Francis, a niece, of Nashville."[30]

A decade later, Nellie Francis, now only known to the public as "a niece, of Nashville," was eighty years old and just as active as she had ever been in her church. But by the end of the decade, her ability to act on her passion to be engaged was beginning to diminish as her fingers painfully stiffened from arthritis, her hearing faded, and her eyesight dimmed, making it impossible for her to continue the secretarial duties at the university that had allowed her to sustain her support of schools in Nashville and St. Paul. For her friends and associates, who marveled at this commitment from the aged and diminutive woman from whom a spark still emanated, the obvious signs of decline may have prompted a recognition of a life well spent. It would be a simple affair meant to honor an old woman whose distant past shone like a light made dim by the foggy mist of day's end. To those who would assemble in the Student Union Center at Fisk University, she would be honored as "a [local] woman" with the added honorific "the widow of William Francis, ambassador to Liberia, West Africa." Her role in this well-intended ceremony would be to sit primly in her deafness, possessing secrets, knowledge, and experience that few in attendance would have expected or fully understood. One person later noted how serene she looked.[31]

Her countenance masked the fact that she had witnessed the unrestrained evil of white men and women lynching blacks or harassing them for living in a white neighborhood, even in progressive Minnesota, home of the great liberal of the U.S. Senate Hubert H. Humphrey. And she had coped with the fragile egos of men and women of high station and of both races. Indeed, hope had seemed to elude her since her return to Nashville. In the thirty-three years since her arrival, the city continued to be governed by leaders whose policy of segregation—supported by white women voters whom Juno had fought to enfranchise—was so pervasive that it left too many of her people accepting their subjugation as an act of nature, or worse—God's will. Yet, even in this circumstance, she remained hopeful, knowing that a courageous and energetic new generation of race leaders had stepped forward. Rosa Parks, an office secretary for Montgomery's branch

Student Diane Nash and Fisk University classmates marching to integrate a segregated Nashville, 1960. Copyright Jack Corn, *Tennessean.* Imagn Content Services, LLC.

of the NAACP, and a young pastor named Martin Luther King Jr. led a movement to secure the right of black people to sit where they wanted on municipal buses, and in doing that claim their own dignity. And right there at Fisk was an English major named Diane Nash who had taken the baton left by Juno, who in the 1940s led colored women in a march to city hall to protest discrimination at the city's largest department stores.[32] Diane followed suit in 1960 after leading sit-in protests against Jim Crow in downtown businesses and confronting Mayor Ben West on the courthouse steps, who conceded that discrimination was wrong. Of the young leaders, one imagines, it was she to whom Nellie would have most related, for, like herself, Diane had been raised in the sheltered environment of a strong matriarch who instilled her with refined manners, articulation, and a composed confidence that, when joined with a burning sense of racial justice, gave impetus to her leadership role. She was born to do this work.

As for the honoree, her own work began when she was seventeen, inspired by memories of her father speaking before an attentive Nashville crowd that had assembled not far from where she now sat, nearly a hundred years earlier, and later by the partnership she had with her beloved Billy in the courtroom and in the court of public opinion and during their promenade in the parlor in their house on old St. Anthony, as well as, of course, the Seay women who had nurtured her and in turn were nurtured by her. They all had provided her with her own modest prelude to this moment when the sense of urgency for justice again filled the streets and the conscience of America. One imagines that these were the ruminations that filled her with hope as she took in the sun's rays for as long as she could, hearing and cherishing the ancient Negro chorus of perseverance:[33]

> If you want to get to heaven, I'll tell you how,
> Keep your hand right on that plow.
> Hold on, hold on
> Keep your hand right on the plow,
> Hold on.
>
> Keep on plowing and don't you tire.
> Ev'ry row grows high'r and high'r,
> Keep your hand on the plow,
> Hold on.

Epilogue

Until 1865, with the end of the Civil War, free blacks and slaves were buried next to whites in private white cemeteries that provided resting spots for slaves or loyal black employees, and in the Nashville City Cemetery. After the war, some 1,909 former black soldiers from Union army regiments were buried here. But soon after, local whites did not want blacks in private cemeteries, and as disease spread throughout black enclaves around the city, owing in part to congested housing, lack of sanitation, and malnutrition, the mortality rate spiked and the black community was confronted with a crisis of how to dispose of the dead.

In 1869, to provide a safe place where the dead of the city's blacks could be honored when they were laid to rest, a group of black leaders and a few white donors pooled their resources to establish Mount Ararat Cemetery. A young Thomas Griswold, who had become a successful merchant and city councilman, became secretary. Over time, because of periodic epidemics, the death rate increased, and with it the need for more land, which would become Greenwood Cemetery. It would be the place where Nellie would bring Billy for his final resting place, the place her father had helped to establish.

Born in Indianapolis, coming of age and living his adult life in St. Paul, Nashville was Billy's new adopted home. According to the Nashville *Tennessean,* he was survived by his wife Nellie, "his" grandmother Nellie Seay, aunts Alice West (nurse) and J. P. Pierce (educator), Alice's husband James West (physician), and cousins John West (Indianapolis), L. A. West (Memphis physician), and T. G. West (Nashville physician). His funeral was at First Baptist Church. Nothing in his obituary indicated to Nashville readers that, other than Liberia, he had spent his entire adult life in St. Paul. "Since the diplomat's wife intends to stay in Nashville, the body was brought to this city for burial."[1] This was to be his new "home" just as it would be for her. Although Nellie would periodically visit St. Paul over the next few decades, she stayed in the Saint Paul Hotel rather than with old friends. The trips were likely primarily visits to the gravesites of her mother, father, and sister Lula, who were all interred in St Paul's Oakland Cemetery, where they would remain, possibly because she could not afford to bring them all home. To bring Billy to Nashville, she needed an act of Congress.

With Billy's interment, she had reason to leave St. Paul for good. Although she continued to have a circle of friends in the city, some of whom she would later visit in California, her sense not just of St. Paul as home but of who she knew herself to be—someone committed selflessly to public service—was forever changed by the frustrating and corrosive effect of "the snares of petty discord." Her intellect, talents, and physical traits had opened up avenues of opportunity, but even her modest reserve and willingness to fill a supporting role were not enough to mollify critics who voiced all their grievances against her when she mishandled the Detroit resolution. During that dark moment, only her family stood by her.

She gave herself wholeheartedly to the campaign for suffrage, hoping that through that work she could help to realize the spirit of the Detroit resolution that called for racial unity; and she faced a leader in Clara Ueland who seemed equally committed. But what Nellie found was the nettlesome presumptions of race and privilege among white liberals who seemed incapable of recognizing that women's suffrage alone would not wipe away the racial prejudice against black women. The self-flattery of claiming one's innocence, good intentions, and social class allowed them to not see their responsibility to get at the root of racial discrimination. Instead, they considered that it was only black people who made race matter during those volatile times, that it was up to them to ignore their racial interest for the good of the whole. She appreciated their support in passing a needed law, but noted that they were nowhere when the mob threatened them for not knowing their place on St. Anthony Street.

The last known image of Nellie Francis, 1924.
Courtesy of the Minnesota Historical Society.

In moving to Nashville at the age of fifty-three, Nellie had retired from public service, to live whatever years she had left with the family she had left behind. She continued to serve her community and her church, touching many lives despite her deafness and blindness, until she could do so no longer. Seven years after she was recognized at Fisk by the Nashville chapter of the National Council of Negro Women, on Saturday, December 13, 1969, she died. It took four days of preparation for the K. Gardner Funeral Home to prepare her body to lie in state and accommodate the throngs of mourners who were expected to attend. She would lie in state from noon Wednesday until Thursday evening. She was ninety-seven years old.[2]

Notes

PROLOGUE

1. "Mrs. Francis Paid Tribute by Council," (Nashville) *Tennessean,* November 26, 1962, 18.

1. NO FLOWERS

1. Larry Millet, "St. Paul's Early and Unusual Megachurch Went up in Flames—Twice," *Minneapolis Star Tribune,* July 28, 2017. http://www.startribune.com/st-paul-s-early-and-unusual-megachurch-went-up-in-flames-twice/437190703/.
2. St. Paul *Dispatch,* June 12, 1891, 3 ("the school's largest graduating class"); "A History of Central High School," (St. Paul: St. Paul Public Schools 2007), https://www.spps.org/domain/2108; accessed April 21, 2018; "From the Past to the Present: An Inventory of Saint Paul Public School Facilities," Jene T. Sigvertsen, ed. (St. Paul: Saint Paul Public Schools 2006), 11–11A; Elizabeth Lorenz-Mayer and Nancy O'Brien Wagner (Bluestem Heritage Group), "Onward Central: The First 150 Years of St. Paul Central High School" (St. Paul: Transforming Central History Committee, September 12, 2016) (digital), 9–10, found in Minnesota Historical Society (hereafter, MHS), "Ramsey County: St. Paul: School Records: Central High School," Catalogue ID number, 001734734, Location No. 131.D.19.10F, and Internet. Between 1870 and 1890, the population of St. Paul had grown from 20,030 to 133,156.
3. *Dispatch,* June 12, 1891, 3.
4. "Takes One of the Class Honors at the High School Commencement," *The Appeal,* June 13, 1891, 3.

5. St. Paul *Globe*, June 12, 1891, 2; St. Paul Central High School Records, Class of 1891, MHS, 131.D.19.10F.
6. *Dispatch*, June 12, 1891, 3.
7. Recently accumulated evidence suggests that the Great Black Migration from the South to northern cities, a development that greatly advanced African American economic progress, would have occurred decades earlier had immigration restrictions been in place. See William J. Collins, "When the Tide Turned: Immigration and the Delay of the Great Black Migration," *Journal of Economic History* 57 (1997): 607–32. African Americans moved at times and to places where the foreign-born were less prominent (ibid., 629); St. Clair Drake and Horace R. Cayton, *Black Metropolis: A Study of Negro Life in a Northern City* (New York: Harper and Row, 1962). Labor market competition resulting from generous immigration is also said to have resulted in displaced hostility toward African Americans in the late nineteenth century, because they possessed less power to fight back. See Susan Olzak, "The Changing Job Queue: Cases of Shifts in Ethnic Job Segregation in American Cities, 1870–1880," *Social Forces* 63 (1989): 996–1009; Susan Olzak and Suzanne Shanahan, "Racial Policy and Racial Conflict in the Urban United States, 1869–1924," *Social Forces* 82 (2003): 481–517; Frank Morris Sr. and James G. Gimpel, "Immigration, Intergroup Conflict, and the Erosion of African American Political Power in the 21st Century," published by the Center for Immigration Studies (February 1, 2007), https://cis.org/Report/Immigration-Intergroup-Conflict-and-Erosion-African-American-Political-Power-21st-Century; accessed June 11, 2020.
8. *The Appeal*, June 13, 1891, 3.
9. *Pioneer Press*, June 12, 1891, 4. The editor of *The Appeal* referred to the *Pioneer Press* as the leading paper in the Northwest (June 13, 1891, 3). As to the claim that she was the first black student to graduate from Central, the author culled through the lists of all graduating classes since the school's inception. Griswold was the only student with "Negro" penciled next to her name (Ramsey County: St. Paul: Central High School Records, "Senior class lists, 1870–1927," Location No. 131.D.19.10F, MHS).
10. Frank Lincoln Mather, ed., *Who's Who of the Colored Race: A General Biographical Dictionary of Men and Women of African Descent*, vol. 1 (Chicago, 1915), 107.

11. "Ahead of Her Time: A Women's History of Central High School, 1977," 8 (Ramsey County: St. Paul: School Records: Central High School. Location # 131.D.19.10F, MHS).
12. Ibid., 10.
13. Ibid., 14.
14. *Pioneer Press,* June 12, 1891, 4; *The Appeal,* June 13, 1891, 4.
15. *Pioneer Press,* June 12, 1891, 4; *Dispatch,* June 12, 1891, 3; *The Appeal,* June 13, 1891, 4.
16. An Irish republican organization in the United States in the late nineteenth and twentieth centuries, successor to the Fenian Brotherhood (*The Oxford Companion to Irish History,* 2d ed., ed. S. J. Connolly [New York: Oxford University Press, 2002]).
17. *Pioneer Press,* June 12, 1891, 4; *Dispatch,* June 12, 1891, 3; *The Appeal,* June 13, 1891, 4.
18. *Globe,* June 12, 1891, 2.
19. *Pioneer Press,* June 12, 1891, 4; *The Appeal,* June 13, 1891, 3.
20. *Globe,* June 12, 1891, 2.
21. *The Appeal,* June 13, 1891, 4 ("Little Red Riding Hood"); January 9, 1892, 3 ("Magic Mirror"); January 23, 1892, 3 (Mock Trial).
22. *Pioneer Press,* June 12, 1891, 4; *The Appeal,* June 13, 1891, 3. The term "host" has a biblical connotation for "heavenly host," or "angel," "creations of God." In another sense, "Angels grab the attention of many," whose "main purpose . . . is to strengthen and comfort believers." The term would not have been foreign to black churchgoers who frequently used biblical references in both public and political settings. In using the term in reference to Nellie after delivering her graduation speech that called for racial comity during a time of national racial strife, *The Appeal* editor John Q. Adams was making a statement about Nellie's spirit that motivated her to speak on the topic, coupled with her angelic appearance on such a massive stage.
23. Paul Nelson, *Fredrick L. McGhee: A Life on the Color Line, 1861–1912* (St. Paul: Minnesota Historical Press 2002), 52–53; William D. Green, *Degrees of Freedom: The Origins of Civil Rights in Minnesota, 1865–1912* (Minneapolis: University of Minnesota Press, 2015), 253–55; *Pioneer Press,* June 3, 1895, 1.
24. Earl Spangler, *The Negro in Minnesota* (Minneapolis: T. S. Dennison 1961), 78.

25. Green, *Degrees of Freedom,* 87–88, 90, 118, 173–74, 175 (Emancipation Proclamation celebrations), 195–96, 207–9 (cakewalk), 194, 200, 299 (Minnesota Bookerites); *The Appeal,* August 3, 1889, 2 (Emancipation Proclamation celebration). For examples of black beauty, see advertisements found characteristically in *The Appeal* throughout the month of November 1899, in which products are sold that straighten African hair.
26. *The Appeal,* April 16, 1892, 3.
27. *Pioneer Press,* June 12, 1891, 4; *Globe,* June 12, 1891, 2.
28. Theodore M. Brown and Elizabeth Fee, "Walter Bradford Cannon," *American Journal of Public Health* 92(10) (October 2002): 1594.
29. Cannon was indeed a special student, more so than even other white, Anglo-Saxon Protestant boys. The son of a railroad worker and a high-school teacher, he seemed less dramatically luminescent, for as a young man fully dedicated to his studies he found solace in the introspective pursuits of writing and exploring the relationship between science and religion. He already exhibited acumen in the biological sciences. But it was also during his high-school years that he read about the debates between traditionalists and Darwinists, especially those involving William Wilberforce, bishop of Oxford, and Thomas Huxley. Out of view of his high-school community, he became so affected by the perceived conflict between science and religion that he eventually announced that he no longer believed in the ideals of the Calvinist church, the faith of his family. He was subsequently referred to his minister, about whom he later remarked, "The clergyman took precisely the wrong course in dealing with my difficulties: he wanted to know what right I had, as a mere youth, to set up my opinion of great scholars who supported the church doctrines. This appeal to authority did not appeal to me at all, because I knew that there were great scholars in the opposition. Furthermore, I had the feeling that I was entitled to my independent judgment" (ibid.,1594–95). See also Edric Lescouflair, "Cannon, Walter Bradford (1871–1945)," Harvard Square Library: Digital Library of Unitarian Universalist Biographies, History, Book, and Media, http://www.harvardsquarelibrary.org/biographies/walter-bradford-cannon-2/. Saul Benison and A. Clifford Barger, "Cannon, Walter Bradford," Complete Dictionary of Scientific Biography. Encyclopedia.com

(April 18, 2018), https://www.encyclopedia.com/people/medicine/medicine-biographies/walter-bradford-cannon#2830904846.

30. For correspondence between Cannon and Newson, see "Series VIII. Personal and Biographical Correspondence, 1892–1945," Box 145, Folders 2037–2055. See also Edric Lescouflair, "Cannon, Walter Bradford (1871–1945)," Harvard Square Library: Digital Library of Unitarian Universalist Biographies, History, Book, and Media, http://www.harvardsquarelibrary.org/biographies/walter-bradford-cannon-2/; Benison and Barger, "Cannon, Walter Bradford."

31. Four of his most noteworthy publications were Walter B. Cannon, *Mechanical Factors of Digestion* (1911), with an introduction by Horace W. Davenport (Canton, Mass,: Science History Publications, 1986,) vol. 8; *Bodily Changes in Pain, Hunger, Fear and Rage: An Account of Recent Researches into the Function of Emotional Excitement* (1915) (Eastford, Conn.: Martino Fine Books, 2016); *Traumatic Shock* (New York: D. Appleton and Company, 1923); and with coauthor Arturo Rosenbleuth, *Autonomic Neuro-Effector Systems* (New York: Macmillan, 1937).

32. He declined deanships at Harvard in 1908 and a second time in 1916, and at Minnesota in 1913. For references to his activities in international relief efforts, see Cannon Papers (Russian) Series III. International Activities, "Correspondence and Related Records, 1905–1945," Boxes 37–67, Folders 459–904, and "Russian Correspondence," 1920–1945, Boxes 37–39, Folders 459–508; (China) "China Correspondence, 1921–1945," Boxes 40–44, Folders 409–578; and (Spain) "#2 Aid to Spain and Spanish Refugee Relief Correspondence, 1922–1945," Boxes 45–46, Folders 579–609; "Correspondence, 1936–1945," Boxes 47–54, Folders 610–712. In his work on civil liberties, democracy, and intellectual freedom, see "J.'National Organizations for Civil Liberties, Democracy, Intellectual Freedom Correspondence, 1938–1942,'" Box 87, Folders 1185–1202.

33. Cannon Papers, "Series IX. Diaries, Scrapbooks, and Memorabilia, 1892–1945," undated, Box 165, "Farewell reception in honor of Miss Mary Jeanette Newson, May 28, 1925, hosted by the Parent–Teacher Association," Ramsey County: St. Paul: Central High School Records. Location # 131.D.19.10F, MHS.

34. *Dispatch,* June 12, 1891, 3.

35. *Pioneer Press,* June 12, 1891, 4.
36. *The Appeal,* June 13, 1891, 3.

2. THE LEGACY

1. "Allen, Robert (1778–1844)," Biographical Directory of the United States Congress, 1774–Present, http://bioguidecongress.gov/scripts/biodisplay.pl?index=A000142; accessed April 29, 2018; "Robert Allen," Genealogical Notes and Anecdotes: Descendants of Robert Allen (ABT 1674–ABT 1775), https://web.archive.org/web/20131122145650/http:/gennotes.150m.com/rallen.html; accessed April 15, 2018.
2. 1820 U.S. Federal Census; 1830 U.S. Federal Census; 1840 U.S. Federal Census; Census Place: Smith, Tennessee, 230; Ancestry.com. 1840 U.S. Federal Census [database online] Provo, Utah: Ancestry.com Operations, Inc. 2010; Sixth Census of the United States, 1840 (National Archives and Records Administration microfilm publication M704, 580 rolls); Records of the Bureau of the Census, Record Group 29, National Archives, Washington, D.C.
3. Tennessee Marriage Records, 1780–2002.
4. U.S. Find a Grave Index, 1600s–Current; Carol Lynn Yellin and Janann Sherman, "Frankie Pierce," in Ilene Jones-Cornwell, ed., *The Perfect 36: Tennessee Delivers Woman Suffrage* (Nashville: Vote 70 Press, 2013); "Our History: Nashville First Baptist Church," http://nashvillefirst.org/about/history/; accessed April 30, 2018. For reference to Rev. Merry's status as a free man, see John Cimprich, "The Beginning of the Black Suffrage Movement in Tennessee, 1864–65," *Journal of Negro History* 65(3) (summer 1980): 187. For a history of the church and its remarkable leader, Nelson Merry, see "Church History," in *History of Nashville, with Full Outline of the Natural Advantages, Accounts of the Mound Builders, Indian Tribes, Early Settlement, Organization of the Mero District, and General and Particular History of the City down to the Present Time* (Nashville: Publishing House of the Methodist Episcopal Church, 1890), 479.
5. Seay, born in 1815, one year after Nellie, was the son of James Seay (white) and Harriet Hunter (black) of Hillsboro, Tennessee, https://www.findagrave.com/memorial/172625860/nellie-seay.
6. https://www.findagrave.com/memorial/131393568/maggie-griswold.
7. 1910 U.S. Federal Census.

8. Yellin and Sherman, *The Perfect 36*.
9. Christine Kreyling, "Nashville, Past and Present," in *The Plan of Nashville: Avenues in a Great City* (Nashville: Vanderbilt University Press, 2005), 7.
10. Since 1822, about four thousand free and enslaved black people were buried in the Nashville City Cemetery. Other slaves were interred in white family and church cemeteries. After the federal government established the National Cemetery in 1866, 1,909 former black soldiers from Union Army regiments were buried there, with tombstones imprinted USCT (United States Colored Troops). However, soon white residents began rejecting black bodies in white cemeteries, especially in the midst of mounting mortality rates caused by cholera, pneumonia, intestinal diseases, poverty, poor housing, malnutrition, alcohol consumption, and other ailments. All of this created a need for black undertakers and cemeteries, which Griswold and his colleagues provided. Griswold became secretary of Mount Ararat (Bobby L. Lovett, "Mount Ararat and Greenwood Cemeteries" [1869], http://library3.tnstate.edu/library/DIGITAL/mount.htm).
11. 1880 U.S. Federal Census (Nashville, Davidson County, Tennessee).
12. Bobby L. Lovett, *The African-American History of Nashville, Tennessee, 1780–1930: Elites and Dilemmas* (Fayetteville: University of Arkansas Press, 1999), 71–73; 1880 U.S. Federal Census, Nashville, Davidson, Tennessee, Roll 1249, Page: 1068; Enumeration District: 040.
13. John Cimprich, "The Beginning of the Black Suffrage Movement in Tennessee, 1864–65," *Journal of Negro History* 65(3) (summer 1980): 186–88.
14. William Edward Hardy, "Farewell to All Radicals: Redeeming Tennessee, 1869–1870," PhD dissertation, University of Tennessee, 2013, 9–10; Cimprich, "The Beginning of the Black Suffrage Movement in Tennessee, 1864–65," 192.
15. Hardy, "Farewell to All Radicals," 10.
16. Eric Foner, *Reconstruction: America's Unfinished Revolution, 1863–1877* (New York: Harper and Row, 1988), 96, 326.
17. Hardy, "Farewell to all Radicals," 26–27, 30.
18. Ibid., 47; Alrutheus A. Taylor, *The Negro in Tennessee, 1865–1880* (Washington, D.C.: Associated Publishers, 1941), 59–60; William Gillespie

McBride, *Blacks and the Race Issue in Tennessee Politics, 1865–1876* (Nashville: Vanderbilt University Press, 1989), 282–87; Unknown Author, *Journal of the Proceedings of the Convention of Delegates: Elected by the People of Tennessee, to Amend, Revise, or Form and Make a New Constitution, Assembled in the City of Nashville, January 10, 1870* (Classic Reprint) (Ann Arbor: University of Michigan, October 14, 2017).

19. Selena Sanderfer, "Tennessee's Black Postwar Emigration Movements, 1866–1880," *Tennessee Historical Quarterly* 73(4) (winter 2014): 254, 259.
20. Walter L. Fleming, "'Pap' Singleton, the Moses of the Colored Exodus," *American Journal of Sociology* 15(1) (July 1909): 61.
21. Sanderfer, "Tennessee's Black Postwar Emigration Movements, 1866–1880," 268; Fleming, "'Pap' Singleton," 61, 63–64.
22. Fleming, "'Pap' Singleton," 65–66.
23. "John W. Morton Passes Away in Shelby," *Tennessean*, November 21, 1914, 1–2.
24. Sandefer "Tennessee's Black Postwar Emigration Movements, 1866–1880," 263.
25. Kreyling, "Nashville Past and Present," 8.
26. To get a sense of Edgefield, see the attached reproduction and description "City of Nashville and Edgefield (1860)," maps at the Tennessee State Library and Archives, http://teva.contentdm.oclc.org/cdm/ref/collection/p15138coll23/id/249.
27. The reference to Singleton's exodus in 1873 is in Lovett, *The African-American in Nashville, Tennessee, 1780–1930*, 94; Fleming, "'Pap' Singleton," 64–65. Nellie's middle name was "Frances."

3. MR. GRISWOLD

1. Mark B. Riley, "Edgefield: A Study of an Early Nashville Suburb," *Tennessee Historical Quarterly* 35(2) (summer 1978): 143–44.
2. Bobby L. Lovett, *The African-American History of Nashville, Tennessee, 1780–1930: Elites and Dilemmas* (Fayetteville: University of Arkansas Press, 1999), 108.
3. Lovett, *The African American History of Nashville*, 134 (regarding the education of free blacks).
4. *Northwestern Bulletin Appeal* (St. Paul), January 10, 1925, 1, 4.
5. Ibid., 4.

6. Carter G. Woodson mentions the prevalence of private education of black children in Tennessee, and in its largest cities in particular (*The Education of the Negro* [Brooklyn: A & B Publishers Group, 1998], 73–74). See also Lovett, *The African American History of Nashville*, 131–37.
7. Lovett, *The African American History of Nashville*, 134.
8. *Nashville Directory*, vol. 16 (Nashville: Marshall and Bruce, 1880), 246.
9. *Nashville Republican Banner*, July 17, 1867.
10. Lovett, *The African American History of Nashville*, 108.
11. This is mentioned in the preceding chapter (Lovett, "Mount Ararat and Greenwood Cemeteries").
12. Lovett, *The African American History of Nashville*, 108. The City Market-house was described as "being unequaled in extent, convenience, and elegance by any similar building in the United States, except Boston, Mass., which cost $500,000" (J. Woolbridge, ed., *History of Nashville, Tennessee, Natural Advantages, Accounts of the Mound Builders, Indian Tribes, Early Settlement, Organization of the Mero District, and General and Particular History of the City Down to the Present Time* [Nashville: Publishing House of the Methodist Episcopal Church, 1890], 116).
13. Lovett, *The African American History of Nashville*, 220.
14. Ibid., 137.
15. Ibid.
16. "Nashville's First Schools and Public Schools System" (Nashville Public Library Blog), September 22, 2018, https://library.nashville.org/blog/2018/09/nashvilles-first-schools-and-public-school-system; accessed April 23, 2019.
17. Woodbridge, *History of Nashville*, 127–28; *Digest of Ordinances of the City of Nashville, to Which Are Prepared the State Laws Incorporating, and Relating to, the City with an Appendix Containing Various Grants and Franchises*, compiled by Claude Waller, City Attorney, and Frank Slemons, Assistant City Attorney (Nashville: Marshall, Bryce Printing, 1893), 769–70; *The Code of Nashville*, prepared and edited by J. C. Bradford (Nashville: Albert B. Tavel Law Publisher and Stationer, 1885), 276–78; Lovett, *The African American History of Nashville*, 219–20.
18. For a reference to Nellie's sacrifice for family, see chapter 8, "Divided Duty."

19. Lovett, *The African American History of Nashville,* 138; "Lula Obituary," *Northwestern Bulletin Appeal* (St. Paul), January 10, 1925, 1.
20. David V. Taylor, "Blacks," in *They Chose Minnesota: A Survey of the State's Ethnic Groups,* ed. June Drenning Holmquist (St. Paul: Minnesota Historical Society Press, 1981), 81; Green, *Degrees of Freedom,* 197.
21. *The Appeal,* July 12, 1890, 3.
22. *U.S. City Directories, 1822–1995*: 1889 (waiter), 578; 1890–91 (waiter), 594; 1891 (waiter), 601; 1893 (porter), 625; 1896 (porter), 618; 1897 (waiter), 614; 1898 (cook), 598; (St. Paul) *Northwestern Bulletin Appeal,* January 10, 1925, 1, 4.
23. *Northwestern Bulletin Appeal* (St. Paul), January 10, 1925, 1, 4.
24. *The Appeal,* July 12, 1890, 3.
25. *U.S. City Directories, 1822–1995*: 1890–91 (waiter), 594.
26. L. Griswold Chapman to J. F. Pierce, February 19, 1921, J. P. Pierce Papers, Tennessee Historical Society.
27. Lovett, *The African American History of Nashville,* 94–95; Betsy Phillips, "It's Time for Nashville to Properly Honor Frederick Douglass: Solving the Mystery of Fred Douglass Park," *Nashville Scene,* February 6, 2017, https://www.nashvillescene.com/news/pith-in-the-wind/article/20851231/its-time-for-nashville-to-properly-honor-frederick-douglass.
28. (St. Paul) *Northwestern Bulletin Appeal,* January 10, 1925, 1, 4.
29. Arthur C. McWatt, "'A Greater Victory': The Brotherhood of Sleeping Car Porters in St. Paul," *Minnesota History* (spring 1997): 204.
30. *Minneapolis Afro-American Advance,* November 25, 1899, 2. See also Patricia McKissack and Frederick McKissack, *A Long Hard Journey: The Story of the Pullman Porter* (New York: Walker and Co., 1989), 23.
31. *U.S. City Directories, 1822–1995*: 1893 (porter), 625; 1896 (porter), 618.
32. McWatt, "'A Greater Victory,'" 205; McKissack and McKissack, *A Long Hard Journey,* 19–22, 44; Jervis Anderson, *A. Philip Randolph: A Biographical Portrait* (New York: Harcourt, Brace, Jovanovich, 1973), 163.
33. McWatt, "'A Greater Victory,'" 205; McKissack and McKissack, *A Long Hard Journey,* 44; Anderson, *A. Phillip Randolph,* 162–63; Jack Santino, *Miles of Smiles, Years of Struggle: Stories of Black Pullman Porters* (Urbana: University of Illinois Press, 1989), 41.

34. "Sexism in the Office," Gender and the Office/Early Clerical Workers/ Early Office Museum, https://www.officemuseum.com/office_gender .htm; accessed May 11, 2018.
35. *Pioneer Press,* June 3, 1895, 1; *Globe,* June 3, 1895, 1; Nelson, *Fredrick L. McGhee,* 52; Green, *Degrees of Freedom,* 253–54.
36. L. Griswold Chapman to editor of the Nashville *Globe,* November 28, 1919 (in memory of Thomas Griswold).
37. "Aberdeen Hotel: The Grandest Apartment Hotel in St. Paul," in *Forgotten Minnesota,* December 9, 2011, http://forgottenminnesota.com/2011/ 12/the-grandest-apartment-hotel-in-the-twin-cities/.
38. Jon Butler, "Communities and Congregations: The Black Church in St. Paul, 1860–1900," *Journal of Negro History* 56(2) (April 1971): 128, 129–30.
39. L. Griswold Chapman to editor of the Nashville *Globe.*
40. *The Appeal,* November 18, 1899, 3.
41. L. Griswold Chapman to editor of the Nashville *Globe.*

4. BILLY

1. *The Appeal,* February 23, 1901, 3.
2. Paul D. Nelson, "William T. Francis, at Home and Abroad," *Ramsey County History* 51(4) (winter 2017): 4.
3. Butler, "Communities and Congregations," 124–25.
4. *The Appeal,* October 15, 1887, 4; Nelson, "William T. Francis, at Home and Abroad," 3.
5. *The Appeal,* August 17, 1893, 3.
6. Lula married Tom King in 1894, and upon his death, she married Richard Chapman in 1900: *U.S. City Directories, 1822–1995*: 1889 (waiter), 578; 1890–91 (waiter), 594; 1891 (waiter), 601; 1893 (porter), 625; 1896 (porter), 618; 1897 (waiter), 614; 1898 (cook), 598.
7. Nelson, "William T. Francis, at Home and Abroad," 3.
8. U.S. Census 1870, Indianapolis, Marion County, Indiana, Third Ward, 125, 20; Nelson, "William T. Francis, at Home and Abroad," 31; U.S. Census 1880.
9. "The Golden Age: 1865 through World War I—Railroads in Minnesota, 1862–1956," U.S. Department of the Interior, National Park Service,

National Register of Historical Places, Continuation Sheet, Section E, 7–8, http://www.dot.state.mn.us/culturalresources/docs/rail/sectione.pdf; accessed May 6, 2018.

10. It was common practice for the stenographer pool to be dominated by men. As economist Dora L. Costa notes, "At the end of the nineteenth century, clerks and secretaries were trusted male employees familiar with the entire operation of the company . . . and employees who could be promoted to the top echelons of the company" (Dora L. Costa, "From Mill Town to Board Room: The Rise of Women's Paid Labor," *Journal of Economic Perspectives* [fall 2000]: 101–22).
11. Nelson, "William T. Francis, at Home and Abroad," 3. See also Frank Lincoln Mather, ed., *Who's Who of the Colored Race: A General Biographical Dictionary of Men and Women of African Descent*, vol. 1 (Chicago: 1915), 107; Angel Kwolek-Folland, *Engendering Business: Men and Women in the Corporate Office, 1870–1930* (Baltimore: Johns Hopkins University Press, 1998); Lisa M. Fine, *The Souls of the Skyscraper: Female Clerical Workers in Chicago, 1870–1930* (Philadelphia: Temple University Press, 1990), 26.
12. *Northwestern Bulletin*, January 10, 1925, 4.
13. 1895 Minnesota Census, 563.
14. *The Appeal*, December 25, 1897, 3.
15. Tom, born in 1852, was twenty-two when Nellie was born. In 1899, Billy was thirty.
16. Northern Pacific Railway Company, Law Department, Corporate Records, 1864–1973, Manuscript Collection. Catalogue ID number: 001719915, Minnesota Historical Society.
17. Nelson, "William T. Francis, at Home and Abroad," 4.
18. Douglas R. Heidenreich, *With Satisfaction and Honor: William Mitchell College of Law, 1900–2000* (St. Paul: William Mitchell College of Law, 1999), 19–20.
19. *The Appeal*, July 19, 1902, 2; Green, *Degrees of Equality*, 260–67; Nelson, *Fredrick McGhee*, 96.
20. Richard Kluger, *Simple Justice: A History of Brown v. Board of Education and Black America's Struggle for Equality* (New York: Vintage Books, 1975), 71.
21. Nelson, *Fredrick McGhee*, 97–98.
22. *The Appeal*, July 19, 1902, 5.
23. Nelson, *Fredrick L. McGhee*, 105; *The Appeal*, July 19, 1902, 3.

24. He was one of two black students to do so that year. The other was a mail carrier by day named James P. Anderson (Heidenreich, *With Satisfaction and Honor,* 20).
25. Nelson, *Fredrick L. McGhee,* 190.
26. Ibid.
27. Ibid.
28. The City Assembly was the upper chamber of city government (*The Appeal,* February 24, 1906, 3); *Pioneer Press*, March 4, 1906, sec. 2, 10; *Dispatch*, May 2, 1806, 1; *The Appeal,* April 14, 1906, 3 (Maggie's death and funeral service).
29. *The Appeal,* April 14, 1906, 3 (Maggie's death and funeral service).
30. Ibid. (Republican endorsement).
31. *The Appeal,* April 21, 1906, 3 (with photo); April 28, 1906, 3–4.
32. *The Appeal,* April 28, 1906, 3 (Citizens' League endorsement).
33. Billy was one of several men asked what he wanted for Christmas. After others mentioned such things as cigars and cuff links, Billy said that he wanted either a boy or a girl (*The Appeal,* December 25, 1897, 4).
34. Douglas Heidenreich, "A Citizen of Fine Spirit," *William Mitchell Magazine* 18(2) (fall 2000): 2.
35. "WILLIAM T. FRANCIS Says Hurrah for People of St. Paul," *The Appeal,* May 5, 1906, 3.
36. *The Appeal,* April 14, 1906, 3.
37. *The Appeal,* July 19, 1902, 5 (Maggie's dress).
38. "A Card of Thanks," *The Appeal,* May 5, 1906, 3.
39. The quotation comes from the *Northwestern Bulletin,* January 10, 1925, 4.

5. A BITTER TASTE STILL LINGERED

1. *Pioneer Press,* June 12, 1891, 4; emphasis added.
2. David Levering Lewis, *W.E.B. Du Bois: Biography of a Race, 1868–1919* (New York: Henry Holt and Company, 1993), 333–34. (The *Constitution* quote can be found on page 333.) *The Appeal* listed some of the newspaper coverage: "Atlanta Disgraces the Nation" *(Brooklyn Eagle),* "Our Disgrace at Atlanta" *(New York Herald),* "The Shame of Atlanta" *(New York World),* "Mob Murder Again" *(Cleveland Leader),* "Atlanta's Massacre" *(Chicago Daily News),* "Atlanta's Race Terrorism" *(Topeka Daily Capital),* "The Atlanta Savagery" *(Chicago Chronicle),* "The Atlanta Butcheries"

(Springfield Republican), and even in southern newspapers: "Atlanta's Reign of Blood" *(St. Louis Globe-Democrat),* "The Atlanta Horror" *(Baltimore News)* (*The Appeal,* September. 29, 1906, 3).

3. *The Appeal,* September 29, 1906, 3.
4. Ibid., 2 (postcards and the comparison of atrocities), 3 (Richmond trip).
5. *The Appeal,* October 20, 1906, 3.
6. *The Appeal,* November 3, 1906, 3.
7. Ibid., 2.
8. *The Appeal,* January 12, 1907, 2.
9. Booker T. Washington, *Up from Slavery* (New York: Oxford University Press, 1995), 2 (Washington's mixed-race parentage), 131 (his felicity with white philanthropists); *The Appeal,* November 24, 1906, 2 (Washington's lifetime pension from Carnegie).
10. Nellie had said in her high-school commencement speech: "May the people of this country, North and South, East and West, early awake to the sense of their duty in this matter and thoroughly realize that the race problem must be settled right, and then will the early rays of the morning sun kiss the fair land of a happy, peace-loving, justice-doing people; and then can all, black and white, American and foreign-born, shout with one glad shout that shall sound and resound from pole to pole, and from sunrise to sunset, this is the land of the free" (*Pioneer Press,* June 12, 1891, 4; *Dispatch,* June 12, 1891, 3; *The Appeal,* June 13, 1891, 4).
11. Washington, *Up from Slavery,* 131.
12. Ibid., 129.
13. *The Appeal,* December 29, 1906, 3; January 5, 1907, 3.
14. Edmund Boisgilbert, M.D. (Ignatius Donnelly), *Doctor Huguet, A Novel* (New York: D. D. Merrill, 1892). The narrator states: "I have made up my mind to tell the whole dreadful story, let the consequences be what they may. I know there are those, among my friends, who will consider it a species of degradation for me to make public the facts that will appear on these pages, while there are others who will urge that the world will never believe so improbable a story as that which I am about to tell. But it seems to me that I have been chosen, by some extra-mundane, super intelligence, out of the multitude of mankind, and subjected to a terrible and unparalleled experience, in order that a great lesson may be taught to the world; and that it is a duty therefore, which I owe to the world, and

which I should not shrink from or avoid, to make known all the facts of that experience, at whatever cost of shame, or agony to myself. Blessed is the man who can feel that God has singled him out from among his fellows, and that the divine hand has shaped his destiny; and yet such men usually bear on their hearts and minds a burden of life-long woe. Those whom God so honors he agonizes" (7–8).

15. Lewis, *W. E. B. Du Bois,* 335.
16. "St. Paul: A Week's Record of Minnesota's Capital," *The Appeal,* July 19, 1902, 5 (Nellie and Lula entertaining Du Bois). Nellie was a member of Pilgrim's choir, which had two sopranos, three contraltos, two tenors, and three basses. Lula served as the accompanist, a role she had filled since the family arrived in St. Paul, and Claude Jackson was director.
17. It is not implausible to surmise that Washington may have been attracted to Nellie. Those in the know understood that she was his type, for she—like Du Bois's gifted and soon-to-be paramour Jessie Faucet—possessed, as Lewis noted, "what shallow folk regarded as the highest Talented Tenth virtues—cosmopolitan, comely, and café au lait" (Lewis, *W. E. B. Du Bois,* 432, 464 [Du Bois's extramarital affairs]). Of course, this does not mean that she knowingly played on his proclivities or that Du Bois or Nellie behaved inappropriately. A year after they met, Du Bois began a long-term affair with Jessie Faucet, who worked with him at *The Crisis* magazine.

    Jessie Redmon Faucet was a person of great accomplishment. Born in Camden County, New Jersey, on April 27, 1882, she was an editor for *The Crisis,* a poet, essayist, novelist, and educator, the first African American woman to graduate from Cornell University (1905) and to be elected to Phi Beta Kappa. She earned her M.A. degree in French from the University of Pennsylvania, and a degree from the Sorbonne. Playing a pivotal role in the literary expression of the Harlem Renaissance, she was dubbed by Langston Hughes as "the Mid-Wife" of African American literature. Her parlor in Harlem came to be a gathering place for a circle of intellectuals and artists. For the program throughout the conference and the final evening, see *The Appeal,* July 19, 1902, 2.
18. *The Appeal,* July 29, 1905, 4 (the Francises, McGhees, and Turners vacationing on Sturgeon Lake); Nelson, *Fredrick L. McGhee,* 190–91.
19. *The Appeal,* February 2, 1907, 3.

20. *The Appeal,* May 11, 1907, 3 (listed at reception); February 24, 1900, 3 (certificate of osteopathy).
21. *The Appeal,* October 12, 1907, 3.
22. *The Appeal,* January 18, 1908, 3.
23. *The Appeal,* February 1, 1908, 3.
24. *The Appeal,* February 8, 1908, 2.
25. *The Appeal,* February 15, 1908, 3.
26. Ibid.
27. Ibid.
28. *The Appeal,* March 7, 1908, 3.
29. *The Appeal,* May 30, 1908, 3.
30. Others included in *The Appeal,* for example, were the Ladies' Catholic House Club, sponsoring a social (June 2, 1906, 2); Olive Leaf Whist Club (June 2, 1906, 3); Lula was in the Federation during its second anniversary on July 25–27 in Duluth, when she was associate editor (August 8, 1906, 8); Social and Literary Club (November 2, 1907, 3); M. T. C. Art Club (November 2, 1907, 3); The Prize Drill (of which Billy was a member) (November 9, 1907,3); Promenade Social (November 16, 1907, 3); forty-fourth anniversary of Pilgrim (November 16, 1907, 3); Mecca Club (November 30, 1907, 3); entertaining Dr. and Mrs. Curtis Chapman of Kansas City (October 10, 1908, 3)
31. *The Appeal,* October 10, 1908, 3.
32. *The Appeal,* July 11, 1908, 4.
33. *The Appeal,* March 14, 1908, 4; May 30, 1909, 3.
34. *The Appeal,* April 18, 1908, 3 (getting depositions).
35. *The Appeal,* October 31, 1908, 3 (as president); April 18, 1908, 3 (introducing McKibbens).
36. *The Appeal,* April 25, 1908, 2; May 2, 1908, 3 (returned from Chicago).
37. *The Appeal,* September 5, 1908, 3 (began tour to eastern cities); October 3, 1908, 3 (return to St. Paul).
38. Butler, "Communities and Congregations," 126.
39. Ibid.
40. Between 1900 and 1910, Minnesota's black population increased from 4,959 to 7,084. See Earl Spangler, *The Negro in Minnesota* (Minneapolis: T. S. Denison & Company, 1961), 64; John A. Kineman and Richard C.

Browne, *America in Transition* (New York: McGraw-Hill, 1942), 190; *United States Census, Abstract,* 1910 (Washington, D.C., 1913), 601.

41. The black community had grown steadily since 1870 when the population was 180, to 470 in 1880; 1,500 in 1890; 2,300 in 1900 (Butler, "Communities and Congregations," 126). See also Taylor, "Blacks," 80–81.
42. Green, *Degrees of Freedom,* 223–29.
43. For a discussion of gender and marital status of the general black population in St. Paul in contrast to church membership, see Butler, "Communities and Congregations," 126–27.
44. *The Appeal,* December 19, 1908, 3.
45. Ibid.
46. *The Appeal,* January 2, 1909, 3.
47. *The Appeal,* January 9, 1909, 3.
48. *The Appeal,* February 6, 1909, 3.
49. *The Appeal,* January 26, 1909, 3 (winning a suit in probate court); February 27, 1909, 3 (successfully conducting several suits on behalf of North Pacific Railway); March 13, 1909, 3 (taking depositions in Peoria). For examples of his civic work, see February 6, 1909, 3 (arranged a minstrel show); February 13, 1909, 3 (participated in the presidential inauguration festivities for Taft); February 20, 1909, 3 (performed as young Lincoln as a lawyer); February 27, 1909, 3 (attended the Ramsey County Bar Association annual dinner, the only black in attendance).
50. "Mock President's Election and Inauguration at Pilgrim Baptist—A Contest of Colors," *The Appeal,* March 20, 1909, 3, March 27, 1909, 3.
51. Ibid.,March 20, 1909, 3.
52. *The Appeal,* June 12, 1909, 3.
53. Lewis, *W. E. B. Du Bois,* 306.
54. *The Appeal,* May 16, 1908, 3ff.
55. *The Appeal,* April 24, 1909, 3.
56. Ibid.
57. *The Appeal,* June 12, 1909, 3.
58. Juno Pierce to Nettie Napier, February 14, 1926, Nettie Langston Napier Letters, Tennessee Historical Society (Nashville).

6. SISTERHOOD

1. *The Appeal,* October 8, 1910, 3; November 26, 1910, 3.
2. Booker T. Washington, *The Negro in Business,* "Chapter XIX: Philip A Payton Jr. and the Afro American Realty Company" (Boston and Chicago: Hertel, Jenkins & Co., 1907), 197–207.
3. Jonathan Gill, *Harlem: The Four Hundred Year History from Dutch Village to Capital of Black America* (New York: Grove Press, 2011), 172.
4. Ibid., 177.
5. Washington, "Chapter XIX," 203–4.
6. Ibid., 203.
7. *The Appeal,* November 26, 1910, 3.
8. *The Appeal,* December 3, 1910, 3
9. *The Appeal,* October 8, 1910, 3; December 10, 1910, 3.
10. *The Appeal,* December 31, 1910, 3.
11. *The Appeal,* January 7, 1911, 3.
12. *The Appeal,* January 14, 1911, 3.
13. "Mock Debate on Women's Suffrage," *The Appeal,* January 21, 1911, 3.
14. The John Brown Monument Association was formed in St. Paul in 1894 "for the purpose of erecting a marble shaft to the memory of that [white] hero, [the abolitionist] John Brown." A year later, the organization decided that a better way to honor Brown was to erect "an orphans' home and training school." Mrs. T. H. Lyles of St. Paul urged women across the country to "raise a collection to assist in building the said orphans' home and industrial school" by passing the basket at their churches. Moreover, the group "[paid] for scholarships for students in the South and [sent] boxes of ready-made sheets, pillow-slips and table linen, etc., to needy schools in the South."

    The Adelphai Club, formed in 1899 by women from Minneapolis and St. Paul, assisted in furnishing the reception room at the Jean Brown Martin home for children and gave assistance to the Crispus Attucks home for elderly African Americans in many ways, including supplying milk for the children when the home housed both children and elderly adults. The Ladies' Book Club of Duluth raised seventy dollars in 1906 to aid a member who, being afflicted with tuberculosis and ordered to a warmer climate, was financially unable to go. The Adelphai Club contributed a sum of money each month to two elderly ladies, and in 1936, it would establish a scholarship of fifty dollars, awarded once every three years, for African American students pursuing higher education (Records of the National Association of Colored Women's Clubs, 1895–1992, Part 1: Minutes of National Conventions, Publications, and President's Office Correspondence: A Microfilm Project of University Publications of America, Microfilm Reels, Lillian Serese Williams and Randolph Boehms, Consulting editor [Bethesda, Md.: University Publications of America, 1994], Reels 1, 6, 92, http://www.lexisnexis.com/documents/academic/upa_cis/1555_RecsNatlAssocColWmsClubPt1.pdf; accessed June 24, 2018.

15. Taylor, "Blacks," 80.
16. I am defining the "African American middle class" as people who are married with a single breadwinner, homeowners, and churchgoers. It did not necessarily mean that the family had acquired enough wealth to be above the poverty line.
17. Records of the National Association of Colored Women's Clubs, Reel 8.
18. Mary Dillon Foster, *Who's Who among Minnesota Women: A History of Women's Work in Minnesota from Pioneer Years to Date* (St. Paul: Self-published, 1924), 205; David Taylor, "Pilgrim's Progress: Black St. Paul and the Making of the Urban Ghetto, 1870–1930," PhD dissertation, University of Minnesota, 1977, 179–80; Paul D. Nelson, "Orphans and Old Folks: St. Paul's Crispus Attucks Home," *Minnesota History* (fall 1998): 104.
19. *The Appeal,* August 4, 1906, 8.
20. *The Appeal,* July 19, 1902, 5 (a photo of Ruffin at Lula's home); July 19, 1902, 2 (the schedule for Ruffin's address).
21. Records of the National Association of Colored Women's Clubs, 2.
22. Heidenreich, *With Satisfaction and Honor,* 19.
23. For example, the following clubs routinely appeared: the Ladies' Catholic House Club (June 2, 1906, 2); Olive Leaf Whist Club (June 2, 1906, 3); Social and Literary Club (November 2, 1907, 3); M. T. C. Art Club (November 2, 1907, 3); The Prize Drill (of which Billy was a member) (November 9, 1907, 3); Promenade Social (November 16, 1907, 3); 44th anniversary of Pilgrim (November 16, 1907, 3); Mecca Club (November 30, 1907, 3).

24. The state federation was founded on January 8, 1905. Notice of Maggie's improved condition and Billy's speech appeared in *The Appeal,* January 14, 1905, 3.
25. *The Appeal,* January 18, 1908, 1.
26. Records of the National Association of Colored Women's Clubs, 1895–1992, Part 1, 2. For reference to women graduates of the St. Paul College of Law, see Heidenreich, *With Satisfaction and Honor.*
27. *The Appeal,* January 28, 1911, 3 (planning committee); June 24, 1911, 3 (seventh annual meeting); March 2, 1912, 3 (executive board meeting for eighth annual meeting).
28. *The Appeal,* August 5, 1911, 3; August 12, 1911, 3; November 4, 1911, 3.
29. *The Appeal,* September 30, 1911, 3 (entertaining McCard); "Early Attorneys of the Arch Social Club," in *Alexander Hemsley: A Glimpse into the Utility of the Odd Fellows and Other Secret Societies* (Baltimore: Maryland State Archives 1998), https://msa.maryland.gov/msa/stagser/s1259/121/6050/html/11416000.html; accessed June 25, 2018.
30. *The Appeal,* April 20, 1912, 3.
31. *The Appeal,* May 18, 1912, 3 (election to represent Mars Lodge, host banquet, entertain dignitaries); May 25, 1912, 3 (entertained Bishop I. B. Scott, Bishop of Africa, Dr. W. J. Lyons of Baltimore, ex-minister to Liberia, Dr. W. H. Brooks, pastor of St. Mark's Church, New York, Dr. J. W. Bowen, president of Gammon Theological Seminary, Atlanta, and Mr. E. H. McKissack, ex-secretary and treasurer of the Odd Fellows Endowment Bureau of Mississippi).
32. *The Appeal,* June 22, 1912, 3.
33. *The Appeal,* June 29, 1912, 3.
34. Ibid.
35. *The Appeal,* July 6, 1912, 3.
36. *Twin Cities Star,* July 6, 1912, 1; *The Appeal,* July 6, 1912, 3.
37. *The Appeal,* July 13, 1912, 3
38. *The Appeal,* August 3, 1912, 3. Influential American neurologist Silas Weir Mitchell developed the rest cure in the late 1800s for the treatment of hysteria, neurasthenia, and other nervous illnesses. It became widely used in the United States and the United Kingdom, but was prescribed more often for women than men. It was frequently used to treat anorexia nervosa. The treatment kept some patients alive and others out

of asylums, though some patients and doctors considered the cure worse than the disease.

The rest cure usually lasted six to eight weeks. It involved isolation from friends and family. It also enforced bed rest and nearly constant feeding on a fatty, milk-based diet. Patients were force-fed if necessary—effectively reduced to the dependency of an infant. Nurses cleaned and fed them and turned them over in bed. Doctors used massage and electrotherapy to maintain muscle tone. Patients were sometimes prohibited from talking, reading, writing, and even sewing.

Mitchell believed that the point of the rest cure was physical and moral. It boosted the patient's weight and increased blood supply. It also removed the patient from a potentially toxic social atmosphere at home. However, the implicit point was the neurologist breaking his (almost always female) patient's will. Some outspoken and independent women received the rest cure, among them writers Virginia Woolf and Charlotte Perkins Gilman. They reacted fiercely against the treatment and doctors practicing it, and wrote about the experience. Later feminist scholars argued that the rest cure reinforced an archaic and oppressive notion that women should submit unquestioningly to male authority because it was good for their health. See http://broughttolife.sciencemuseum.org.uk/broughttolife/techniques/restcure.

39. Victor L. Streib and Lynn Sametz, "Executing Female Juveniles," *Connecticut Law Review* 22 (1989): 25. See also Derryn E. Moten, *A Gruesome Warning to Black Girls: The August 16, 1912 Execution of Virginia Christian* (Iowa City: University of Iowa Press, 1997), 45–49.

40. Leigh Lundin, "Virginia, Virginia," in *Capital Punishment,* Criminal Brief (September 26, 2010), http://criminalbrief.com/?p=14100. Charlotte Christian's letter to the governor reads:

My dear [Mr.] governor

Please [forgive] me for Bowing low to write you a few lines: I am the mother of [Virginia] Christian. I have been [paralyzed] for more than three years and I could not and Look after Gennie as I wants too. I know she dun an awful [wicked] thing when she kill Miss Belote and I hear that the people at the [penitentiary] wants to kill her but I is praying night and day on my knees to God that he will soften your heart so that She may spend the rest of her days in prison. they say that the whole thing is in yours Hands and I know if you will [only] save my child who is little over sixteen years old God will Bless you [forever] . . . If I was able to come to see you I could splain things to you better but I [can't] do nothing but pray to God and ask him to help you to [sympathize] with me and my [trouble].

I am your most [humble subject],
Charlotte Christian

41. William Loren Katz, "Racism through Rose-Colored Glasses" (December 12, 2013), https://consortiumnews.com/2013/12/12/racism-through-rose-colored-glasses/.
42. *The Appeal,* July 27, 1912, 3 (Nellie's photo included).
43. Virginia Department of Corrections, State Penitentiary, Series 11, Prisoner Records, Subseries E, Execution Files, Box 373, Folder 3, Accession 41558; Roger Christman, Senior State Records Archives, "Virginia Christian: The Last Woman Executed by Virginia," September 14, 2010, http://www.virginiamemory.com/blogs/out_of_the_box/2010/09/14/virginia-christian-the-last-woman-executed-by-virginia/.
44. David Baker, "Black Female Executions in Historical Context," *Criminal Justice Review* 33(1) (2008): 64–88; Victor L. Streib, "Death Penalty for Female Offenders, January 1, 1973, through December 31, 2011," no. 66 (2012): 7, https://deathpenaltyinfo.org/documents/FemDeathDec2011.pdf; accessed June 22, 2018.

7. LADY PRINCIPAL

1. Ione Gibbs was elected as vice president (*The Appeal,* August 19, 1912, 3).
2. *Twin City Star,* September 7, 1912, 2; "Visiting Home People (in Nashville)," *Nashville Globe,* September 13, 1912, 7.
3. Jacqueline Anne Rouse, "Out of the Shadow of Tuskegee: Margaret Murray Washington, Social Activism, and Race Vindication," *Journal of Negro History* 81(1–4) (winter–fall 1996): 31–32.
4. Ibid., 32.
5. Ibid.
6. His first wife of two years was Fannie Smith (1882–84) and his second wife was Olivia Davidson (1886–95), who introduced him into her circle of New England philanthropic reformers.

7. Mary Martha Thomas, *The New Woman in Alabama, Social Reformers and Suffrage, 1890–1920* (Tuscaloosa: University of Alabama Press, 1992), 74–78; Rouse, "Out of the Shadow of Tuskegee," 32n9.
8. Cynthia Neverdon-Morton, *Afro-American Women of the South and the Advancement of the Race, 1895–1925* (Knoxville: University of Tennessee Press, 1989), chapter 6.
9. Rouse, "Out of the Shadow of Tuskegee," 34.
10. Thomas, *The New Woman in Alabama*, 72.
11. Ibid., 76–77; M. M. Washington, "The Tuskegee Women's Club," *Southern Workman* (August 1920): 368.
12. Rouse, "Out of the Shadow of Tuskegee," 45nn10, 15.
13. Jacks is quoted in V. P. Franklin, *Living Our Stories, Telling Our Truths: Autobiography and the Making of the African American Intellectual Tradition* (New York: Oxford University Press, 1996), 74–75.
14. Rouse, "Out of the Shadow of Tuskegee," 36.
15. Jacqueline A. Rouse, *Lugenia Burns Hope, Black Southern Reformer* (Athens: University of Georgia Press, 1989), 5–7.
16. Rouse, "Out of the Shadow of Tuskegee," 46n28, citing *NACW's Petition to Congress concerning the Congo Situation, National Notes* (1918).
17. "International Council Holds Public Meeting," *Chicago Defender*, August 16, 1924, 1.
18. Rouse, "Out of the Shadow of Tuskegee," 45n20, citing Margaret Washington, "The Negro Home," a speech delivered before the Women's Interracial Conference, Memphis, Tennessee, October 20, 1920, 4–5, Margaret Murray Washington papers.
19. See Rouse, "Out of the Shadow of Tuskegee," 46n32.
20. Ibid., 46n33.
21. Ibid., 42.
22. *Twin City Star*, August 10, 1912, 2; August 17, 1912, 7.
23. Rouse, "Out of the Shadow of Tuskegee," 46n38, citing Margaret Washington on working for the ballot, *National Notes* (1914), 5, Margaret Murray Washington papers.
24. Ibid., 43 and 46n39, citing Margaret Washington on lynching, *National Notes* (1921), 9, Margaret Murray Washington papers.
25. Ibid., 46n37, citing Margaret Washington on working for the ballot, *National Notes* (1914), 5, Margaret Murray Washington papers.

8. DIVIDED DUTY

1. *Twin City Star,* April 18, 1913, 2.
2. Nelson, *Fredrick L. McGhee,* 200.
3. Nelson, "William T. Francis, at Home and Abroad," 4.
4. Nelson, *Fredrick L. McGhee,* 194–98.
5. Green, *Degrees of Freedom,*.253.
6. *The Appeal,* October 5, 1912, 3; Nelson, *Fredrick L. McGhee,* 205.
7. *The Appeal,* October 5, 1912, 3.
8. *The Appeal,* February 8, 1913, 3 (Odd Fellows and Wilson's inaugural ceremonies); February 22, 1913, 3 (counsel for the P. H. Haid estate).
9. *The Appeal,* March 15, 1913, 3.
10. Nelson, "William T. Francis, at Home and Abroad," 4. In Minnesota at the time, the NAACP was initially called the Society for the Advancement of Colored People, perhaps in an effort to sidestep the controversy associated to the organization in a state where the Bookerite imprint still had impact.
11. In July, he would be going to Philadelphia for the convening of the Odd Fellows Supreme Court, for which he served as clerk (*Twin City Star,* July 11, 1913, 3).
12. The legislature adjourned on April 24, 1913.
13. In her will, Mrs. Eliza Collins left $185,000, "much interested in the education of Afro-Americans," and five thousand dollars to Dr. and Mrs. Booker T. Washington (*Twin City Star,* August 10, 1912, 3).
14. For a notice of Jasper Gibbs being Minneapolis manager of the paper, see *The Appeal,* February 7, 1914, 2.
15. "Lawyer Francis' Opinion": Comments on problem with a circuit court decision in St. Paul *(Dr. J. W. Thompson v. Pullman Company, et al.)* that says that states' rights doctrine to create state-rate regulation is a problem for interstate commerce and analogizes the matter with the problem of states' rights over civil-rights law. If the high court rules in favor of states' rights over railroad rates regulation, it will be used to thwart civil rights in Jim Crow states: " If we are not able to destroy the effect of Jim Crow laws upon the interstate commerce theory then we are indeed in a helpless condition, and the case of Thompson v. Pullman Company recently argued in the United States circuit court of appeals at St. Paul, must fail.' (Editor writes) Attorney Francis was for many years chief clerk

of the legal department of the Northern Pacific railway, and on account of his broad knowledge of the history of the rate cases we hold his opinion as valuable information to our readers" (*Twin City Star,* July 4, 1913, 3).

16. Ibid.
17. *Twin City Star,* July 11, 1913, 3 (trip to Odd Fellow Supreme Court); July 25, 1913, 2 (stopovers in subsequent cities); August 1, 1913, 2 (Billy's comment about the trip).
18. *Twin City Star,* July 18, 1913, 1 (activities of national chapters); July 18, 1913, 3 (Gibbs trip to Philadelphia).
19. *Twin City Star,* September 2, 1913, 4 (public letters); October 10, 1913, 3 (a call for a day of prayer against bad laws).
20. *Twin City Star,* October 24, 1913, 2.
21. *Twin City Star,* November 8, 1913, 4 (probate hearings); November 28, 1913, 2 (two criminal cases).
22. *The Appeal,* August 2, 1913, 2 (Napier resignation); October 25, 1913, 3 (petition against Wilson segregation policy).
23. Born in the 1850s before the Civil War, Amanda Lyles learned how to style both African American and Caucasian women's hair. She established her first business, the Hair Bazaar, in 1880, later renaming it Mrs. T. H. Lyles Hair Emporium. Amanda operated her hair-styling business from 1880 until at least 1902. She worked closely with her first husband in his business and took over management of his funeral home operation after his death in 1920. She also worked in public service, including supporting the Red Cross, and was an activist for what today would be known as civil rights. Amanda organized literary societies for African Americans in St. Paul. She spoke out on race relations and gave speeches across the nation in support of antilynching laws. She also spoke up about the importance of women's right to vote. She spoke for prohibition and the end to job and housing discrimination, and raised funds to establish an orphanage and schools for black children in Chicago. She was buried in an unmarked grave next to her first husband, Thomas. The Hall of Fame committee is hoping to raise the funds to provide for a headstone ("Minnesota Chapter of the National Association of Women Business Owners," http://minnesotabusiness.com/minnesota-businesswomen-be-celebrated; Dave Kenney, *Northern Lights: The Stories of Minnesota's Past,* 2d ed. [St. Paul: Minnesota Historical Society Press, 2003], 199).

24. *The Appeal* reported: "As everyone knows Mrs. [J. E.] Johnson's palatial residence is an ideal one for a big social function and its capacity was tested on this occasion. The hostesses were assisted in receiving by Mesdames Grace Booker, G. E. Bresley, F. D. Parker, J. Q. Adams, Valdo Turner, T. H. Lyles, W. T. Francis, C. E. James, R. H. Anderson, and O. C. Hall. Misses Alberta C. Bell and Adina Adams performed at the piano during the evening . . . Mr. O. C. Hall followed with a very pleasing talk. Dainty refreshments were served. Wednesday afternoon Mrs. Terrell addressed the ladies of the B. L. Club which held its meeting at the home of Mrs. Valdo Turner. After the reception Mrs. Terrell was entertained by the card club at the residence of Mrs. G. W. James of St. Anthony Avenue. She left for the East on a later train" (November 15, 1913, 3; Terrell's visit).
25. Ida B. Wells, *Crusade for Justice: The Autobiography of Ida B. Wells,* ed. Alfreda M. Duster (Chicago: University of Chicago Press, 1970), 253–55.
26. Ibid., 255.
27. "Porter Awarded Damages: Lawyer Francis Gets Verdict Against the Pullman Company," *Twin City Star,* February 27, 1914, 2. In a later report, the amount was less than requested, but Francis stated that his client would not appeal (*Twin City Star,* July 17, 1914, 3).
28. *The Appeal,* January 10, 1914, 4 (Billy wins a divorce case in Minneapolis); February 21, 1914, 4 (probate case); *Twin City Star,* February 6, 1914, 2 (Billy is special administrator representing the Trust Co., who are the general administrators of an estate worth fifteen thousand dollars).
29. *The Appeal,* March 28, 1914, 3.
30. The *Twin City Star* reports a recent speech by H. S. Jordan of the University of Virginia in an article in *Popular Science* magazine: "The United States has, in addition to its negro problem, a mulatto problem . . . Prof. Jordan, after a careful discussion of the subject, both from a biological and political standpoint, reaches the conclusion that the mulatto is on the whole superior to the negro, and that in the presence of some two millions of them among us we have the key to the solution of our race problem" (July 18, 1913, 4).
31. "Nannie Helen Burroughs," https://en.wikipedia.org/wiki/Nannie_Helen_Burroughs; accessed October 30, 2018.

32. Nannie Helen Burroughs (1879–1961) was an orator, religious leader, civil-rights activist, feminist, and businesswoman who came to prominence at the National Baptist Convention in 1900. In 1909, she founded the National Training School for Women and Girls in Washington, D.C., where she worked until her death (*Twin City Star,* April 25, 1914, 3, referring to Nellie as "porcelain dol").
33. *The Appeal,* April 25, 1914, 4
34. In June, Lula returned fully rested from a five-month retreat to Paris, Texas, where she had spent the winter for her health, in the company of her aunt Juno, with whom she had stayed (*Twin City Star,* February 6, 1914, 2; June 19, 1914, 2).

9. JUNO

1. *Twin City Star,* June 26, 1914, 1.
2. Ibid.
3. *Twin City Star,* June 26, 1914, 2.
4. Ibid.
5. Lovett, *The African-American History of Nashville, Tennessee, 1780–1930,* 232.
6. Carole Stanford Bucy, "Juno Frankie Pierce," Tennessee Encyclopedia (Nashville: Tennessee Historical Society (October 8, 2017), https://tennesseeencyclopedia.net/entries/juno-frankie-pierce/; accessed June 26, 2018.
7. For reference to her march on city hall, see "J. Frankie Pierce and the Tennessee Vocational School for Colored Girls (1923–1919)," http://ww2.tnstate.edu/library/digital/pierce.htm; accessed June 26, 2018. Among her many accomplishments, Pierce and the members of Nashville Federation of Colored Women's Clubs and the Committee of the Blue Triangle League of the YWCA successfully advocated for department store restroom facilities for black women, resulting in Montgomery Ward's providing the first such facilities in Nashville ("Find-A-Grave: Juno Frankie Seay Pierce," https://www.findagrave.com/memorial/172449485/juno-frankie-pierce; accessed June 26, 2018).
8. *Twin City Star,* June 26, 1914, 2.
9. Ibid.

10. Ibid.
11. "Federated Clubs Resign," *Twin City Star,* July 3, 1914, 2.
12. *The Appeal,* July 3, 1914, 2 (masthead), 4 (list of withdrawn clubs and new federation officers); *Twin City Star,* August 12, 1916, 2 (reference to Jasper as Ione's son: "Successful young businessman").
13. *Twin City Star,* September 18, 1914, 2 (Juno leaves St. Paul for home).
14. *Twin City Star,* July 31, 1914, 2; *The Appeal,* August 22, 1914, 3; *Twin City Star,* August 29, 1914, 3; *Twin City Star,* September 4, 1914, 1; *The Appeal,* September 5, 1914, 3; *Twin City Star,* September 11, 1914, 2.

10. FROM WILBERFORCE TO THE HOUSE ON ST. ANTHONY

1. *Twin City Star,* August 14, 1914, 1, 2; *The Appeal,* August 8, 1914, 3.
2. *Twin City Star,* August 14, 1914, 1, 2; *The Appeal,* August 8, 1914, 3.
3. Records of the National Association of Colored Women's Clubs, 1895–1992, Part 1, 3, Frame No. 0406, http://www.lexisnexis.com/documents/academic/upa_cis/1555_RecsNatlAssocColWmsClubPt1.pdf; accessed July 28, 2018.
4. *Twin City Star,* August 14, 1914, 1, 2; *The Appeal,* August 8, 1914, 3.
5. NACWC-1, 3; *Twin City Star,* August 14, 1914, 2.
6. Wells, *Crusade for Justice,* 229–30.
7. Rosalyn Terborg-Penn, "Afro-Americans in the Struggle for Women Suffrage," PhD dissertation, Howard University, 1977 (University Microfilms International, Ann Arbor, Michigan), 285; Giddings, *When and Where I Enter,* 126.
8. Ellen Carol DuBois, *Feminism and Suffrage: The Emergence of an Independent Woman's Movement in America, 1848–1869* (Ithaca, N.Y.: Cornell University Press, 1978), 174.
9. Giddings, *When and Where I Enter,* 126.
10. Elizabeth Cady Stanton et al., *History of Woman Suffrage,* vol. 4 (Rochester, N.Y.: National American Woman Suffrage Association, 1881–1922), 5:6; Barbara Stuhler, *Gentle Warriors: Clara Ueland and the Minnesota Struggle for Woman Suffrage* (St. Paul: Minnesota Historical Society Press, 1995), 6.
11. Aileen S. Kraditor, *The Ideas of the Women Suffrage Movement, 1899–1929* (Garden City, N.Y.: Anchor Books, 1971), 107; Giddings, *When and Where I Enter,* 124.

12. "Universal Suffrage," *Rochester Post,* February 10, 1866; William D. Green, *The Children of Lincoln: White Paternalism and the Limits of Black Opportunity, 1860–1876* (Minneapolis: University of Minnesota Press, 2018), 261; emphasis added.
13. Terborg-Penn, "Afro-Americans in the Struggle for Women Suffrage," 298.
14. John Hope Franklin and Evelyn Brooks Higginbotham, *From Slavery to Freedom: A History of the African Americans,* 9th ed. (New York: McGraw Hill, 2011), 375.
15. Giddings, *When and Where I Enter,* 127–28 (Wells at the NASWA march in 1913); Herbert Aptheker, ed., *The Correspondence of W. E. B. Du Bois* (Amherst: University of Massachusetts Press, 1973), 1:127.
16. Rosalyn Terborg-Penn, *African American Women in the Struggle for the Vote, 1850–1920* (Bloomington: Indiana University Press, 1998), 119.
17. *Minneapolis Journal,* November 1900; Stanton et al., *History of Woman Suffrage, 1881–1922,* vol. 4, 358–59; Terborg-Penn, *African American Women in the Struggle for the Vote,* 119.
18. Terborg-Penn, *African American Women in the Struggle for the Vote,* 118.
19. *The Appeal,* August 15, 1914, 2.
20. *Minneapolis Tribune,* May 3, 1914, 1, 3, 14; Stuhler, *Gentle Warriors,* 82–84.
21. Stuhler, *Gentle Warriors,* 86.
22. *Twin City Star,* August 14, 1914, 1 and 2. They traveled to Cincinnati, Toledo, Chicago, and Wisconsin.
23. Stuhler, *Gentle Warriors,* 78–79.
24. *Twin City Star,* September 18, 1914, 2.
25. Stuhler, *Gentle Warriors,* 85.
26. *Twin City Star,* September 18, 1914, 2.
27. Stuhler, *Gentle Warriors,* 85.
28. *Twin City Star,* September 18, 1914, 2.
29. "A Suffrage Meeting on Monday Night," *Twin City Star,* October 9, 1914, 2; *The Appeal,* October 10, 1914, 3.
30. "Suffrage Meeting," *The Appeal,* November 7, 1914, 4.
31. Stuhler, *Gentle Warriors,* 80. See also Rhoda R. Gilman, "'A Beautiful, High-Minded Woman,': Emily Gilman Noyes and Woman Suffrage," *Ramsey County History* 32(3) (fall, 1997): 18–20.
32. Stuhler, *Gentle Warriors,* 81.

11. FLICKERING

1. The census records her death on January 10; the newspaper accounts mentioned January 12.
2. *Twin City Star,* January 16, 1915, 2 (Hattie's declining moments and A. H. Lealtad's eulogy).
3. *The Appeal,* January 16, 1915, 3 (Hattie's dying moments and Rev. H. P. Jones's eulogy).
4. *The Appeal,* January 16, 1915, 3; "Hattie A. Davenport," U.S. Find a Grave Index, 1860s–Current, https://www.findagrave.com/memorial/173005940.
5. *Twin City Star,* January 16, 1915, 2 (Hattie's Louisville birthplace); Emma Lou Thornbrough, *The Negro in Indiana before 1899: A Study of Minority* (Bloomington: Indiana University Press, 1993), 7–15, 23–24, 30–50, 69–70; "Indiana Minorities: People of African Descent" and "Indiana-Slavery and Bondage," (truncated history and migration of black residents), https://www.familysearch.org/wiki/en/Indiana_Minorities#INDIANA.2C_.5BCOUNTY.5D-_SLAVERY_AND_BONDAGE.
6. For reference of James Francis, see 1870 U.S. Federal Census. For William Bell, see 1880 U.S. Federal Census.
7. U.S. Colored Troops Military Service Records, 1863–65.
8. "Hattie Francis," 1880 U.S. Federal Census.
9. See chapter 3.
10. One cause for the antiblack sentiment of native- and foreign-born workers springs from the fear, often real, that black laborers will take jobs from whites. In the case of labor tensions broiling in northeastern Minnesota, miners fought with management to improve working conditions. It was during this time that advertisements appeared in the *Twin City Star* seeking to induce black laborers to "job opportunities in Duluth." The notices appeared more frequently when the miners' strike began in 1916 (*Twin City Star,* September 2, 1916, 2).
11. Every neighbor on their block was white and half were immigrants from Ireland, Germany, England, and Canada (1895 Minnesota Census, 563; Minnesota, Territorial, and State Censuses, 1849–1905, Ramsey, Part 5—City of St. Paul, Wards 7–8).
12. "Abraham Davenport," in the Minnesota Marriages Index, 1849–1950 (1900); Census Place: St Paul, Ward 4, Ramsey, Minnesota; page: 6;

Enumeration District: 0083; FHL microfilm: 1240783. See 1907, 1909, 1912, 1913, U.S. City (St. Paul) Directories. *U.S. City Directories, 1822–1995*.

13. *Twin City Star,* March 5, 1915, 2 (new office space); April 3, 1915, 2 (clients); June 5, 1915, 2 (verdicts).
14. *Twin City Star,* January 23, 1915, 2; *The Appeal,* January 23, 1916, 2 (suffrage meeting).
15. *The Appeal,* January 23, 1915, 3.
16. *Twin City Star,* March 12, 1915, 2. For Westlake's profile, see Legislators Past and Present, Minnesota Legislative Reference Library, https://www.leg.state.mn.us/legdb/fulldetail?ID=12063; accessed August 28, 2018.
17. Stuhler, *Gentle Warriors,* 267n2.
18. *Twin City Star,* June 19, 1915, 3.
19. *Twin City Star,* June 26, 1915, 1; July 3, 1915, 2.
20. *Twin City Star,* July 3, 1915, 2. (Only the names of officers were mentioned; photo of Hicks, 4.)
21. *The Appeal,* June 26, 1915, 3
22. *Twin City Star,* July 31, 1915, 2.

12. FLARE-UP: AN INSULT TO HATTIE'S MEMORY

1. *The Birth of a Nation* (1915), https://www.youtube.com/watch?v=I3kmVgQHIEY.
2. William Monroe Trotter was an uncompromising advocate of equal rights for black people. An 1895 graduate of Harvard, he was the first African American elected a member of Phi Beta Kappa, he founded the *Guardian* newspaper, devoted to civil rights. In 1905, he and Du Bois cofounded the Niagara Movement, but when it became the NAACP, Trotter withdrew, objecting to the presence of whites in leadership and its dependence on white financing. He created an alternative organization, the National Equal Rights League.
3. Unnamed, "'The Birth of a Nation' Sparks Protest" Mass Moments, April 26, 2005, https://www.massmoments.org/moment-details/the-birth-of-a-nation-sparks-protest.html.
4. "Negro Women Offer to Die to Stop Film," *Boston Herald,* April 26, 1915; "'The Birth of a Nation' Sparks Protests," https://www.massmoments

.org/moment-details/the-birth-of-a-nation-sparks-protest.html; accessed August 19, 2018.

5. "'The Birth of a Nation' Sparks Protests."
6. "The New Governor," *Twin City Star,* May 1, 1915, 4.
7. "Equal Rights League Exercises," *Twin City Star,* May 21, 1915, 1.
8. "'The Clansman' Removed," *Twin City Star,* May 21, 1915, 1.
9. "Frank Pictures Viewed with Disfavor by Censor," *Twin City Star,* July 17, 1915, 1.
10. John D. Bessler, *Legacy of Violence: Lynch Mobs and Executions in Minnesota* (Minneapolis: University of Minnesota Press, 2003), 201.
11. *Glencoe Enterprise,* July 1917, 1 (court testimony of the hoods); Elizabeth Dorsey Hatle, *The Ku Klux Klan in Minnesota* (Charleston, S.C.: History Press, 2013), 15.
12. Matt Reicher, "Minnesota Commission of Public Safety," MNOPEDIA Minnesota Historical Society, http://www.mnopedia.org/group/minnesota-commission-public-safety#; accessed November 1, 2018; Theodore C. Blegen, *Minnesota: A History of the State,* 2d ed. (Minneapolis: University of Minnesota Press, 1975), 471; Ehsan Alam, "During World War I, Minnesota Nativists Waged an All-out War on German Culture in the State," MINNPOST, January 5, 2016, https://www.minnpost.com/mnopedia/2016/01/during-world-war-i-minnesota-nativists-waged-all-out-war-german-culture-state/; accessed October 31, 2018; Carl Chrislock, *The Progressive Era in Minnesota* (St. Paul: Minnesota Historical Society Press, 1971), 159.
13. Billy would begin by responding to invitations by ethnic groups. In January, he would speak to the Men's Club of the German Methodist Church, whose members included "a number of the pioneers and substantial people of the city" (*The Appeal,* January 22, 1918, 2).
14. Noel Ignatiev, *How the Irish Became White* (New York: Routledge, 1995), 31.
15. *The Appeal,* August 28, 1915, 2; September 4, 1915, 2 (a photo of Talbert); September 11, 1915, 3 (Nellie entertained Talbert).
16. *The Appeal,* September 4, 1915, 3; *Twin City Star,* September 4, 1915, 2.
17. *Twin City Star,* October 16, 1915, 2.
18. Ibid.; "'Birth of a Nation' Film Will Be Barred Unless Kicks Are Withdrawn," *Minneapolis Journal,* October 17, 1915, 12.

19. "1000 Invited Censors See 'Birth of Nation,'" *Minneapolis Tribune,* October 28, 1915, 5; "Dr. Spaulding O.K.'s 'Birth of a Nation,'" *Minneapolis Tribune,* October 17, 1915, 9.
20. "1000 Invited Censors See 'Birth of Nation,'" 5.
21. "Opposition to Film Pictures Unabated," *Minneapolis Tribune,* October 30, 1915, 9.
22. "'Birth of a Nation' Hearing Continued," *Minneapolis Tribune,* November 2, 1915, 7.
23. "It Pays to Agitate," *The Appeal,* November 13, 1915, 2.
24. "A Damnable Photo-Play," *Twin City Star,* October 16, 1915, 4.
25. "A Peaceful Protest," *Twin City Star,* October 16, 1915, 4.
26. The ordinance prohibited "the display of moving pictures and theatrical performances, which tend to create race and religious hatred. It makes it a misdemeanor punishable by the imprisonment in the county jail for each offense" (*The Appeal,* November 6, 1915, 2).
27. Ibid., 4.
28. Ibid., 3 (the meeting); Stuhler, *Gentle Warriors,* 80 (Ueland's regard for the Women's Welfare League); Green, *The Children of Lincoln,* 391 (John Davidson).
29. "It Pays to Agitate," 2.
30. The *Twin City Star* listed those who led the St. Paul effort. "The enacted ordinance prohibited exhibitions which tend to incite riot or create race or religious prejudice, or purport to represent any hanging, lynching, burning, or placing in a position of ignominy any human being, the same being incited by of inducive to race or religious hatred" (November 27, 1915, 4).
31. *The Appeal,* January 22, 1918, 2 (speech before the Men's Club of the German Methodist Church).
32. L. Chapman to J. Pierce, February 25, 1918, F. J. Pierce Papers, Tennessee Historical Society.

13. MRS. GREY AND THE SPIRIT OF DETROIT

1. *The Appeal,* January 22, 1916, 3, 4.
2. For a discussion of Emily Grey, see Emily O. Goodridge Grey, "The Black Community in Territorial St. Anthony: A Memoir," ed. Patricia C. Harpole, *Minnesota History* 49 (summer 1984): 42–53.

3. For a full account of the incident, see William D. Green, "Eliza Winston and the Politics of Freedom in Minnesota, 1854–60," *Minnesota History* (fall 2000): 106–22.
4. *Twin City Star,* January 8, 1916, 3.
5. Green, *The Children of Lincoln,* 278, 369, 389–90 (regarding Minnesota's partial woman suffrage law for school board); *Twin City Star,* January 8, 1916, 4 (reference to the *Independent*).
6. *The Appeal,* January 22, 1918, 2 (speech before the Men's Club of the German Methodist Church); February 12, 1916, 4 (semiannual meeting of state federation); *Twin City Star,* March 11, 1916, 2 (divorce case); February 19, 1916, 1 (personal injury decision); *The Appeal,* February 19, 1916, 3 (Burnquist's association); *Twin City Star,* April 8, 1916, 2 (Lula's hospitalization).
7. "On to Baltimore," *The Appeal,* April 29, 1916, 2.
8. Ibid.
9. Kayomi Wada, National Association of Colored Women's Clubs, Inc. (1896), http://www.blackpast.org/aah/national-association-colored-women-s-clubs-inc-1896. "On to Baltimore" had also appeared in the *Twin City Star,* April 22, 1916, 4.
10. "On to Baltimore," *Twin City Star,* April 22, 1916, 4.
11. *Twin City Star,* May 13, 1916, 3.
12. Terborg-Penn, *African American Women in the Struggle for the Vote, 1850–1920,* 126, 127.
13. "Stands by Negroes," *Twin City Star,* May 6, 1916, 2.
14. *Twin City Star,* July 1, 1916, 2.
15. "National Association of Colored Women's Clubs," *The Appeal,* May 13, 1916, 4; *Twin City Star,* July 8, 1916, 1. The editors of both newspapers titled Nellie's statement as if it had been endorsed by the National Association, when it in fact hadn't. It would lead to her dismissal from her national post.
16. "Federated Clubs in Session," *Twin City Star,* July 1, 1916, 2.
17. *Twin City Star,* June 17, 1916, 1. Billy's campaign article notes that he has practiced before the state supreme court and the U.S. Supreme Court and is married to Nellie, who, as Smith noted, "is a national character in civic, clubs and social uplift work" (*Twin City Star,* May 6, 1916, 2; "Francis Is a Winner," July 1, 1916, 2).

18. "Will Represent Minnesota Clubs," *Twin City Star,* July 8, 1916, 2.
19. *Twin City Star,* June 24, 1916, 2 (Seymour lecture): May 6, 1916, 2 (Fisk Jubilee Singers); July 8, 1916, 3 (*The Birth of a Nation* returns).
20. *Twin City Star,* July 22, 1916, 1 (Mrs. Washington's Minnesota trip); ibid. ("Mrs. Chapman Much Improved" (Lula in recovery); August 5, 1916, 2 (Nellie's tour before Baltimore).
21. *Twin City Star,* September 2, 1916, 1; *The Appeal,* August 5, 1916, 2 (photograph of lynching in Waco).
22. *Twin City Star,* September 2, 1916, 2.
23. Ibid. (U.S. Steel advertisement for black laborers); November 11, 1916, 1 (Billy's electoral loss); ibid., 2 (Billy's letter of appreciation to voters); November 18, 2 (Donovan's resignation).
24. The United States officially entered the war on April 6, 1917.
25. *The Appeal,* December 9, 1916, 4; "Negro Women Attend Convention," *Twin City Star,* December 9, 1916, 2.
26. Emily O. Goodrich Grey, "The Black Community in Territorial St. Anthony: A Memoir," ed. Patricia C. Harpole, *Minnesota History* (summer 1984): 50.
27. Ibid., 53.

14. AFTER BALTIMORE

1. *Twin City Star,* January 13, 1917, 1.
2. Paula C. Giddings, *When and Where I Enter: The Impact of Black Women on Race and Sex in America* (New York: Quill/William Morrow, 1984), 138.
3. *Twin City Star,* January 13, 1917, 1.
4. Ibid., 1; *The Appeal,* July 14, 1917, 2; August 12, 1916, 3; December 9, 1916, 3 (Hardy as Talbert's sister).
5. Giddings, *When and Where I Enter,* 97.
6. Ibid.
7. *The Appeal,* July 8, 1916, 3 (announced Washington's pending arrival); July 22, 1916, 3 (Washington meets black and white club members, and Nellie).
8. *The Appeal,* July 22, 1916, 3 (Washington's visit; marching in the Prohibitionist parade). The resolution appeared twice before Maggie came to town ("National Association of Colored Women's Clubs," *The Appeal,* May 13, 1916, 4; *Twin City Star,* July 8, 1916, 1).

9. *The Appeal,* November 11, 1916, 4 (Lula's hospitalization; Richard dinner); *The Appeal,* November 18, 1916, 3 (Sunday school party).
10. *Twin City Star,* March 10, 1917, 4 (noted white women in the Douglass home initiative).
11. *Twin City Star,* July 14, 1918, 1.
12. *The Appeal,* July 14, 1917, 4 (Billy and Richard meet their wives at the lake); *Twin City Star,* August 4, 1917, 8; August 11, 1917, 3 (at the Bumble Bee Cottage).
13. Green, *The Children of Lincoln,* 187–252 (history of Pilgrim Baptist Church).
14. "Mrs. Francis Makes Strong Appeal," *The Appeal,* April 27, 1918, 3; *Twin City Star,* April 27, 1918, 4.
15. For a full account of how Minnesota's black community considered the war effort, see Peter J. DeCarlo, "Loyalty within Racism: The Segregated Sixteenth Battalion of the Minnesota Home Guard during World War I," *Minnesota History* 65(6) (summer 2017): 208.
16. W. E. B. Du Bois, "Close Ranks," *The Crisis* 16(3) (July 1918). See also John Hope Franklin and Evelyn Brooks Higginbotham, *From Slavery to Freedom: A History of African Americans,* 9th ed. (New York: McGraw-Hill, 2011), 331.
17. Stuhler, *Gentle Warriors,* 150–52.
18. DeCarlo, "Loyalty within Racism," 211; *Twin City Star,* July 21, 1917, 1 (commission appointment); *The Appeal,* August 18, 1917, 3 (appointment by the adjutant general); "Attorney Francis Appointed War Orator," *The Appeal,* July 13, 1918, 3.
19. Lula Chapman to Juno Pierce, August 28, 1918, Pierce Papers, Tennessee Historical Society, Nashville, Tennessee (regarding tensions between Nellie and Billy over Billy's assignment)
20. "Mine Eyes Have Seen," *The Appeal,* July 20, 1918, 3 (Nellie sings Negro "folk" songs).
21. W. E. B. Du Bois, *The Souls of Black Folk* (New York: Fawcett World Library, 1969), 17.

15. A GLORIOUS PERFORMANCE IN THE PARLOR

1. "Mandy," by Irving Berlin, Eddie Cantor singing, from *Ziegfeld Follies* (1919), https://www.youtube.com/watch?v=gCgUEzsovrA.
2. "Atty. and Mrs. W. T. Francis Celebrate the Twenty-fifth Anniversary of Their Wedding," *The Appeal,* August 17, 1918, 3; *Twin City Star,* August 17, 1918, 3.
3. "Atty. and Mrs. W. T. Francis Celebrate the Twenty-fifth Anniversary of Their Wedding," *The Appeal,* August 17, 1918, 3.
4. *The Appeal,* July 27, 1918, 3.
5. "A Distinguished Visitor," *Twin City Star,* August 17, 1918, 3 (profile of Hallie Q. Brown).
6. *The Appeal,* August 3, 1918, 3; August 17, 1918, 3 (Nellie and Brown went to the play at Como Park).
7. *The Appeal,* August 17, 1918, 3.
8. "Mr. and Mrs. W. T. Francis Have Useful Public Careers in this Community," *The Appeal,* August 24, 1918, 3.
9. Ibid.
10. *The Appeal,* August 17, 1918, 3.
11. *Twin City Star,* August 10, 1918, 5.
12. *The Appeal,* August 31, 1918, 3 (Nellie at Bumble Bee Cottage); September 7, 1918, 3; September 21, 1918, 3; September 28, 1918, 3; *Twin City Star,* September 28, 1918, 5 (Billy travels to eastern cities); "Odd Fellows Hold Successful Meeting: W. T. Francis of St. Paul Elected Deputy Grand Master," *Twin City Star,* September 14, 1918, 1.
13. *The Appeal,* November 9, 1918, 4; emphasis added.
14. Nellie and Everywoman's Suffrage Club were listed in the St. Paul subscription to the *Woman Citizen,* from January 1 to December 1, 1918, Minnesota Woman Suffrage Association/Manuscript Collection, Correspondence and Related Records, January 1918–March 1918, 10 of 162. Location 308.C.15.98, Box. 2.

16. THIS BROAD UNITED STAND

1. "Mrs. W. T. Francis/Praises Stand Taken by the Women Suffragists," *The Appeal,* October 12, 1918, 3; emphasis added.
2. *The Appeal,* November 2, 1918, 3 (lunch between Francis and Kenyon); Stuhler, *Gentle Warriors,* 123, 132, 133.

3. *The Appeal,* December 7, 1918, 3; "The Suffrage Delegation," *Twin City Star,* December 14, 1918, 3.
4. The original Susan B. Anthony Amendment's enforcement clause read: "Congress shall have the power, by appropriate legislation to enforce the provisions of this article."
5. Terborg-Penn, *African American Women in the Struggle for the Vote, 1850–1920,* 127, citing *The Crisis* 17 (November 1918), 25.
6. Ibid.
7. Ibid., 128; Stanton et al., *History of Woman Suffrage,* 5, 1900–1922, 645–46.
8. An image of the leaflet can be seen in Terborg-Penn, *African American Women in the Struggle for the Vote, 1850–1920,* 129.
9. Ibid., 128.
10. Nellie's intent in supporting the Detroit women's effort to join black and white organizations was not to frustrate the NAWSA complicity with white southern supremacists, but rather to breach the barrier of discrimination within their community. The goals, if not the tactics, were, in a word, different.
11. Giddings, *When and Where I Enter,* 161. During this time, other federations were growing in number by consolidating with other state federations. "Mrs. M. Moseley Withers, the talented young woman from Minneapolis, who is deputy organizer for the Northwestern Federation, has injected so much enthusiasm in the work that the federation is steadily growing, and it was through her efforts that such an ideal meeting place (in Grand Forks) was secured." *The Appeal* published a series of articles that detailed the dissolution of the Minnesota federation that would result in the various clubs joining other federations from Wisconsin, Iowa, Illinois, Wyoming, Kansas, Indiana, Missouri Colorado, and even Arizona ("Third and Last Call," *The Appeal,* June 7, 1919, 5; June 14, 1919,4). In a tribute to Mrs. Ethel Howard Maxwell, outgoing president, corresponding secretary Mrs. Lula M. Lee said, "No other President had accomplished in so short a time such good work. She brought together clubs that had been dormant and did that work in a manner the Master taught us to do—made peace and brought harmony." Although it may not have been intended as a dig against Nellie, she had reason to take it that way ("Federation Aftermath," *The Appeal,* July 5, 1919, 3).

12. In contrast to the image promoted by Harper, Anthony's tactics during the 1866 suffrage campaign in Kansas raised eyebrows when she invited George Francis Train, a Democratic demagogue and racist, to join her, knowing that his advocacy would undercut the Republicans' efforts to win suffrage rights for the African Americans of the state (Ellen Carol DuBois, *Feminism and Suffrage: The Emergence of an Independent Women's Movement in America, 1848–1869* [Ithaca, N.Y.: Cornell University Press, 1999], 93, 95, 96–97, 99); Green, *Children of Lincoln,* 271–73.
13. Giddings, *When and Where I Enter,* 161–62.
14. Ibid., 162, citing Elizabeth C. Carter to Ida Hustad Harper, April 10, 1919 (NAACP files, Suffrage, Library of as well as the amendment in Congress, Washington, D.C.).
15. "Woman's Suffrage Wins," *The Appeal,* June 7, 1919, 3; June 14, 1919, 3.
16. Stuhler, *Gentle Warriors,* 167; *The Appeal,* January 25, 1919, 3.
17. Stuhler, *Gentle Warriors,* 168.
18. Ibid., 168n14.
19. Ibid., 169, citing Stanton et al., *History of Woman Suffrage,* 6:325; [Clara] Ueland report, March 19, 1919, 14:761, MWSA Records; *St. Paul Daily News*, March 24, 1919, 1.
20. Stuhler, *Gentle Warriors,* 175n31, 176; *Message of Gov. J. A. A. Burnquist to the Special Session of the Legislature of Minnesota, September, 1919* (St. Paul, 1919), 1 (Minnesota Historical Society); Senate and House Journal, Extra Session, 1919, 1, 13 (Minnesota Historical Society); Stuhler, "Organizing for the Vote: Leaders of Minnesota's Woman Suffrage Movement," *Minnesota History* (fall 1995): 301.
21. Stuhler, *Gentle Warriors,* 176; Giddings, *When and Where I Enter,* 163.
22. Giddings, *When and Where I Enter,* 163; Rebecca L. Price, "The True Story of Tennessee Suffragettes," nashvillelifestyle.com, December 26, 2015, https://nashvillelifestyles.com/living/community/the-true-story-of-tennessee-suffragettes/.
23. Giddings, *When and Where I Enter,* 164.
24. Ibid., citing Mary White Ovington to Alice Paul, July 9, 1920 (NAACP files, Suffrage, Library of Congress, Washington, D.C.).
25. Carole Stanford Bucy, "Juno Frankie Pierce," Tennessee Encyclopedia, Tennessee Historical Society, https://tennesseeencyclopedia.net/entries/juno-frankie-pierce/; accessed September 29, 2018.

26. Rosalyn Terborg-Penn, "Afro-Americans in the Struggle for Woman Suffrage," PhD dissertation, Howard University, 1977 (University Microfilms International, Ann Arbor, Mich.), 293; Giddings, *When and Where I Enter,* 165.
27. Price, "The True Story of Tennessee Suffragettes"; Bucy, "Juno Franklin Pierce."
28. Anna Dickie Olesen, press releases dated June 11, 1919, 6:427 and June 10, 1916, 6:337–38, MWSA Records, Minnesota Historical Society, in Stuhler, *Gentle Warriors,* 173.
29. See the letter from Ueland to state legislators (June 10, 1919) seeking support for "a special session in order to vote upon the ratification of the federal Suffrage Amendment": correspondence and Related Records, May 1919–1921, June 2–10, 1919 (digital). 81/110, Location #308.B. 15.9B Box 3, MWSA Manuscript Collection, Minnesota Historical Society.
30. Clara Ueland to Andreus Ueland, transcribed by Brenda Ueland, *O Clouds, Unfold! Clara Ueland and Her Family* (Minneapolis: Nodin Press, 2004), 214–15.
31. Mary Ann Firmin, "Brenda Ueland: Early Feminist and Writing Theorist," M.A. thesis, Oregon State University, May 23, 1991, 5. Brenda Ueland describes the household help she grew up with as follows: By the time the Uelands had their third of nine children, they lived in a large and stately three-story house with white Corinthian columns, and a handsomely carved stairway, situated on three acres of land along the south shore of Lake Calhoun. "Two strong fresh-faced girls from Scandinavia had bedrooms on the third floor. There was a hired man—Gus or Alfred or Ole whoever he happened to be—to drive the carriage, to milk the cow and pump water for the large-drinking pail in the kitchen. The barn was also rather architecturally handsome with diamond shaped windows and many gables and a little turret. On the second floor was a hay mow, dim and dusty and fragrant, and here a room had been plastered off for the hired man. It had pretty casement windows opening on the western lawn" (in Ueland, *O Clouds, Unfold!,* 42, 44–45).
32. Clara Ueland to Andreas Ueland, in Ueland, *O Cloud, Unfold!,* 215.
33. Ibid., 68.
34. Ibid.

35. *The Appeal,* May 6, 1916, 2; Nelson, "William T. Francis," 12n16 (Nellie brings singers to the Shubert Club).
36. Clara Ueland to Andreus Ueland, in Ueland, *O Clouds, Unfold!,* 214–15.
37. Everywoman was listed as an affiliate in 1919, consisting of four members—Nellie Francis (president), Mrs. S. L. Maxwell (secretary), Mrs. H. High (vice president), and Mrs. W. H. Howard (treasurer). (Suffrage Club, 1912–19), MWSA 6/103.
38. For an example of a letterhead sent out in 1920, see Ueland to Board Members (June 26, 1920, correspondence and Related Records, May 1919–1921), June 2–10, 1919 (digital), 81/110, Location #308.B.15.9B Box 3, MWSA Manuscript Collection, Minnesota Historical Society.
39. A Notice for Suffrage Week in Albert Lea, January 27–28, Pro-Suffrage Materials: Programs and Notices of Events, undated and 1916–1920 (digital), 2/117, Location #308.C.15.8F Box 5, MWSA records, Minnesota Historical Society, http://www2.mnhs.org/library/findaids/00756.xml.
40. "Minnesota's Disgrace," *The Appeal,* June 19, 1920 (Duluth lynchings).

17. UNDER THE SHADOW OF THE BRIGHT NORTH STAR

1. Ann Juergens, "Lena Olive Smith: A Minnesota Civil Rights Pioneer," *William Mitchell Law Review* 397 (2001): 412; Sean Dennis Cashman, *African Americans in the Quest for Civil Rights, 1900–1990* (New York: New York University Press, 1991), 29.
2. Cashman, *African Americans in the Quest for Civil Rights, 1900–1990,* 29.
3. Ibid., 30.
4. C. Vann Woodward, *The Strange Career of Jim Crow,* 2d ed. (New York: Oxford University Press, 1966), 114–15.
5. John Hope Franklin, *The Two Worlds of Race: A Historical View, in Race and History: Selected Essays, 1938–1988,* 145; Juergens, "Lena Olive Smith," 412.
6. Franklin, *The Two Worlds of Race,* 145.
7. Duluth Lynchings website, "Background," http://www.mnhs.org/duluthlynchings/background.php.
8. William D. Green, "To Remove the Stain: The Trial of the Duluth Lynchers," *Minnesota History* (spring 2004): 23–24.

9. *Minneapolis Tribune,* June 18–20, 1920, 1 (all three days); Michael Fedo, *The Lynchings in Duluth,* reprint ed. (St. Paul: Minnesota Historical Society Press, 2000), 112–13, 122, 131.
10. For a summary of indictments and links to selected documents, see the Legal Proceedings page of the Duluth Lynchings Online Resource: http://collections.mnhs.org/duluthlynchings/.
11. *Duluth Herald,* July 13, 1920, 1; *Minneapolis Tribune,* June 18, 1920, 1; *Labor World* (Duluth), June 17, 1920, 2; *Duluth Herald,* June 18, 1920, 8.
12. W. F. Rhinow to Governor J. A. A. Burnquist, August 5, 1920, 2 (cover letter to his investigative report), Minnesota Governor Records (Burnquist), Subject file 648c, roll 1, Minnesota Historical Society; *The Appeal,* June 26, 1920, 4
13. *The Appeal,* June 26, 1920, 4.
14. *Duluth Herald,* July 7, 1920, 1; July 14, 1920, 12; July 21, 1920, 1, July 24, 1920, 1; Fedo, *The Lynchings in Duluth,* 4–5; Fred W. Friendly, *Minnesota Rag* (New York: Random House, 1981), 9.
15. On the streetcar strike and police wages, see the *Duluth Herald,* July 21, 1920, 1; July 22, 1920, 1; July 26, 1920, 11. On Magney, see the *Duluth Herald,* September 14, 1920, 3; September 16, 1920, 13.
16. *Duluth Herald,* August 30, 1920, 1.
17. *The Appeal,* July 10, 1930, 3.
18. *Duluth Herald,* August 31, 1920, 1; September 1, 1920, 1.
19. *Duluth Herald,* September, 3, 1920, 1.
20. *Duluth Herald,* September, 6, 1920, 1. Rozon's defense counsel had attended Stephenson's trial.
21. *Duluth Herald,* June 25, 1920, 3; June 28, 1920, 11; September 4, 1920, 1; September 11, 1920, 1; September 13, 1920, 1.
22. Green, "To Remove the Stain," 28.
23. *Duluth Herald,* September 11, 1920, 1, 2.
24. *Duluth Herald,* September 16, 1920, 1, 3.
25. *Duluth Herald,* September 17, 1920, 1.
26. Green, "To Remove the Stain," 29.
27. *Minnesota v. Hammerberg,* trial transcript, 31–33, 35, 36, 38, copies in Minnesota State Reformatory for Men, Inmate Case Files, State Archives, Minnesota Historical Society; *Duluth Herald,* September 15, 1920, 6. For Cant's assessment of Hammerberg's mental capacity, see

Hammerberg sentencing transcript, Duluth Lynchings microfilm, roll 1, 81–83, 91.

28. Hammerberg trial transcript, 62.
29. Ibid.
30. Ibid., 71, 74–76.
31. *Duluth Herald,* November 3, 1920, 4; Fedo, *The Lynchings in Duluth,* 150; *Chicago Evening Post,* quoted in the *Duluth Herald,* June 19, 1920, 8. Stephenson and Dondino were sent to the Stillwater State Prison after exhausting all appeals, and Hammerberg went to the St. Cloud Reformatory. For a summary of the sentences and time served, plus links to court documents, see the Incarcerations page of the Duluth Lynchings website.
32. *The Appeal,* July 3, 1920, 3.
33. Duluth Lynchings website, "Afterwards," Minnesota Historical Society.
34. Green, "To Remove the Stain," 35n43.
35. Dibell, a Duluth attorney until 1918 when he was appointed to the court, wrote: "It is common knowledge that colored men are not easily distinguished in daytime and less readily in the dark or in the twilight. Young southern negroes, such as these, look much alike to the northerner. The proof is in the case" (*State of Minnesota vs. Max Mason,* 189 NW 452, 454 [1921]).
36. Duluth Lynchings website, "Incarcerations," Minnesota Historical Society.
37. *Duluth Herald,* December 2,1920, 1.

18. SHUN THE SNARES OF PETTY DISCORD

1. For references to the mob action that harassed the home of Nellie and Billy Francis, see Nelson, "William T. Francis, at Home and Abroad," 6, 12n24; *St. Paul Daily News,* December 7, 1924, section 2, 1 (Oscar Arneson, president of the Cretin Improvement Association, first offered the Francises one thousand dollars to give up their house, which Nellie and Billy declined. He then initiated harassment in order to move the couple out. This will be discussed in the epilogue); Heidenreich, "A Citizen of Fine Spirit," 5, 9. The NAACP reported that over a thirty-one-year period—1889–1919—2,549 black men and fifty-one black women were lynched. During the year 1919, seventy-eight Negroes were

lynched; eleven of the black men were ex-soldiers, one was a woman, and fourteen were burned at the stake. Twenty-eight cities staged race riots in which more than a hundred black people were killed (*The Crisis* 19[5] [March 1920]: 243), https://www.marxists.org/history/usa/workers/civil-rights/crisis/0300-crisis-v19n05-w113.pdf.

For a general history on the spread of white supremacy throughout the South during Reconstruction and after, see Eric Foner, *Reconstruction: The Unfinished Revolution, 1863–1877* (New York: Harper & Row, 1988); Lewis, *W. E. B. Du Bois.*

2. "Political Pointers," *The Appeal,* October, 16, 1920, 3; October 23, 1920, 3, 4 (addressed a meeting of colored Minneapolis women at a voting demonstration); November 6, 1920, 3 (her invitation to speak at the League of Women Voters).
3. *The Appeal,* November 6, 1920, 4.
4. "'Gramma' Nellie Seay," (Nashville) *Tennessean,* January 6, 1924, 39; Delois Wilkinson, "Black Women Oppose Three Foes—racism, sexism, and poverty," *Tennessean,* February 23, 1987, 8.
5. "'Gramma' Nellie Seay," 39.
6. *Tennessean,* April 14, 1877, 4; June 8, 1895, 6.
7. *The Appeal,* November 20, 1920, 3; November 27, 1920, 4; December 25, 1920, 3; January 1, 1921, 3.
8. *The Appeal,* November 27, 1920, 3.
9. *The Appeal,* December 4, 1920, 3.
10. Bucy, "Juno Frankie Pierce."
11. *The Appeal,* December 4, 1920, 3.
12. *The Appeal,* December 11, 1920, 2 (speaks at the two white churches); January 29, 1921, 3 (speaks at the Adelphai Club).
13. "League of Women Voters," *The Appeal,* December 18, 1920, 2.
14. "Minnesota Federation of Women," *The Appeal,* December 18, 1920, 3.
15. Walter White, "The Work of the Mob," *The Crisis*18(8) (September 1918): 222; Ismail Akwei, "How a Pregnant Mary Turner Was Brutally Lynched by a White Mob in 1918," *Face2Face Africa,* May 21, 2018, https://face2faceafrica.com/article/how-a-pregnant-mary-turner-was-brutally-lynched-by-a-white-mob-in-1918–2; accessed June 4, 2019; Julie Buchner Armstrong, "A Hundred Years after Her Lynching, Mary Turner's Memorial Remains a Battleground," *Zocalo* (May 15,

2018), https://www.zocalopublicsquare.org/2018/05/15/hundred-years-lynching-mary-turners-memorial-remains-battleground/ideas/essay/; accessed June 4, 2019.

16. "Minnesota Federation of Women," *The Appeal,* December 18, 1920, 3.
17. Ibid.
18. *The Appeal,* February 28, 1921, 3; "Women in Philanthropy and Charity in Cleveland and Northeast Ohio," Western Reserve Historical Society (2018), "Lethia C. Fleming," https://www.wrhs.org/research/library/library-exhibits/women-in-philanthropy/; accessed October 17, 2018.
19. *The Appeal,* February 26, 1921, 2.
20. *The Appeal,* "Mrs. W. T. Francis," March 19, 1921, 2.
21. *The Appeal,* December 18, 1920, 2.
22. "Mrs. W. T. Francis Meets President Harding," *The Appeal,* March 19, 1921, 2.
23. Ibid.
24. Donald Lee Grant, *The Way It Was in the South: The Black Experience in Georgia* (Athens: University of Georgia Press, 2001), 336.
25. NAACP, *Thirty Years of Lynching in the United States, 1889–1918* (New York: National Association for the Advancement of Colored People, April 1919), 7; Walter White, *Rope and Faggot: A Biography of Judge Lynch* (New York: Alfred A Knopf, 1929), 232; Christopher C. Meyers, "Killing Them by Wholesale: A Lynching Rampage in South Georgia," *Georgia Historical Quarterly* 90(2) (summer 2006): 214, 217.
26. *Acts and Resolutions of the General Assembly of the State of Georgia, 1893* (Atlanta, 1894), 128. The bill passed in the House 88–0 and in the Senate 30–0.
27. Meyers, "Killing Them by Wholesale," 217.
28. Ibid., 217–18.
29. "Everywoman Progressive Council," *The Appeal,* April 9, 1920, 3 (her report to the council).
30. "Citizen Mass Meeting," *The Appeal,* December 11, 1920, 3.
31. "A Prediction Verified," *The Appeal,* February 5, 1921, 3.
32. Timothy J. Greene, "Teaching the Limits of Liberalism in the Interwar Years: The NAACP's Antilynching Campaign," *OAH Magazine of History* 18(2) (January 2004): 28–30; William F. Pinar, "The NAACP and the Struggle for Anti-Lynching Federal Legislation, 1917–1950,"

Counterpoints 163 (2001): 683–752; "Lynchings by Year and Race," University of Missouri-Kansas City School of Law; "Statistics Provided by the Archives at Tuskegee Institute," accessed September 7, 2010.

33. John D. Bessler, *Legacy of Violence: Lynch Mobs and Executions in Minnesota* (Minneapolis: University of Minnesota Press, 2003), 216.
34. "Big Anti-Lynching Mass Meeting at St. James AME," *The Appeal*, April 9, 1921, 2.
35. Bessler, *Legacy of Violence,* 217, 226; *Minnesota House Journal, 1921*, 1171; *Minnesota Senate Journal, 1921*, 1216; Robert Zangrando, *The NAACP Crusade against Lynching, 1909–1950* (Philadelphia: Temple University Press, 1980), 13, 20; *Session Laws of the State of Minnesota Passed during the Forty-second Session of the State Legislature,* chapter 401, H.F. No. 785; "Minnesota Anti-Lynching Bill," *The Crisis* 22 (June 1921): 67; Steven R. Hoffbeck, "Victories Yet to Win: Charles W. Scrutchin, Bemidji's Black Activist Attorney," *Minnesota History* (summer 1996): 74.
36. "Minnesota's Anti-Lynching Law," *The Appeal,* April 23, 1921, 2.
37. "The Anti-Lynching Mass Meeting," *The Appeal,* April 23, 1921, 3.
38. "To Whom This May Concern," *The Appeal,* April 23, 1921, 3.
39. "St. Paul Honors Mrs. W. T. Francis," *The Appeal,* May 7, 1921, 3.
40. Ibid.
41. Ibid.
42. Ibid.; emphasis added.
43. Ibid.
44. Ibid.

19. HOLD ON

1. Juno held title to the property. See Heidenreich, "A Citizen of Fine Spirit," 5.
2. Nelson, "William T. Francis, at Home and Abroad," 6, 12n24. See also the *St. Paul Daily News,* December 7, 1924, section 2, 1 (Arneson's quote); Heidenreich, "A Citizen of Fine Spirit," 9.
3. MHP Connect: "Housing Discrimination Revealed: History of Race and Real Estate in Minneapolis" (July 24, 2018), https://mhponline.org/blog/connect/855-housing-discrimination-revealed-history-of-race-real-estate-in-minneapolis-bus-tour.

4. "Home Stoned in Race Row," *Minneapolis Tribune*, July 16, 1931, 1.
5. U.S. Department of the Interior, National Park Service, "Lee, Arthur and Edith, House," National Register of Historic Places Registration Form "Summary Paragraph," Section 8 page 11, 23, 24 (January 14, 2014).
6. *Corrigan v. Buckley*, 271 U.S. 323 (1926).
7. *The Appeal*, January 22, 1918, 2 (speech before the Men's Club of the German Methodist Church).
8. *Northwest Bulletin*, January 10, 1925, 1 (Lula's death notice).
9. Nelson, "William T. Francis, at Home and Abroad," 10.
10. Ibid.
11. Ibid., 8–9.
12. Ibid., 10.
13. Heidenreich, "A Citizen of Fine Spirit," 6.
14. Nelson, "William T. Francis, at Home and Abroad," 10–11.
15. "Negro Diplomat's Funeral to Be Held Thursday," *Tennessean*, August 14, 1929, 1.
16. Nellie may have sought what would later be called "Lump Sum Death Benefit" (LSDB). The origin of the LSDB was in 1935 legislation, although it was not intended to be a "burial benefit." The concern in the 1935 act was the equity of individuals who died prior to retirement age (sixty-five at the time). And because there were no survivor benefits in the original program, a provision was added to award an LSDB to the survivors in the amount of 3.5 percent of the individual's covered earnings. LSDB payments were made from 1937 through 1939, and because the maximum covered earnings during these years was three thousand dollars per year, the maximum LSDB payment that could have been made was $315, although virtually all of the payments were considerably less. In December 1939, the average LSDB was $96.93 (Larry DeWitt, "The History and Development of the Lump Sum Death Benefit," SSA Historian's Office, September 7, 2006, https://www.ssa.gov/history/lumpsum.html; accessed November 15, 2018).
17. "Denied Congressional Gratuity of Late Husband," *Northwest Monitor*, July 8, 1930, 1, 3.
18. "$10,000 to Mrs. Nellie Francis for work she did at the Tennessee Vocational School for Colored Girls. The work was performed, the legislature

pointed out in passing the bill, with the understanding that compensation would be made at a later date because the state was financially unable to compensate her at the time" (*Tennessean,* July 10, 1966, 14).

19. "Denied Congressional Gratuity of Late Husband," 1, 3.
20. "117 Year-Old Former Slave Dies Here," *Tennessean,* February 12, 1931, 5.
21. "Nellie Seay Bible Study Club," *Tennessean,* February 21, 1972, 32.
22. Tennessee Historical Society, J. Pierce Book entry, September 2, 1932, 42.
23. *Twin Cities Herald,* September 30, 1932, 3; "Minnesotan Living in Quake Zone Is Reported Safe," March 3, 25, 1933, 1, 6.
24. N. Francis to J. Pierce, April 2, 1933, J. Pierce Papers, Tennessee Historical Society.
25. Melvin Joseph Maas: An Inventory of His Papers, Manuscript Collection, Minnesota Historical Society File no. 00985, Location P1530, Box 1, http://www2.mnhs.org/library/findaids/00985.xml; Paul Nelson, "Maas, Melvin (1898–1964)," MNopedia, Minnesota Historical Society, http://www.mnopedia.org/person/maas-melvin-1898-1964.
26. "Would Get Pension under Bill in Congress," *Twin Cities Herald,* December 10, 1932, 1; Heidenreich, "A Citizen of Fine Spirit," 6; Nelson, "William T. Francis, at Home and Abroad," 11.
27. *Tennessean,* December 16, 1969, 29.
28. Both women lived in Gramma's house at 1210 Phillips Street (*Tennessean,* March 30, 1954, 24 [Juno's address]; February 12, 1931, 5 [Gramma's residence]; *U.S. City Directory, 1943,* 261 [as housekeeper]). She would continue working at Tennessee State throughout the decade. *U.S. City Directories (Nashville), 1953,* 317; *1955,* 317; *1958,* 324; *1959,* 319; Paul Nelson, "Francis, Nellie (1874–1969)," MNopedia, Minnesota Historical Society, http://www.mnopedia.org/person/francis-nellie-1874-1969.
29. *Brown vs. Board of Education of Topeka,* 347 U.S. 483 (1954). The decision was handed down on May 17, nearly two months after Juno died.
30. "Mrs. Pierce, Negro Civic Leader Died," *Tennessean,* March 30, 1954, 24.
31. "Mrs. Francis Paid Tribute by Council," *Tennessean,* November 26, 1962, 18.
32. For her march on city hall, see "J. Frankie Pierce and the Tennessee Vocational School for Colored Girls (1923–1919)," http://ww2.tnstate.edu/library/digital/pierce.htm; accessed June 26, 2018. Among her

many accomplishments, Pierce and the CWC successfully advocated for department store restroom facilities for black women, resulting in Montgomery Ward's providing the first such facilities in Nashville. See "Find-A-Grave: Juno Frankie Seay Pierce," https://www.findagrave.com/memorial/172449485/juno-frankie-pierce /; accessed July 26, 2018.

33. The lyrics are traditional, set to the theme of *Eyes on the Prize*.

EPILOGUE

1. "Negro Diplomat's Funeral to Be Held Thursday," *Tennessean,* August 14, 1929, 1.
2. Obituary, *Tennessean,* December 15, 1969, 38; "Mrs. Francis Rites Tomorrow," *Tennessean,* December 16, 1969, 29.

Index

Page numbers in italic refer to illustrations.

William D. Green is M. Anita Gay Hawthorne professor of critical race and ethnic studies and professor of history at Augsburg University in Minneapolis. His previous books published by the University of Minnesota Press include *A Peculiar Imbalance: The Fall and Rise of Racial Equality in Minnesota, 1837–1869*; *Degrees of Freedom: The Origins of Civil Rights in Minnesota, 1865–1912*, winner of the 2016 Hognander Minnesota History Award; and *The Children of Lincoln: White Paternalism and the Limits of Black Opportunity in Minnesota, 1860–1876*, winner of the 2020 Hognander Minnesota History Award.